GOD'S FRIENDS

Called to Believe and Belong

Wesley W. Nelson

Developed and Produced
by the
Departments of Christian Education and Publication
The Evangelical Covenant Church

COVENANT PUBLICATIONS

ISBN 0-910452-59-8

Copyright © 1985 by Covenant Publications (formerly Covenant Press)
3200 W. Foster Avenue, Chicago, IL 60625
Printed in the United States of America
Design & Layout: David R. Westerfield
Production assistants: Gregory Sager, Janice Carlson, Naomi Wood

Foreword

The rite and practice of confirmation in the Church has been around for a long time. Its form and meaning reach back to antiquity, but its relevance for the upcoming generations within the Church was never more apparent. The reason for this revision, update, and contemporization of confirmation materials is to assure that Covenant youth and youth in other churches will receive the spiritual enlightenment necessary to secure a commitment to Christ and his Church, and do so in the context and thought-forms where life is currently being lived and experienced in the crucial adolescent years of identity discovery.

Wesley Nelson, while neither sacrificing the integrity or the authority of the Word of God nor taking anything from it, has re-interpreted that Word for contemporary youth. Here is the current, living, and solid biblical witness that unfolds the riches and depth of spiritual truth even while it speaks convincingly to the problems and complexities faced by the young of this generation.

The reason for Confirmation remains unchanged in the Covenant. Aaron Markuson said it well in his 1954 foreword to *According to Thy Word:* " . . . The purpose is to make the message clear, and to secure a commitment of young lives to Jesus Christ and his Church."

As we recognize our indebtedness to the author and the committee assigned the task of working with him to produce this two-part study—an excellent basis for Christian understanding—let us also praise God for the talent, time, and work offered up by all who had a hand in producing it.

Milton B. Engebretson, *President*
The Evangelical Covenant Church

Preface

Confirmation has long occupied a place of special importance in the ministry of The Evangelical Covenant Church. Considering the broad range of educational activities in the Church, confirmation continues to be a unique teaching and learning experience for pastors and students.

God's Friends: Called to Believe and Belong is the story of God's mighty acts—retold through fresh, contemporary approaches. But it is still the same wonderful old story. Integrating Bible history, church history, and Christian doctrine, the text is more than a vehicle for instruction. It is also a call to confirm one's friendship with God, through faith in Jesus Christ.

The appreciation of the Covenant Church is extended to many who shared in this project—including participants in early consultations and the sixteen congregations which tested the work in pilot experiences. Major thanks, of course, is given the members of the task force, who with writer Wesley W. Nelson and project director Bruce Lawson were responsible for the conception and development of all aspects of the program. They were: Bonnie Agard, Frances Anderson, Robert Ash, Edwin Hallsten, Donald Njaa, David Noreen, and David Wilder. It was a unique team experience, with Nelson and Lawson giving untold hours to coordination of text and lesson plans. Appreciation is also given our office support personnel: Judy Isaacson, typist; Gregory Sager, typesetter; and David Westerfield, who was responsible for design and layout. Credits are given in the back of the book for photos used, where we are aware of the source. Any credits missed will be corrected in future reprintings.

God's Friends: Called to Believe and Belong is presented as a gift to the Covenant in our centennial year. It is offered, in love, to the youth and their teachers of our second century. May many new friends of God find their own places of service within the continuing story of his people.

David S. Noreen, Executive Secretary
Department of Christian Education

James R. Hawkinson, Executive Secretary
Department of Publications

Chicago, 1985

CONTENTS
Part One

Part Two

Part One

Getting Started

CHAPTER 1
Beginning with Mixed Feelings

As our Confirmation course begins, we all have mixed feelings because we don't know just what to expect.

CHAPTER 2
Mixed Feelings about God

We discover that it is okay to have mixed feelings about God. We don't know him very well yet. He wants to reveal himself to us through the Bible and through his Son, Jesus.

CHAPTER 3
Getting Acquainted with Your Bible

The Bible is an exciting and important book, and we need to know some things about it in order to make the best use of it.

CHAPTER 4
The Bible, God's Special Message to Us

Through the Bible we learn how we can be God's friends and how we can live in a good relationship with him and with one another. The Bible is God's Word and God's promise to us. It tells us about his Son, Jesus Christ and what he has done for us. The Bible is also the story of people like us, who responded to God's message in different ways. We can see ourselves in them, and we can learn from them.

CONFIRMATION

Your Picture

Beginning with Mixed Feelings

1

In Class

1. GETTING TO KNOW EACH OTHER

Welcome to confirmation! It will help us to feel more comfortable and more welcome if we get to know one another a little better. I shall begin by telling a few things about myself.

I was born in 1910 (what a long time ago!) in Iowa. I was named Wesley because my parents knew a famous man by that name.

When I was your age:

The thing I did best was *study*.

The thing that embarrassed me most was that *I was called "Limpy" because I limped*.

The food I liked best was *mashed potatoes*.

The food I hated most was *squash*.

The thing I liked best about school was that *I had a nice teacher*.

The thing I hated most about school was that *some girls teased me*.

The animal I like best for a pet is a *dog* because *dogs forgive me no matter what I do*.

The thing I hate most about myself is that *I leave things lying around the house*.

The thing I like most about myself is that *I like people*.

The thing that frightens me most is *writing this book*.

* * * * * * * * * *

Now that you know a little about me, please write some things about yourself by filling in the following blanks:

I was born in the year _____ in _____ .

I was named _____ because _____ .

The thing I do best is _____ .

The thing that embarrasses me most is _____ .

The food I like best is _____ .

The food I hate most is _____ .

The thing I like best about school is _____ .

The thing I hate most about school is _____ .

The animal I like best for a pet is _____ because _____ .

The thing I hate most about myself is _____ .

The thing I like best about myself is _____ .

The thing that frightens me most is _____ .

2. MIXED FEELINGS

Whenever we begin a new experience we usually have mixed feelings about it. Writing this book is a new experience for me, and I am nervous about doing it. I feel nervous because I want you to like me. I want you to find this book to be interesting.

It is possible that you, too, have mixed feelings and are somewhat nervous about beginning this course. It will help you to know that other people also have mixed feelings and are nervous whenever they begin something new. During this course we hope to discover how much God cares about our mixed feelings and how concerned he is about helping us to feel comfortable and secure. Part of being a Christian is discovering how much God is interested in us and in what happens to us.

3. THE MEANING OF CONFIRMATION

The word "confirm" means "to make sure." The purpose of this course is to help you to become sure about what it means to be a Christian and to live the Christian life. As you become a "confirmed" Christian you will know more about God and Jesus and the Bible, but you will also know more about yourself and your feelings. One thing you will discover is that it is okay to have mixed feelings about yourself. Of course, becoming a "confirmed" Christian is something that will go on through your entire life. Some of you may begin your Christian life during this course. Others have been followers of Jesus as long as you can remember. In either case, this course is intended to help you begin the process of learning to know what it means to be a Christian, which includes knowing yourself and your feelings as well as knowing God and his feelings toward you.

Working together with your teacher will make the class interesting, and during this time you will become very good friends. You will learn to appreciate your teacher and other members of your class more and more as the weeks go by, and they will learn to appreciate you. When it is over, I hope you will look back on this time together as one of the most helpful experiences of your entire life.

I hope this book will become your own special book. There are places in it for you to write what you are feeling and thinking, and I believe you will enjoy referring to it in years to come.

4. WRITING YOUR FEELINGS ABOUT CONFIRMATION

These are my feelings as I begin this Confirmation study: _____

_____

_____

_____

_____

_____

_____

_____

_____

_____

_____

Mixed Feelings about God

2

BIBLE READING: Psalm 100
Other suggested Bible readings: Psalm 136:1-9; Psalm 139:1-12; Matthew 6:25-32.

CATECHISM

For some of the classes of this course you will be asked to memorize the answers to certain questions about the Christian faith. Questions and answers such as these have been used in teaching the Christian faith for many centuries. They are known as the "catechism." You will not just memorize them; they will become a part of the class discussion, and they will help you to understand what Christians believe. Since we learn about the Christian faith from the Bible, each answer will include a Bible verse.

WHO IS GOD?

God is personal, eternal Spirit, creator of the universe, Father of our Lord Jesus Christ, and our Father.

Lord, you have been our dwelling place throughout all generations. Before the mountains were born or you brought forth the earth and the world, from everlasting to everlasting you are God.

Psalm 90:1, 2, NIV

HAVE YOU EVER WONDERED WHAT GOES ON IN THE MIND OF YOUR DOG?

If my wife and I are discussing whether or not to take our dog for a walk or for a ride, or to give her some scraps from the table, she keeps looking from one of us to the other, trying to figure out how the conversation is going. Her eyes light up and her tail wags when we are speaking in her favor, and she looks

dejected when the conversation goes against her.

At times like these I find myself yearning to be able to talk with her. I long to have her tell us what she is thinking about. This, of course, is impossible. Though there is often a great deal of understanding between us and our pets, there is a gap between us that nothing can bridge. No matter how much we learn about animals, and no matter how well we understand them, we shall never know just how they think or feel.

THERE IS A FAR GREATER DIFFERENCE BETWEEN US AND GOD

If it is this hard for two different creatures to understand each other, think how great a problem it must be for us to relate to God, who is so much greater than we. Is he sitting up in heaven looking at us? How does he feel about us? Will he be angry about what we are do-

ing? Does he have anything to do with the terrible things that are happening in the world? Does he really care? How much will he forgive? Why do some people get by without being punished for what they are doing? Questions like these cause us to have mixed feelings about God.

MIXED FEELINGS ABOUT GOD ARE NORMAL

You may remember the story of three blind persons who could not agree on what an elephant is like because one of them had felt only an ear, another had felt only a leg, and the third had felt only the trunk. This story may help us understand why we have so many different ideas about God. Since he is so much greater than we, none of us can know him fully.

How difficult it is even to think about a Being who has no beginning and no end. We find it hard to understand how he can be all-powerful and still appear to be very gentle—as, for instance, when he came in the form of his Son, Jesus. How can he have control of the whole world and still give us the right to make our own choices? He is a Spirit; no one can see him. Yet it is possible to know him personally, and he wants us to be his friends.

Because there is such a great difference between God and us, we may expect to become confused about what he is like

and to have mixed feelings about him. This is a normal part of learning to know him and of learning to understand him better while we grow as Christian persons.

GOD WISHES TO REVEAL HIMSELF

As we seek to learn about God, he is also seeking to reveal himself to us. Therefore we must be careful about forming our own ideas of what he is like. He may be just the opposite of what we expect, and we might not recognize him. We must depend on him to reveal himself to us. The two chief ways in which God reveals himself are through the Bible and through his Son, Jesus.

The Catechism for this chapter tells us some things that God has revealed about himself.

1. God is personal (Psalm 139:1-6).

This means that he is a person, just as we are persons. He thinks, and he has feelings. Most of all, the Bible teaches us that God is loving and caring.

2. God is eternal Spirit (Galatians 6:7, 8).

Since he is eternal, he does not change, and we can depend on him at all times. Since he is Spirit, we cannot see him, but this means that he can be with us wherever we are.

3. God is the Creator of the universe (Genesis 1:1).

Even though he is an unseen Spirit, he knows about the things around us that can be seen because he made them all.

4. He is the Father of our Lord Jesus Christ (1 Peter 1:3).

This gives us the most help for getting to know God. Jesus lived among us as a human being, and we can learn about him from the Bible. By learning about Jesus we learn about God, because God is his Father. Jesus said, "He who has seen me has seen the Father."

5. He is our Father (Ephesians 4:1-6).

Jesus taught us to think of God as our Father. We can all understand what a loving father should be like, even though some people are not fortunate enough to have such a father.

God knows that mixed feelings are normal for us. Because he wishes to reveal himself, he wants to help us deal with them. We shall depend on him to help us in this Confirmation class to get to know him better and trust him more.

Check Yourself

1. According to this chapter, what are the two chief ways in which God reveals himself?

2. What are some things that God has revealed about himself?

3. If God is so great and we are so small, how do we know he cares about us?

In Class

1. To me the most important idea about God is

_____

_____

_____

_____

_____

2. Where does the Bible tell about this idea?

_____

_____

_____

_____

_____

3. I chose this idea because _____

_____

_____

_____

_____

4. How do the words "mixed feelings" apply to your feelings about God?

_____

_____

_____

_____

_____

_____

Getting Acquainted with Your Bible 3

ASSIGNMENT: Memorize the books of the Old Testament.

BOOKS

If you look at the top of any page of your Bible you will see a word which is the name of the "book" of which that page is a part. The Bible is really a library of sixty-six books, which were all written separately. After a long time these books were put together to form the Bible as we have it today. On page 13 you will find the books of the Bible as though they were standing in order on a library shelf.

CHAPTERS

Each book is divided into chapters. In most Bibles the chapter number appears at the top of the page, right after the name of the book. Sometimes there are two numbers, which means there are parts of two chapters on that page. Leaf through the book to which you have turned and see how many chapters it has.

VERSES

If you look carefully at a page, you will notice little numbers that have been inserted into the printing. They begin at the beginning of each chapter and increase until the end of the chapter. These numbers indicate verses. The books of the Bible have been divided into chapters and verses in order to help us find what we wish. For instance, if I were to say, "Turn to John 3:16," you would first find the Book of John. Then you would turn to the third chapter and find the sixteenth verse. Chapter and verse numbers were not part of the books of the Bible as they were originally written down.

THE INDEX

Now turn to the index in the front of the Bible. This will help you find the book you wish. As your assignment for this chapter you are to be memorizing the books of the Old Testament. The more familiar you become with these books, the more quickly you will be able to find them.

Dead Sea scrolls discovered in Qumran in 1947.

The Library of the Bible

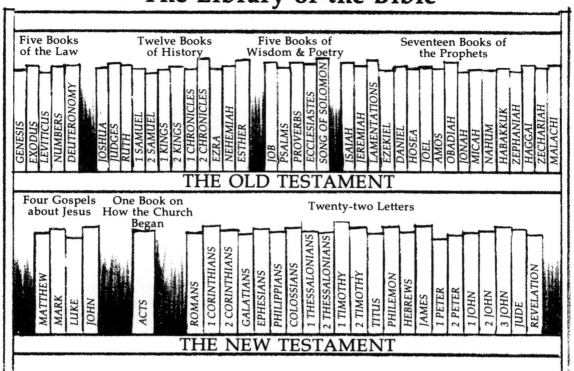

Five Books of the Law: GENESIS, EXODUS, LEVITICUS, NUMBERS, DEUTERONOMY

Twelve Books of History: JOSHUA, JUDGES, RUTH, 1 SAMUEL, 2 SAMUEL, 1 KINGS, 2 KINGS, 1 CHRONICLES, 2 CHRONICLES, EZRA, NEHEMIAH, ESTHER

Five Books of Wisdom & Poetry: JOB, PSALMS, PROVERBS, ECCLESIASTES, SONG OF SOLOMON

Seventeen Books of the Prophets: ISAIAH, JEREMIAH, LAMENTATIONS, EZEKIEL, DANIEL, HOSEA, JOEL, AMOS, OBADIAH, JONAH, MICAH, NAHUM, HABAKKUK, ZEPHANIAH, HAGGAI, ZECHARIAH, MALACHI

THE OLD TESTAMENT

Four Gospels about Jesus: MATTHEW, MARK, LUKE, JOHN

One Book on How the Church Began: ACTS

Twenty-two Letters: ROMANS, 1 CORINTHIANS, 2 CORINTHIANS, GALATIANS, EPHESIANS, PHILIPPIANS, COLOSSIANS, 1 THESSALONIANS, 2 THESSALONIANS, 1 TIMOTHY, 2 TIMOTHY, TITUS, PHILEMON, HEBREWS, JAMES, 1 PETER, 2 PETER, 1 JOHN, 2 JOHN, 3 JOHN, JUDE, REVELATION

THE NEW TESTAMENT

THE OLD TESTAMENT AND THE NEW TESTAMENT

By this time you know that the Bible is divided into the Old Testament and the New Testament. The Old Testament was written before the time of Jesus, and it speaks of things that happened and of people who lived before he came. The Old Testament was the Bible that was used by Jesus and the first Christians. The New Testament was written after Jesus came. It tells us the things we need to know about Jesus and about being his followers.

PRACTICE IN USING THE BIBLE

Leaf through the Bible near the middle until you find the Book of Psalms. This was the songbook, or the hymnbook, of God's ancient people, who used it in their worship. Many of our hymns are based on the Psalms.

Turn to Psalm 117. This is the middle chapter of the Bible, and it is also the shortest chapter in the Bible.

Turn ahead to Psalm 119. This is the longest chapter in the Bible.

Close your Bible and then see how quickly you can find the shortest and the longest chapter.

Fill in the following blanks, using the index when you need it:

1. The number of books in the Old Testament is _____

2. The number of books in the New Testament is _____

3. The number of verses in the shortest chapter is _____

4. The number of verses in the longest chapter is _____

5. The shortest verse is John 11:35. What does it say? _____

6. The longest verse is Esther 8:9. How many words does it contain? _____

7. Find and read Proverbs 17:14. This verse is about _____

8. How many people are mentioned in Numbers 2:32? _____

9. What is the last word in Galatians 6:18?

_____

THE CONCORDANCE

A concordance is a book that is used to look up passages which we might not

13

otherwise be able to find. A concordance has the words of the Bible listed in alphabetical order, with the chapter and verse number and part of the verse after each word. For instance, if we did not know where to find the words "Jesus wept," we might look in a concordance under the word "wept." There we would find it, with the reference, John 11:35. Large concordances have all the words of a certain translation of the Bible, smaller concordances have only the words that are used most often. It is possible to buy a Bible with a small concordance in the back.

HOW THE BIBLE CAME TO US

Long ago, God called certain people to become such close friends of his that they were able to speak his message just as he intended it to be spoken. They did this even though they used their own language and their own way of expressing themselves.

They also wrote God's message, and these writings became the books of the Bible, also known as "The Holy Scriptures." In a similar way, some of Jesus' followers were chosen by God to write the books of the New Testament. These writings were also used by the early Christians. Gradually, all these books were brought together and became our Bible.

The way in which God made it possible for these persons to give God's message as he intended is called "inspiration." This word means that God's Spirit inspired the writers of the Bible so they could write his message. Turn to 2 Timothy 3:16 and read what it says about the writing of the Scriptures.

Bibles were copied by hand before the time of the printing press. The work was done so carefully that the differences which crept into the various copies are not important enough to make any real differences in our faith and life. As we study the Bible and seek to understand its true meaning, we may trust it to bring us the message that God intended.

Check Yourself

1. Read 2 Timothy 3:16. What does it tell you about how God gave us the Bible?

2. What is meant by "inspiration"?

3. Why is it important for Christians to know how to use the Bible?

In Class

Which scripture passage, used during this session, is most meaningful to you?

_____

_____

_____

Rewrite that passage in your own words _____

_____

_____

_____

What does it mean?_____

_____

_____

_____

_____

The Bible: God's Special Message to Us   *4*

BIBLE READING: Psalm 119:89-96
Other suggested Bible Readings: All of Psalm 119

CATECHISM: WHAT DO WE BELIEVE ABOUT THE BIBLE?

We believe in the Holy Scriptures, the Old and New Testaments, as the Word of God and the only perfect rule for faith, doctrine, and conduct.

All Scripture is inspired by God and is useful for teaching the truth, rebuking error, correcting faults, and giving instruction for right living.

2 Timothy 3:16, TEV

Once there were two very good friends who became separated because one was persuaded to break off the friendship. In spite of this, the other remained faithful and made great sacrifices to win the unfaithful friend back. As a result of these sacrifices, the two friends were finally united.

If we let one of these friends represent God and the other represent the people whom he created, then this story will help us understand how the Bible describes the relationship between God and human beings. They became unfaithful to the true God and turned to false gods. The true God longed to reveal himself and to let them know how much he loved them. He made great sacrifices to win them back to himself. In the first book of the Bible, the book of Genesis, God and human beings became separated. In the last book of the Bible, the book of Revelation, those who returned to him are united with him to enjoy life together forever.

Of course, this is no ordinary friendship. Because God is our Creator, we worship him and pay him our highest respect. Yet the Bible also teaches us to think of God as our friend. One reason God created human beings is that he wanted creatures so much like himself that he could love them and have a relationship with them.

THE BIBLE, THE WORD OF GOD

When we say to someone, "I have a word for you," we mean, "I have a message for you." In the Bible God says, "I have a message for you, I want to be your friend, and I want to explain to you how you can be my friend." Since the Bible is God's special message to us, it is called "the Word of God." When we say, as we do in the catechism for this chapter, that "we believe in the Holy Scrip-

tures as the Word of God," we mean that we believe the Bible is God's special message to us. The purpose of this message or this "Word" is to make it possible for us to have a relationship with God.

"THE ONLY PERFECT RULE"

The best way to explain the word "rule," as it is used here, is to say that it is a "guide to follow." "The only perfect rule" means "the only perfect guide to follow."

"FOR FAITH, DOCTRINE, AND CONDUCT."

"Faith, doctrine, and conduct" are three things that are necessary for everything we do. For instance, if we are going to take an airplane trip:

1. We must have faith in the airplane. If we do not trust the plane to stay up in the air, we will not go on board.
2. "Doctrine" means "teaching which we must believe." We must learn from a timetable or from someone at the airline company what the schedule is, where to get the ticket, which plane goes to the place where we want to go, and where to get on that plane. These are "doctrines" or "teachings" that we must know and believe, and we must follow them or we will not get on the plane in time for our trip.
3. "Conduct" means "the way we behave." There is a certain way to behave while

we are on an airplane. For instance, we must stay in our seats with our seat belts fastened for take-off and landing, we must not take a seat assigned to someone else, and we must not walk in the aisles when the air is bumpy.

"Faith, doctrine, and conduct" are also necessary in order to have a relationship with God, and the purpose of the Bible is to tell us how we may have this relationship. We need to have "faith" in him. We need to know and believe and follow certain "doctrines" or "teachings" about him, about ourselves, and about what he has done to make it possible for us to have a relationship with him. We also need to know what kind of "conduct" is expected of us. The Bible is our "only perfect rule" or guide for these three things: faith, doctrine, and conduct.

"THE WORD" THAT IS GOD'S PROMISE

When we say to someone, "I give you my word," we also mean, "I give you my promise." The Bible has the most wonderful good news, that God has promised to be with us and never to give up on us. As we study the Bible we shall see that he has made great sacrifices because he loves us so much and wants us to be his friends. When we say, "The Bible is the Word of God," we mean that God has said to us, "I give you my promise."

"THE WORD" THAT IS A STORY

The Bible contains stories of many people and of many things that happened to them. These were real people, who had experiences very much like ours. From them we see what happens when people respond in different ways to God's message. We can see ourselves in these people and in what happened to them, and we can learn from them and from the different relationships they had with God and with one another.

"THE WORD" THAT IS A PERSON

There is no better way to bring a message to people than to go to them, be-

come one of them, and live among them. God came to us in the form of his Son, Jesus Christ. In him we have God's most complete message to us. From the Bible we learn how he related to sinners and to people who thought they were very good people. We learn how he related to sincere people and to hypocrites. We learn how he related to rich and respected people and how he related to poor and des-

pised people. We also see how he related to God.

In Jesus we have God's most complete message to us. Therefore, Jesus is also called "The Word of God."

SUMMARY

1. The Bible is "the Word of God."

It is God's message, saying to us, "I want to be your friend," and it tells us how we may have a relationship with him.

2. The Bible is God's Word of promise to us.

It is possible to have a relationship with God because he has promised to be faithful.

3. The Bible is God's Word in story form.

In its stories of many other people, we see ourselves.

4. The Bible tells us of God's Word as a Person.

God sent his message to us in the form of a Person, his own Son, Jesus, and tells us how we may have a personal relationship with him.

Check Yourself

1. State, in your own words, what we mean when we say, "The Bible is the Word of God."

2. What do we mean when we say, "The Word is a Person?"

3. If you believe that God really wants to be your friend, what are some ways in which this belief will affect your life?

In Class

1. Write definitions to the following words from the catechism.

a. We believe _____

_____

b. Holy Scriptures _____

_____

c. Old Testament _____

_____

d. New Testament _____

_____

e. Word of God _____

_____

f. Perfect Rule _____

_____

g. Faith _____

_____

h. Doctrine _____

_____

i. Conduct _____

_____

Make a mark on each of the lines below, in the middle or toward either end, where it best indicates your feelings about the Bible:

The Bible is:

Out of date _____	For use today
For me _____	For my parents
Dull/boring _____	Good/alive!
For use in confirmation _____	For use at home

REVIEW OF UNIT ONE

Unit One was about getting started in our class. We discovered that it is okay to have mixed feelings toward one another as well as toward God. We learned that Confirmation study will not only be about God; it will also be about ourselves.

The Bible is important to us, and we need to know how to use it. The reason it is important to us is that it is the Word of God and God's message and promise to us.

The Beginning of All Things

UNIT TWO

CHAPTER 5
God, the Creator

That God made all things means many things to us. It means, especially, that he cares for us and for everything he created.

CHAPTER 6
Human Beings: God's Special Creation

What is special about us as human beings is that we were created in God's image or likeness and he wants us for his special friends.

CHAPTER 7
All Creation
Working Together

God created all things to work together. We humans have the choice of whether or not to be God's friends by working in harmony with him, with other people, with ourselves, and with God's creation as a whole.

CHAPTER 8
"Adam and Eve,
Where Are You?"

Adam and Eve disobeyed God, and this was just the beginning of sin in the world. The steps that led them into sin are just like the steps that lead us into sin. Though we have sinned, God keeps calling us back to be his friends again.

CHAPTER 9
Sin Begins
to Take Over

Sin became an epidemic, filling the whole world with violence and evil. Sin brings God's judgment, but he cares for us and has promised to forgive us if we will return to him.

God, the Creator

BIBLE READING: Genesis, Chapters 1 and 2

CATECHISM: WHAT IS GOD'S RELATIONSHIP TO THE WORLD?

God created the world by his Word, sustains it by his power, and entrusts it to the care of human beings.

The earth is the Lord's and the fulness thereof, the world and those who dwell therein.

Psalm 24:1

"IN THE BEGINNING GOD CREATED THE HEAVENS AND THE EARTH"

With these words, the Bible introduces God to us as the Creator of all things. The word "Genesis" means "beginnings," and the first two chapters of Genesis tell us of the beginning of everything.

THE TWO CREATION ACCOUNTS

If we read these two chapters carefully we discover that they really contain two accounts of creation. The second, which begins at Genesis 2:4, places a greater emphasis on the creation of human beings. The Bible, in other places as well as this, uses more than one account of the same event. For instance, Matthew, Mark, Luke, and John, in the New Testament, all contain accounts of the life of Jesus, and each includes some details the others leave out. (In class you may have an opportunity to examine these two accounts of creation and to compare them.)

WHAT IT MEANS TO US THAT GOD IS CREATOR

1. That God is our Creator means that he has the power to do what he says.

As we read the first chapter of Genesis we note the words, "God said," appearing over and over. We learn from the Bible that while our world was coming to be, God was commanding it all to happen. He needed only to speak and things were created. God has the power to make everything he says come true. In our world, where so many things fail us, it is important to know that we have a God on whose Word we can depend. What he says and what he does are always exactly the same.

2. It means that God brings order out of confusion.

God took six days to finish his creation. In the beginning everything was dark and disorderly. Then step by step, in six days, God brought order out of the confusion. On the first day he created light, on the second he separated the sky from the earth, and so on, until, on the

ORDER

sixth day, he created human beings. As this wonderful world appears, we see that God's purpose is to bring order and beauty out of disorder and confusion and that God is working to fulfill his purpose.

We need not concern ourselves with whether or not these were ordinary twenty-four hour days or whether they had some other meaning. If those who study the earth discover that it took much longer to form the earth, we need not quarrel with them. This account was not intended to tell us the age of the earth. What is important is that God had a purpose in his work of creation. and he worked according to that purpose. It is important for us to know that God is still working according to his purpose of bringing order and beauty out of confusion. When things around us seem confusing, it is good to know that God is still working out his purpose.

3. It means that God's creation is to be enjoyed.

What a great universe this account describes, from the vast world of space to

the things so small that they cannot even be seen! What a variety we discover in creation! What beauty we find in the world around us! God certainly did not want a dull creation. He intended for us to marvel at its greatness and to enjoy its variety and beauty.

4. *It means that God considers rest to be important.*

Although God is usually described as being busy, this account includes a seventh day, in which God rested after he had finished his work of creation. This account says that everything God had done was "very good." He had done a good job, and he was satisfied, and then he rested. God has given rest to us as a gift. He not only gave his people a day of rest, but he also gives us rest from worry and guilt when we trust in him. When we are tired and troubled we may put ourselves in his hands and relax. Rest is a wonderful gift which God has given us.

5. *It means that God cares for his creation.*

God gave human beings the responsibility of caring for the earth. He is concerned about his creation and wants us to be careful about how we use it. Most of all, he is concerned about us. He cares for us and loves us.

6. *It means that we belong to God*

Because God created us, we belong to him, and the whole world in which we live belongs to him. This means that we may trust him to care for us and to fulfill his promises. It also means that we are responsible to him, to live as he wishes us to live.

CREATION AND SCIENCE

When we listen to many scientists speak, we find that they do not seem to give credit to God for creating the earth. This does not necessarily mean that they lack faith in God. Weather forecasters do not usually give credit to God for bringing rain, but this does not mean that they disbelieve in God or that God is not behind the natural causes of rain. Scientists make discoveries by studying the earth itself. As a result of their studies they change their views from time to

time. The message of the Bible, on the other hand, deals with things that do not change. We respect the work of scientists and make use of their discoveries, but nothing the scientists may learn about the earth will prove that God was not there from the beginning as its Creator. In fact, it is quite impossible to imagine how it could have happened without him.

In general, science seeks to discover how the earth came to be and how we can learn from it in order to use its resources. The purpose of the Bible, on the other hand, is to tell us why the earth was created and what meaning it has for us. Therefore, science and the Bible have different purposes, and even though they do not always seem to recognize one another, this does not mean that they are opposed to one another.

Some scientists believe in God and some do not, but their scientific study cannot destroy our faith in God. He has given us the ability to believe in him if we are willing to do so. Therefore, our faith need not be affected by people who do not seem to give God credit for creating the earth. We recognize him as the one who caused all things to exist, and we continue to live as people who belong to him.

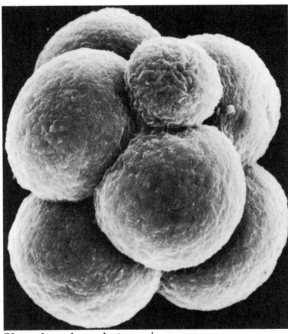

Photo through an electron microscope.

Check Yourself

1. List three statements describing what it means to us that God is Creator.

2. The Bible and science have different purposes in explaining creation. What are they?

3. What differences does it make in our lives if we believe in God as the Creator of all things?

In Class

In the space below, write a prayer thanking God for his creation:

_____

_____

_____

_____

_____

_____

_____

_____

_____

_____

Human Beings: God's Special Creation 6

BIBLE READING: Psalm 8:5, 6; Genesis 1:27
Other suggested Bible readings: Genesis 2:4-25

ASSIGNMENT: Memorize the first article of the Apostle's Creed and Martin Luther's explanation of it.

"THE APOSTLES' CREED"

A simple statement of what Christians believe came into use during the first five centuries after the time of Jesus. This statement is known as "the Apostles' Creed." It has three paragraphs or "articles." The first article is about God.

An explanation of the meaning of the Apostles' Creed was written by a church leader named Martin Luther, of whom we shall learn later.

This first article about God, and the explanation of it, fits very well with this chapter, in which we are learning that human beings are God's special creation.

What is the first article of the Apostles' Creed?

I believe in God the Father Almighty, Maker of Heaven and Earth.
What does this mean?
I believe that God has created me and all that exists. He has given me and still preserves my body and soul with all their powers.

He provides me with food and clothing, home and family, daily work, and all I need from day to day. God also protects me in time of danger, and guards me from every evil.

All this he does out of fatherly and divine goodness and mercy, though I do not deserve it.

Therefore, I surely ought to thank and praise, serve and obey him.

This is most certainly true.

We learn from the story of creation that God gave much more attention to the creation of human beings than he did to the rest of creation. The special care which God gives to human beings is described in the explanation of the first article of the Apostles' Creed. From Gene-sis 1:27 we learn that God created human beings in his own image or "likeness." It is because we are so much like God that we are able to be his friends. Following are some of the things it means to be created in God's likeness or image:

Creation of Adam, by Michelangelo

1. WE ARE TO BE CREATIVE

To be created in God's likeness means that we, like God, can be creative. Though we are not able to make something out of nothing, as God does, we are able to create many things from the resources he has given us. Take a few moments to think of a few of the things people have created from the materials found in the earth.

2. WE CAN MAKE MANY CHOICES

To be created in God's likeness also means that we are able to think and plan, and then, to make choices. Among these choices, we are able to choose between right and wrong.

3. WE WERE CREATED MALE AND FEMALE

Although God is spoken of as "he," the Bible describes him as having the characteristics of both male and female. For instance, he can fill the place of both father and mother to us. As males and females together, therefore, we were created in God's likeness. To be male or female as a human being means much more than to be male or female among other living creatures. Because of our abilities to think and plan and to converse with one another, we are capable of having more meaningful and fulfilling relationships. The creation of human beings as male and female contributes to the beauty and purpose of God's world. We can relate to one another in a variety of ways. For instance, friendships, social activities, and youth groups are much more satisfying when they include both boys and girls or men and women.

The Bible clearly indicates that it is God's will that sex be shared only in marriage. It is in the relationship of husband and wife that God has intended for men and women to reproduce themselves in their children and to bring up these children in the loving care of a family.

4. WE ARE TO CARE FOR AND USE THE EARTH

In the Bible reading for this chapter we saw how God placed Adam and Eve in a beautiful garden and gave them the responsibility to care for it. Since we were created in the likeness of God, we have

27

the ability to care for the earth. From it we receive our food, and we use its resources to make life pleasant and comfortable, and God has put it under our control, to care for it for him.

5. WE CAN RETURN GOD'S LOVE

Most of all, to be created in God's likeness means that we can return his love and be his friends. Only with human beings can God satisfy his longing to love and be loved in return, and only with God can human beings satisfy their deepest longings for someone like God to care for and love them. We were made to be friends of God, and we can be fully satisfied only as we become his friends.

Check Yourself

1. What are some things that are special about human beings that other creatures do not have?

2. How does the responsibility for making decisions make life easier or harder?

3. Suggest some ways in which human beings may return God's love.

In Class

What does it mean to be created in the likeness of God?

_____

_____

_____

_____

_____

_____

_____

_____

_____

_____

_____

_____

_____

All Creation Working Together

BIBLE READING: Psalms 8:3-8
Other suggested Bible reading: Read again Genesis 1:26-30 and Genesis 2:4-25

CATECHISM: WHAT DOES IT MEAN TO BE A HUMAN BEING?

To be a human being is to be created by God in his likeness, free and responsible in relation to God, the world, neighbor, and self.

Then God said, "And now we will make human beings; they will be like us and resemble us. They will have power over the fish, the birds, and all animals, domestic and wild, large and small."

Genesis 1:26, TEV

THE PARTS OF OUR BODIES WORKING TOGETHER

Reach out your hand and pick something up from the table. Notice how your arm and hand and fingers work together. Walk around the room and notice how your legs and feet cooperate. When you want to change direction, they turn you around. When they get the signal that you want to run, they work together in an entirely different way. We are well and happy when all parts of our bodies

take their share of the responsibility.

This is true in all creation, not only in our bodies. From each planet and star to the tiniest insect, all have their places to fill. When God had finished creating the universe, he looked at all the parts working together and "saw that it was very good" (Genesis 1:31). Our world is good when everything and everyone work together as God intended.

THE EARTH AND ITS PEOPLE WORKING TOGETHER

Think of all the cooperation that is required to provide a meal for you or me. The sun, the rain, and the soil cooperate to produce vegetables and grain. The farmer cultivates the soil and harvests the crops and cares for his cattle, from which come milk and butter and beef. Food packagers, truck drivers, wholesalers, and grocers all have a part. In order for them to do their work, they must have others to manufacture and care for the machinery and equipment they use. Thus we could go on and on until we discover that people all around the world depend on each other, and we all depend on the things that God has provided in nature, which also depend on each other.

Whenever anyone fails to do his or her part, or when the weather is not right, or there is a storm, the whole process is affected.

LIVING AS FRIENDS OF THE EARTH

It is important for all God's creatures that we human beings learn to live as friends of the earth which he has given us to enjoy. When there were fewer people, this was not much of a problem because the earth was not affected by the bad treatment it received. Now, however, since there are so many more of us, and since we have so many different kinds of industries, it has become much more important for us to live as good friends of the earth. These are a few of the things we need to remember:
• Our resources are here to use wisely. Some of them have taken countless thousands of years to produce, and when they are gone, there will be no more of them.
• We need pure air to breathe. If we keep releasing poisons into the air, even breathing will become a health hazard.
• Pure drinking water is something we take for granted, but it will not remain pure if we dump wastes where they can seep into the water supplies.
• The soil can be polluted so it cannot produce, or poisons in the soil or water can make farm produce or other food poisonous.
• We can destroy the balance of nature by killing off certain kinds of animal or plant life.
• We can injure our own and other people's ears by forcing them to listen to loud sounds.
• We can destroy the beauty of the earth by leaving junk lying around.

If we become enemies of the earth by our carelessness, it cannot continue to be our friend, and we shall suffer. Therefore, in order to enjoy the friendship of the earth, let us make sure we are living as its friends.

OUR CHOICE: SHALL WE WORK TOGETHER AS HUMAN BEINGS?

Most of creation works together naturally. We human beings, however, have been given the choice of whether or not we will take our share of the responsibility and work together with others. The world would be a harmonious place if all its people would live and act as God intended. The reason for most of the pain and suffering in the world is that we have not always acted as responsible people. When we fail to do as we should we are unhappy, and we cause others to be unhappy. We ourselves, as well as others, are much more happy when we act as God intended.

LIVING AS GOD'S FRIENDS

The catechism for this chapter tells us that we were created both free and responsible. We are free to enjoy friendship with God, and we are also responsible to keep good relationships in four directions:

1. We keep a good relationship with God by treating him with respect because he is our Creator.

2. We keep a good relationship with other people by treating them with respect because God created them. Our neighbors are not only those who live next door but people all around the world.

3. We keep a good relationship with the world by caring for it and for all its creatures because God created them all.

4. We keep a good relationship with ourselves by taking care of our bodies and minds and by loving and serving God, our Creator.

Check Yourself

1. List the steps of cooperation needed in order to mail a letter to a friend.

2. What is the reason for most pain and suffering in the world?

3. What does it mean to be "free and responsible?"

In Class

What is my responsibility:

TO GOD _____

_____

_____

TO WORLD _____

_____

_____

TO NEIGHBOR _____

_____

_____

TO SELF _____

_____

_____

I can be more responsible in the following ways:

_____

_____

_____

_____

_____

"Adam and Eve, Where Are You?" 8

BIBLE READING: Genesis 3:1-24

CATECHISM: WHAT IS SIN?

Sin is all in thought, word, and deed that is contrary to the will of God.

Everyone has sinned and is far away from God's saving presence. But by the free gift of God's grace all are put right with him through Christ Jesus, who sets them free.

Romans 3:23, 24, TEV

Back near the beginning of this book we told the story of two good friends, representing God and human beings. We shall be using this story through this whole course to help us understand how much God wants us to be his friends. We have now come to the time when the two friends, God and human beings, became separated.

Nothing could have been more pleasant for Adam and Eve than to continue to live in the beautiful garden that God had provided. Here they could spend their days caring for the garden, eating of its fruits, and enjoying God's company. Meanwhile, the whole earth was theirs to control and to enjoy. There was only one

thing they must not do. God had told them not to eat of the tree of the knowledge of good and evil. Of course, this became the one thing they wanted to do. Why is it that disobedience seems so much more enjoyable than obedience?

The tempter came in the form of a snake, who persuaded them to disobey God. After you have read the Bible passage for this chapter, go through the steps that led to their fall and see if these steps are not very much like the steps that cause you and me to fall for temptation. These were the steps:

1. *Eve saw the tree*

She looked at it and realized that the fruit was there for her to enjoy just by picking it. The reason she looked at the tree so longingly was that the tempter had already put a doubt in her mind by asking, "Did God really say you should not eat of it?"

2. *The Fruit looked good*

It seemed so attractive and beautiful. Certainly nothing as delightful as this could be wrong! The tempter had already told her that God was not telling her the truth, that he was not really going to punish her.

3. *In fact, it no longer seemed bad. It really was good.*

The tempter had convinced her that it would really be good for her, that it would make her wise.

These are the three steps that usually

lead us into temptation. We do not usually do things that we think are bad while we are doing them. We make ourselves believe that they really are good. "It can't be bad enough to hurt you," or "Everybody's doing it," we say. The Bible warns us of an evil tempter who comes to us and, by steps like these, persuades us to disobey God.

As a result of these three steps a number of things happened:

1. The sin was committed. Eve ate the fruit and gave some of it to Adam.
2. They became ashamed when they realized that they had done wrong.
3. They tried to make excuses. Adam blamed Eve, and Eve blamed the snake.
4. They tried to hide from God. Gone was the happy friendship with God. Now he had to look for them. He came calling to them, "Where are you?" but they were hiding from him because of a bad conscience.
5. They had to suffer the consequences.

God forced them to leave the beautiful garden, and they had to face the results of their sin.

Life became hard for Adam and Eve after they had to leave the beautiful place where they had lived. Never since then has life been perfectly good for any human being. Adam's sin created a huge chasm separating human beings from God. Because of all this we have all sinned, and we all have suffered for it.

GOOD NEWS FOR ALL WHO HAVE SINNED

Fortunately this is not the end of the story. Ever since then God has been looking for human beings, calling, "Where are you?" He loves us just as much as if we had not sinned, and he keeps longing for us to be his friends again.

We shall follow the story as God continues to look for his friends. We shall learn of many who knew him as their friend and trusted him and believed what he had promised. When the right time came, God fulfilled his promise by sending his Son, Jesus, who made it possible for us to have the life which Adam and Eve had lost when they disobeyed God.

"For God so loved the world that he gave his only Son, that whoever believes in him should not perish but have eternal life" (John 3:16).

After we have become God's friends by responding to his love and believing in Jesus, we want to please him. Then, when some temptation to disobey him becomes very strong, he will help us overcome it. "God is faithful; he will not let you be tempted beyond what you can bear. But when you are tempted, he will also provide a way out so you can stand up under it" (1 Corinthians 10:13, NIV).

Check Yourself

1. List the three steps that led Eve to sin.

2. How did Adam and Eve's relationship with God change after they ate the fruit?

3. Why did God send Jesus into the world?

In Class

Let me tell you about a sin I committed when I was about eight years old. My father had told me I must not use some drills he had in his shop. After he had left for work, I suddenly realized how much I needed a hole in a piece of wood. The more I looked at that piece of wood, the more important it seemed to me to have a hole in it. Certainly it could do no harm. I would be very careful with the drills and be sure to put them back in their place when I was finished. My father did not really mean I should not use them. He just wanted to be sure I did not break or lose them. Then I began to think about how much I would learn by drilling the hole in the wood and how useful it would be for the thing I was making. By this time it did not seem at all like disobedience for me to use the drills.

I shall never forget the terrible feeling that came over me when the drill broke. When my father returned, I stayed out of his sight. I was miserable for several days and did not go close to him. Every day I was afraid he would find the broken drill, and yet I wished he would find it so I could get it over with. When he did find it, I tried to excuse myself by telling him how much I needed it, but that did not help. He punished me, but he also forgave me, and we became friends again.

See if you can find the same three steps that led Adam and Eve to fall for temptation in this story of a sin I committed. You will find them in the first paragraph. Compare this with some temptation for which you have fallen.

Sin Begins to Take Over

BIBLE READING: Genesis 4:1-15 Genesis 6:11-8:22

CATECHISM: WHAT ARE THE RESULTS OF SIN?

The results of sin are broken relationships, a weakening of ability to obey God, and finally, eternal separation from him.

For the wages of sin is death, but the gift of God is eternal life in Christ Jesus our Lord.
Romans 6:23, NIV

"SIN!"
"SIN - What an interesting word!"
"SIN - What an exciting word!"
"SIN - is fun!"
"SIN! What a strange word! What does it mean?"
"Sin is everything that is contrary to the will of God."
"Even if I just say it and don't do it?"
"Even if you only *think* it."
This means that I am faced with a choice. Do I think and say and do what God wants or what I want? That is a tough choice to make.

What makes sin so appealing is that it is just what we want to do. Sin is what Adam and Eve did when they ate the fruit that God had forbidden them to eat. They were tempted because it seemed such a good thing to do. Because they wanted to do it so much, they no longer considered it important that God had told them not to do it.

Sin is like an epidemic that has made slaves of all of us, because we have all sinned. As the Bible says, "None is righteous, no, not one" (Romans 3:10). Sin seems like such good news at first, but it always ends up as bad news. As the catechism for this chapter tells us, it weakens us so we cannot know or do God's will. This means that the temptation to sin gets stronger and stronger and we get less and less able to do what God wants us to do. We get farther and farther away from God until sin finally leads to everlasting separation from him. This is what is meant by "hell."

We need only look at the world around us to see how much pain and suffering is

"What's that?"
"Oh, it's sin."
"I don't believe in that."
"Me either."

"What are you doing?"
"Oh, I'm binding you in sin."
"I don't believe in that."
"Me either."

"Who are you anyway?"
"Oh, I'm Satan."
"I don't believe in that."
"Me either."

caused by people who once were gentle and beautiful babies, but who grew up to be slaves of sin. The important thing to remember about sin is that it always takes over; and sin is always bad news!

SIN BEGAN TO TAKE OVER FROM THE VERY BEGINNING

When Adam and Eve disobeyed God and were forced to leave the garden which God had given them, this was only the beginning. Now, in the next generation, we have the first murder.

Cain, the oldest son of Adam and Eve, was a farmer, and Abel, his brother, was a shepherd. Cain brought God an offering of farm produce, and Abel brought meat. God rejected Cain's offering and accepted Abel's. We are not told why God would not accept Cain's offering, but we do know that there was something wrong in Cain's heart because he immediately became jealous of his brother, whose offering God had accepted. God told Cain that his sin was like a wild animal that was ready to pounce on him. He warned him that he must overcome his sin or it would take control of him. Obviously Cain did not pay any attention to God, because he murdered

Abel at the first opportunity.

Then, when God inquired about Abel, Cain lied and said, "I don't know where he is." He even asked God sarcastically, "Am I supposed to take care of my brother?" If he had admitted his guilt and asked God to forgive and help him, there would have been some hope for him, but he refused to admit that he had done wrong, and sin took more and more control of him. His wrong attitude turned to jealousy, which led to murder. Then, to cover up his murder, he lied and became bitter and sarcastic toward God. This is an illustration of the way sin can take over in our lives.

SIN BECAME AN EPIDEMIC

From the time of Cain and Abel, the population of the earth continued to increase, but sin increased just as fast, until the whole earth was filled with violence. The human race was so infected with sin that hardly anyone was able even to think of anything but evil.

Then God determined to destroy all the people except Noah and his family, who were the only friends God had left. God commanded Noah to build a large boat on dry land. Then Noah brought one pair

of each kind of all the animals into this boat, which was known as "the ark." After Noah and his wife and his three sons and their wives had gone into the boat, God shut the door, and it began to rain. It rained forty days and nights, and all life was destroyed except for Noah and his family and the animals that were with him in the boat. After the water had dried away, Noah and his family took the animals out of the boat and a new life began on the earth.

The Holocaust Memorial, a reminder of modern-day sin, helps people remember the six million Jews who were executed during World War II.

LESSONS FROM CAIN AND ABEL AND NOAH

From Cain and Abel and from Noah we can learn three lessons:

1. Sin is like an epidemic.

Every time we sin it becomes easier for us to sin, and every time we sin, we influence other people to sin also.

2. Sin brings God's judgment.

Although God is patient with sin, there comes a time when he must bring judgment. It was only after people had become hopelessly infected with sin that God decided to destroy them.

3. God's judgment is done in love.

It was God's concern for Noah and his family and for the human race as a whole that caused him to bring judgment on the earth. He wanted people to be able to live in a world where they had a chance to choose to be his friends without being influenced by so much evil around them. Therefore, though God found it necessary to act severely, he acted in love. Let us remember that God never wants to bring judgment. He wants us to turn to him and give him a chance to forgive us.

THE RAINBOW IN THE SKY

After Noah and his family had settled on the earth again, God made a sacred agreement with him never to destroy the earth with any more floods. He had taught us the lesson we needed to learn—that he wants us to be his friends, but he wants this friendship to be by our own choice.

Check Yourself

1. What three lessons does this chapter teach us about sin?

2. What was God's warning to Cain, and what was Cain's response?

3. How is God's judgment a sign of his love?

In Class

The first thing we think of when we realize that we have done something wrong is to try to keep other people from finding out about it. We may even lie about it and deny that we have done it. This only increases our sin and makes it worse.

Another thing we are tempted to do is to admit our sin but to think of it as not being very bad. This makes it even harder to give up. Obviously we are not going to give it up if we do not consider it very serious.

We cannot overcome our sin by ourselves. We must turn to God for help. This is what God invites us to do:

1. *Accept God's salvation.* God sent Jesus, who said, "I am the Good Shepherd. The Good Shepherd lays down his life for the sheep" (John 10:11, LB). Jesus gave his life for us in order that we might be forgiven, and he invites us to trust him as our Savior. This is the salvation God has offered to us.

2. *Admit that we have done wrong, and ask for forgiveness.* God will never refuse to forgive us when we come to him in this way, but he will not force us to come. "If we say that we have no sin, we are only fooling ourselves, and refusing to accept the truth. But if we confess our sins to him, he can be depended on to forgive us and to cleanse us from every wrong. (It is perfectly proper for God to do this for us because Christ died to wash away our sins.)" (1 John 1:8, 9, LB).

3. *Continue to be honest and open with Christian friends.* Never try to make excuses for your sins or to hide them from God. Ask your Christian friends to help you, and find useful ways to serve God. "If we are living in the light of God's presence, just as Christ does, then we have wonderful fellowship and joy with each other, and the blood of Jesus his Son cleanses us from every sin" (1 John 1:7, LB).

When we are trusting in Christ, and when we bring our struggles with sin to God, we may be sure that he will forgive us and help us to overcome temptations.

List words describing how you felt before asking forgiveness.

_____

_____

_____

List words describing how you felt after asking for forgiveness.

_____

_____

_____

REVIEW OF UNIT TWO

In the beginning God created everything. Because God created human beings in his own likeness, we are able to choose between right and wrong and to decide about what kind of relationships to have with God, with other people, with ourselves, and with the whole creation. When God finished his creation, it was all good, but evil came into the world when Adam and Eve sinned by choosing to disobey him. All of us have sinned, and sin brings God's judgment. Yet, he has promised never to stop loving us and to keep trying to win us back to himself.

God Chooses a Special People

CHAPTER 10
Abraham: A New Day!

God chose Abraham to be the father of a new nation. He promised to be with Abraham and his descendants, and he called them to be faithful to him. He agreed to bless them if they would obey him. This kind of agreement is called a "covenant." Abraham had faith in God and was faithful to him, but he also had doubts.

CHAPTER 11
God Keeps
His Covenant

God renewed his covenant with Abraham's descendants—Isaac, Jacob, and Joseph. They lived with their families in the land that God had promised to them until they moved to Egypt. During all this time God kept his promise to be faithful to them.

UNIT THREE

ABRAHAM
ISAAC
JACOB
JOSEPH

JESUS

| 2000 BC | 1500 BC | 1000 BC | 500 BC | 4 BC |

Abraham: a New Day!

BIBLE READING: Genesis 12:1-9
Other suggested Bible reading: Genesis 17:1-8, 15, 16

CATECHISM: WHAT IS MEANT BY A COVENANT BETWEEN GOD AND HIS PEOPLE?

A covenant between God and his people is an agreement in which God promises his care and faithfulness as his people respond in faithful obedience.

Know therefore that the Lord your God is God; he is the faithful God, keeping his covenant of love to a thousand generations of those who love him and keep his commands.

Deuteronomy 7:9, NIV

Let us return for a moment to the creation account and watch God as he brings order out of confusion. We stand in amazement as we see sky, water and earth come into focus and as all kinds of living creatures come to be. Our amazement increases as the process goes on, and with each step we might say, "It's a new day!" Those six days of creation were a preview of the way God was to continue to work. Since he is the creator,

we may expect him to do many new things, and we shall not be disappointed. As we go through the Bible and discover him at work, bringing order out of confusion, we shall have reason to say often, "It's a new day!" In this chapter we see that God called a certain person to be his special friend. This was "a new day" because it was a new step in God's plan to win people back to himself. The name of this person was "Abram," but it was later changed to "Abraham." It was a new day for Abraham and it was a new day for the world. Although Abraham lived four thousand years ago, the lives of thousands of people, including our own lives, have been influenced greatly by him. By the time of Abraham, the human race had become proud and disobedient. In Genesis 11:1-9, for instance, we read that people decided to make a name for themselves by building a tower to reach to the skies. This, of course, was impossible, but God was displeased with their pride and confused their language so they could not continue to build. The unfinished tower was called 'Babel,' which means "confusion."

How surprised Abraham must have been when God called him one day to leave his country and his own people and

go to a place to which God would guide him. How strange it must have seemed to hear God promise to make him the father of a great nation and to make him famous and a blessing to many people. We may be sure that, at this time, he had no idea of what all this might mean.

FAITH

One thing it meant was that Abraham must have faith in God and in his promises. Imagine packing up and leaving without even knowing where you are going! All he had was the promise that God would guide him. This took faith! Other people before Abraham also had faith in God, but faith was so much of a part of his life that he became the example, to all God's people, of what it means to live by faith. Abraham helps us to understand what it means to believe in God and to belong to him.

FAITHFUL OBEDIENCE

Real faith always causes us to do something. For instance, if I believed that money would rain in my backyard this evening, I would be sure to stay at home. On the other hand, if I believed that the earth would open up and swallow my house this evening, I would surely go somewhere else. We act in certain ways because of what we believe. This was true of Abraham. His faith in God caused

him to obey God. Faith that causes us to obey God is called "faithful obedience." Nothing pleases God more than faithful obedience.

FAITHFUL OBEDIENCE AND THE COVENANT

God has made an agreement with his people, known as a "covenant," in which he promises to be faithful to them and not forsake them. ★ This covenant means that God will bless his people when they are faithful to him. But it also means that he will still be faithful in punishing them when they disobey him. Therefore, according to this covenant, God will always be faithful to his people. As we trace the history of the descendants of Abraham down through the centuries we are impressed with God's faithfulness. Sometimes God brought them great blessings, and sometimes he was very severe with them, but he never gave up on them, and he never let them go. During all this time, he was showing them his care and faithfulness, as we learn from the catechism for this chapter. God renewed his covenant with Abraham's descendants from time to time. Finally he made a "New Covenant" when he sent his son, Jesus, to earth. In this covenant he has promised to give eternal life to all who trust in him. This means that we who believe in Jesus have a covenant with God and that he is also fulfilling his promise to be faithful to us.

FAITH AND DOUBT

We often misunderstand what faith is like and think that if we have faith we will have no doubts. Faith is trusting God enough to admit that sometimes we doubt, and God honors an honest confession of doubt more than a strong claim of faith that is not really sincere. Abraham, who is an example of faith, also

★ The word, "covenant," which is used here to describe the agreement God made with Abraham and his descendants, is different from the meaning of the word as it is used in the name of the denomination, "The Evangelical Covenant Church," where it refers to an agreement made by the people and churches of the denomination to work together as a family of Christians.

43

struggled with many doubts. Once, for instance, he took a detour through Egypt instead of trusting God to see him through a famine. There he resorted to lying because he thought it was the only way to keep out of trouble. From Abraham we learned that the life of faith is also a struggle with doubt. We need have no fear of doubts as long as we trust God enough to confess them to him. Once a man confessed to Jesus, "I believe, help my unbelief." When he trusted Jesus enough to confess his doubt, Jesus honored his faith.

"DOWN TO EARTH"

Beginning with Abraham we can compare the events of the Bible with events from ancient history. The history of Babylon and Egypt, particularly, runs parallel with the history recorded in the Bible. From now on we shall also be able to trace the events and movements of people on ordinary maps. The geography of the Bible is the same as the geography of this earth on which we live today, although the cities and nations generally have different names and boundaries. Abraham grew up at a place called Ur, near the Persian Gulf, and he traveled through what is now the land of Iraq. God led him to the land of Canaan, which is located on the east shore of the Mediterranean Sea and is now known as Palestine. Find Ur, Haran, and Canaan on the map below. This is the route on which God led Abraham.

HITTITES

• HARAN
PADDAN–ARAM

• NINEVEH
ASSYRIA

MEDIA
(PERSIA)

CYPRUS

MEDITERRANEAN
SEA

SIDON
TYRE
MEGIDDO
SHECHEM
JERUSALEM
GAZA
HEBRON
BEER-SHEBA

• DAMASCUS

• HAZOR

SEA of GALILEE

CANAAN

• JERICHO

DEAD SEA

BABYLONIA

BABYLON •

• SUSA

UR •

ELAM

EGYPT

• KADESH BARNEA

SINAI

ARABIA

PERSIAN
GULF

RED
SEA

THE
OLD TESTAMENT
WORLD

TP-2 © 1980 SPPI

Check Yourself

1. Describe, in your own words, what is meant by a "covenant," as the word is used in this chapter.

2. When God has a covenant with someone, what happens if that person disobeys him?

3. List three examples of faithful obedience from today's world.

In Class

If we are called to be faithful like Abraham was, what does this mean today? Write your answer in the space below:

_____

_____

_____

_____

_____

_____

_____

God Keeps His Covenant 11

BIBLE READING: About Isaac - Genesis 21:1-5
 About Jacob - Genesis 27:1-29
 About Joseph - Genesis 37:1-36
  - Genesis 45:1-15
Other suggested Bible readings: Genesis 28:10-17, Genesis 43, 44

CATECHISM: WHAT IS GOD'S PROVIDENCE?

God's providence is the care by which he upholds all that he has created and guides all according to his wisdom.

Look at the birds of the air: they neither sow nor reap nor gather into barns, and yet your heavenly Father feeds them. Are you not of more value than they?

Matthew 6:26, RSV

"Will lions snatch away our sheep?" "Can we trust the people who were here before us?" "Where will we find pasture for our flocks?" "Will the rain fail this year and will the grazing land dry up?" "Where should we dig another well?" "Where shall we build an altar to worship God?" "We are not permitted to marry the women of the land to which we have come, so how shall we find wives for our sons?" These were the kinds of questions that troubled Abraham and his growing family as they traveled about in the new land to which God had called them. The stories in the Bible about Abraham's son, Isaac, his grandson, Jacob, and his great-grandson, Joseph, are among the most interesting that have ever been written.

These were God's special friends, and through them he planned to bless the whole world. Their children and children's children for centuries to come would repeat the stories of the great things God had done for them. Isaac seemed to be a quiet and well-behaved man. Jacob, on the other hand, was such a schemer and a cheat that I am surprised God even wanted him for a friend.

Joseph was a beautiful person, and the Bible does not have one word of criticism about him.

ISAAC

Isaac was born to Abraham and his wife, Sarah, after they were too old to have children. This was God's way of proving his faithfulness to his covenant. Abraham was given a child by a miracle so he could have the many descendants God had promised him.

It was customary in those days for people to give the god they worshiped the most valuable possession they had by burning one of their own children on an altar as a sacrifice. When Isaac was a boy, God told Abraham to take him up on a mountain and sacrifice him. It must have been frightening to Isaac to be tied up by his father on a stone altar, but just as Abraham took a knife to kill Isaac, he was stopped by God. Abraham had now proven that he was willing to give everything to God. God's people were never permitted to offer human sacrifices. Although God values the willingness to make great sacrifices, he values human

Sacrificing Isaac

Jacob wrestles with God.

life even more.

There is a delightful story in Genesis 24 about the way Isaac's wife was chosen and God's part in the choice. God renewed his covenant with Isaac, and he and his wife, Rebecca, became the parents of God's people who were still to come. When Rebecca left her home to become Isaac's wife, she was given this goodbye greeting by her sisters: "Our sister, may you become the mother of millions! May your descendants overcome all your enemies" (Genesis 24:60, LB).

JACOB

Isaac and Rebecca had two sons, Esau and Jacob. Esau was an outdoor person, and he was his father's favorite, but Rebecca liked Jacob best. Normally Esau should have been the one to inherit the promises of the covenant God made with Abraham. These promises were passed on from the father to the oldest son by a special blessing. It was known as the "birthright." Jacob and his mother tricked Isaac into giving this blessing to Jacob. Esau became furious and threatened to kill Jacob, but Jacob ran away to the home of his uncle, Laban.

On his way to his uncle's home, Jacob had a dream one night that he saw angels going up and down a ladder that reached up into heaven. That night God renewed the covenant with him that he had made with his grandfather, Abraham.

Jacob fell in love with Laban's daughter, Rachel. After Jacob had worked seven

long years for the privilege of marrying Rachel, Laban tricked him into marrying her sister, Leah, instead. Men often had more than one wife in those days, and Jacob loved Rachel so much that he worked another seven years for the privilege of marrying her.

Both Laban and Jacob were schemers, and each of the two men tried to get as much as he could from the other. Some misunderstanding arose between them as to what belonged to Laban and what belonged to Jacob. The feeling between them was so bad that they set up a marker and agreed to stay on opposite sides of it.

God was faithful to the promises he had made to Abraham, and he would not go back on his word in spite of Jacob's failings. God kept on caring for Jacob. One night he came to Jacob in the form of a man, and Jacob wrestled with him. After this Jacob limped. He became a different kind of person, and God renamed him "Israel." We shall know his descendants from now on by the name of "The children of Israel," or "Israelites," or "Israel."

JOSEPH

Jacob had twelve sons, and Joseph was his favorite. This made Joseph's brothers so jealous that they determined to kill him, but they threw him into a dry well instead. Then they sold him to some traders who took him to Egypt where he became the slave of an Egyptian army officer named Potiphar.

Because Joseph refused to go to bed

Joseph and his brothers

with Potiphar's wife, as she requested, she accused him of attacking her. As a result of her accusations he landed in prison. However, he gained the favor of Pharoah, king of Egypt, by interpreting one of his dreams. Pharoah was so impressed that he gave him the highest position in the kingdom and put him in charge of his food conservation program. This program was so successful that it provided all the food that was needed during seven years when the crops would not grow because of lack of rain.

News that there was plenty to eat down in Egypt came to the ears of Joseph's brothers, and they came down to buy food. Joseph disguised himself so they would not recognize him and tested them to see if they were still just as jealous as they had been. Then he made himself known to them and forgave them for all the pain and hurt they had caused him.

Joseph pointed out that God had made all these things work together for their good. His words describe what God had been doing all the time during the lifetimes of Abraham, Isaac, Jacob, Joseph, and his brothers. In spite of all the mistakes that were made, God remained faithful, and he continued to provide for them. In so providing, God had also kept his covenant. The way God keeps on caring for his creation and for his people is described by the word, "providence." The catechism for this chapter is about God's providence, and it is illustrated by the way God cared for Joseph and his brothers.

After this experience Joseph's father and brothers moved to Egypt, and Pharoah gave them a place to live in the province of Goshen.

DATING?

JOB?

COLLEGE?

MARRIAGE?

FAMILY?

"What is my future?"

Check Yourself

1. List one way in which God was faithful to the covenant in each of the three persons mentioned in this chapter.

2. List two events in Joseph's life that seemed bad but turned out good.

In Class

This lesson teaches us that God keeps his promises even when we fail. He even uses our mistakes and the mistakes of others for good. The experience of Joseph is the best illustration of the way God uses things that were intended to be evil and causes good to come out of them. It was fortunate that Joseph was able to see what God had done and to forgive his brothers.

This is a wonderful way to look at things that happen in our lives. It is summed up in Romans 8:28, "We know that in everything God works for good with those who love him." This is what Joseph believed.

Try to think of at least one time in your life when God took something that could have been very bad and caused it to turn out good. Draw an illustration symbolizing that experience.

REVIEW OF UNIT THREE

In Unit Three we saw how God chose Abraham to be the father of a new nation, which was to be God's special people. God made a "covenant" with Abraham and with his descendants, which means that he promised to be faithful to them and that he also called them to faithful obedience to him. God kept his promise to be faithful to Abraham, Isaac, Jacob, and Joseph, and to their families.

Moses and the Wilderness

CHAPTER 12
Strength to Do the Impossible

God called a special friend, named Moses, to free his people from slavery in Egypt. God gave Moses strength to do what he had commanded him.

CHAPTER 13
Life in the Desert

God formed his people into a special nation and taught them to worship him as the true God. He showed them how to make an altar for sacrifice and a meeting place for worship, and he commanded them to gather several times each year for special festivals.

CHAPTER 14
Rules that Make Us Free

God gave his people rules to make it possible for them to keep on living as free people. The rules that are the most important to us are known as "the Ten Commandments."

UNIT FOUR

ABRAHAM
ISAAC
JACOB
JOSEPH

MOSES
Exodus (Leaving Egypt)
40 Years in the desert

JESUS

2000
BC

1300
BC

4
BC

Strength to Do the Impossible

12

BIBLE READING: Exodus 1-3
Other suggested Bible reading: Exodus 11-14

The daughter of Pharoah, king of Egypt, was bathing in the Nile River when she found a basket floating among the weeds near the edge of the water. In the basket was a crying baby. At that moment a little girl appeared, as if she had just happened to be there.

"Oh," we can hear her saying, "A baby! Where did you get it?"

"In the basket, floating on the water."

"What are you going to do with it?"

"Why, keep it, of course!"

"Do you want me to get someone who can nurse it for you?"

"Yes, please do."

Of course we don't know exactly all they said, but we do know that the girl who "just happened" to come by at that moment was the baby's sister, Miriam, who had been watching from a distance to make sure that he would be safe. She ran quickly to get her mother, whom the princess then hired as the baby's nurse, not realizing that she was paying the mother to take care of her own baby. She later named him "Moses."

Many years had passed since Joseph had brought his family to Egypt. Their descendants were known as "Hebrews" as well as "the children of Israel" or "Israelites." They had become so many that the Egyptians were afraid they would take over the whole land. The Egyptians made slaves of them and treated them cruelly, and finally, as a last resort, they began killing the boy babies to keep their population from increasing. Since Moses' parents were Hebrews, they knew that he would be killed as soon as the Egyptians discovered him. This is why his mother smeared tar on a basket to make it waterproof and put it in the water among the weeds by the edge of the river. Then she had her daughter, Miriam, watch from a distance.

Meanwhile, behind the scenes, God was choosing this baby to be another one of his special friends. Through him, God would free his people and make them into a nation, and through them he would influence millions of people, right down to our time.

52

Moses, by Michelangelo

MOSES' EARLY YEARS

After some time, Moses was brought to the palace, where he grew up as the son of Pharaoh's daughter. But he never forgot his own people, and he was greatly troubled about the way they were being treated. No doubt even then he was wondering what he could do to help them.

DOING THE RIGHT THING THE WRONG WAY

However, Moses' first attempt to help his people ended in disaster because he did it in the wrong way. He became so angry when he saw an Egyptian beating a Hebrew that he killed the Egyptian. This was not according to God's purpose, and God gave him no help. To escape from Pharaoh, Moses ran away to a place called Midian, where, for forty years, he worked as a shepherd. During those long days and nights out on the desert, Moses grew and matured. He was going to need both the education he had received as the son of the Egyptian princess and his experience on the desert to prepare him for the big job God had for him.

GOD REMEMBERS HIS COVENANT

While Moses was caring for sheep out in the desert, God was noticing the sufferings of his people as slaves in Egypt. He was not going to forget the covenant he had made with Abraham and his descendants, and he planned to set them free in a way that would be remembered by his people as one of the greatest events in history.

One day, as Moses was going about with his sheep, he saw a bush that kept burning but did not burn up. As he came closer, God spoke to him out of the bush and asked him to go back to Egypt to free his people from slavery and lead them to the land he had promised to Abraham and his descendants.

But Moses remembered his sad failure of forty years before, when he had tried to set his people free and had failed, and he was afraid to try again. God promised to help him this time and to give him the strength to do what would otherwise be impossible. He gave Moses the power to change a stick into a snake and back into a stick again and to perform other miracles. God told Moses to show these miracles to his people back in Egypt to prove to them that God was with him. When Moses objected that he could not speak well enough for this kind of work, God told him to take his brother, Aaron, with him because Aaron was a good speaker.

Upon accepting this special call to set the people free and take them to the promised land, Moses and Aaron called the leaders together and demonstrated God's special power to work miracles. This convinced the leaders that Moses and Aaron were directed by God. Then Moses and Aaron went to Pharaoh and asked him to let the people go into the desert to worship. When Pharaoh refused, they turned their stick into a snake, but this did not impress Pharaoh.

Moses and Aaron then turned the waters of the Nile River into blood, but this did not impress Pharaoh either. Then frogs, by the millions, came up out of the Nile River. They got into the houses, into the food, and into the people's beds. By this time Pharoah began to take Moses and Aaron seriously, and he promised to let the people go out and worship in the desert. As soon as the frogs disappeared, however, he went back on his promise. Next millions of tiny gnats appeared, and this was followed by swarms of flies.

Other catastrophes, sometimes called plagues, followed:
- The cattle grew sick and died.
- Boils broke out on the Egyptians.
- Hail destroyed many of the crops.
- Grasshoppers ate the crops not destroyed by hail.
- Thick darkness covered the land.

After each of these catastrophes, Pharaoh promised to let the people go, but as soon as each one was over he went back on his promise.

Finally God told Moses that he was going to cause the oldest son in every Egyptian family to die. He instructed the Israelites to place blood from a lamb on the door frames of their houses to protect their oldest sons from death. The people dressed and prepared to leave in a hurry, and they roasted and ate the meat of the lamb from which they had taken the blood, together with bitter herbs and bread without yeast.

That very night, when the oldest son in every Egyptian home died, Pharaoh ordered the people to leave, and they left quickly, before he had time to change his mind.

But Pharaoh did change his mind, and his army came charging after the Israelites as they camped by the Red Sea. Again God stepped in and saved them. He sent a strong wind that drove the water back so the Israelites could pass through. The Egyptian Army tried to follow the Israelites, but the water returned and the army was destroyed.

Moses and the people of Israel celebrated their new freedom by singing a song which began: "I will sing to the Lord, for he has triumphed gloriously; the horse and his rider he has thrown into the sea" (Exodus 15:1-18).

This great event by which God saved his people from slavery in Egypt is called "the Passover" because God "passed over" the families of his people when he destroyed the oldest son in every Egyptian home. During this time, God renewed his covenant with his people. He promised to be faithful to them and asked them to obey his commandments and be faithful to him. They agreed to what God asked them to do.

Those were great days for God's people, who had been slaves but now were set free. God proved to his people that he was able to do what he promised and that he gives to those who obey him the strength to do what would otherwise be impossible.

A Jewish family celebrating the Passover today.

Check Yourself

1. What was the main difference between Moses' first attempt to free his people, which failed, and his second attempt, in which he was successful?

2. What is the name of the event which celebrated the Israelites release from Egypt?

3. List three things to which people sometimes become slaves today, and from which they need to be set free.

In Class

From Moses we learn that God gives his special friends the strength to do what he wants them to. Read God's promise in Exodus 3:12. What does this promise mean to you as one of God's friends today? Before you respond, think of something you believe God wants you to do. Some suggestions might be:

- Make friends with someone who is lonely.
- Take your school work more seriously.
- Do or say something you know to be right even though most of your friends may not agree with you.
- Tell someone why you believe in God.

These are just a few suggestions. Now answer the question by completing the statement written below. Remember, God will be with you to help you. "I will be with you....when you

_____

_____

_____

_____

_____

_____

_____

_____

_____

_____

Life in the Desert

13

BIBLE READING: Exodus 15:22-16:36; 23:14-17
Other suggested Bible reading: Exodus 25-27; Leviticus 23

MY PARENTS AND I WERE SLAVES IN EGYPT

Our whole family was forced to work long hours making bricks and constructing buildings for Pharaoh, the great king. There was no time for fun and relaxation, and sometimes my father would be beaten if the slavemaster didn't think our family was working hard enough.

Then, suddenly, one night, we were free to leave Egypt. Moses had forced Pharaoh to let us go. My father had told me about how God had made a covenant with our great ancestor, Abraham, and had promised a land to his descendants where we could live as free people. Now God was going to fulfill his promise, and Moses was going to lead us to this new land of freedom!

The problem was that there was a hot and dry desert between us and that land. The sun kept beating down on me until I got so thirsty that I thought I couldn't stand it any longer. As the days began to pass and there was no water, everyone lost hope and began to complain. We were afraid we were all going to die of thirst, and we began to wish we were back in Egypt.

After three days we arrived at a pool of water, only to find that it was too bitter to drink. By this time we were all sure we were going to die of thirst, and everyone rushed up to Moses, shouting, "What are we going to drink?" But Moses prayed to God, and then he threw a piece of wood into the water, and the water was no longer bitter. What a relief! We all drank until we were satisfied, and our

faith in God and in Moses was restored.

Soon everyone began to complain again because we had no food. "Why have you brought us out in the desert to starve to death?" the people said to Moses. "If we are going to die anyway, why couldn't we have died in Egypt rather than out here in the desert?" Once again God came to our rescue. He caused little flakes to appear on the ground every morning. We didn't know what they were, but they were good to eat, and we called them "manna." So the whole time in the desert we had this "manna" every morning. We got terribly tired of it and complained about it, but it was better than starving to death.

Over and over again during the time in

the desert, we thought God had failed us. We complained to Moses, but God always provided what we needed. There was a cloud in front of us every day, and at night it became a flame of fire. My parents told me that God was in the cloud, leading us through the desert (Exodus 13:21, 22). Let me tell you about some of the things God did for us out in the desert:

1. GOD CHOSE US TO BE HIS VERY OWN NATION

After traveling for three months we came to a mountain called Sinai. There God met with Moses and told him about the new life we were to live as free people. God told Moses that we were to be his very own nation and that we were to obey him. When Moses reported to us what God had said, we all answered, "We will do everything the Lord has said" (Exodus 19:4-8). This was a renewal of the covenant God had first made with Abraham.

2. GOD TAUGHT US ABOUT A DIFFERENT KIND OF LIFE

While we were at Mt. Sinai, God told us about a new and different kind of life we were to live. We were to worship only one God, and we were not to have idols as the other nations had. No images were allowed because the true God could not be formed into images. God gave us many instructions about how to live as free people. We were to be a holy people, and this meant that we were to have a relationship with God and with one another that was different from all the other nations who live around us.

It was hard for us to learn these lessons because all the other people worshiped idols. Even while Moses was talking with God up on Mt. Sinai, the people persuaded Aaron to make an idol shaped like a golden calf. Then we gave thanks to this idol for helping us out of Egypt. A big feast followed, which ended up in a wild and disorderly party. God was angry with us for what we had done, but Moses prayed for the people and God forgave us.

3. GOD TAUGHT US HOW TO WORSHIP HIM

Since God wanted to be our friend, and since he wanted us to be his friends, he taught us how to meet with him through worship. He asked Moses to set apart the whole tribe of Levi to be priests. They became our spiritual leaders. They had charge of our worship, and they also interpreted God's laws and instructions to us. These are some of the things God told us in order to make our worship meaningful:
1) *God told us how to make an altar of sacrifice.*

We had always used altars. Whenever we needed to meet God we would build an altar of stone and worship him by sacrificing an animal. Now, however, God showed us how to make an altar on which we would offer sacrifices as part of our regular worship. The people would bring their animals to the priest, and he would sacrifice them on the altar. My parents explained to me that blood was very sacred because the life of the animal was in the blood. In some ways that I could not understand, the animal gave its life and shed its blood so that the person who had sinned might be forgiven (see Leviticus 17:11).

The tabernacle or the tent of meeting

2) *God gave instructions for making a tent where he would meet his people.*

Under the tent was a room made of boards. This room was divided by a curtain into "the holy place" and "the most holy place." The most sacred of all the furnishings of this tent stood in the most holy place. It was a chest made of wood and overlaid with gold, and it was called "the ark of the covenant." On the cover of the ark of the covenant were two golden angelic figures facing each other. This cover was known as "the mercy seat," and it represented the presence of God among his people.

Around the tent was a courtyard in which stood the altar where sacrifices were made. There were sacrifices for the forgiveness of sin, and there were also sacrifices of thanksgiving.

The tent was made so it could be taken apart and carried by the priests as we continued our journey. When we stopped it was set up again, and the people all camped around it. This tent reminded us that God was always with us, right in the center of the camp, wherever we traveled in the desert.

3) *God told us to gather regularly for special festivals.*

When we got to the promised land, we were supposed to come together at least three times each year in festivals that were like camps or conferences. The first of these festivals was during the spring of the year when we were to celebrate the "Feast of Unleavened Bread." For one week we were supposed to eat bread without yeast. One night during this time we were to eat roasted lamb with bitter herbs, as we had during the night of the Passover in Egypt. All of this was to remind us of how God had freed us from slavery. The second great festival was the "Feast of Harvest," when we were to bring the first of our new crops to the Lord. The third festival was the "Feast of Ingathering," which was to be celebrated when the crops had been harvested. This was also known as the "Feast of Booths," because we had lived in little "booths" or huts when we came out of Egypt (see Exodus 23:14-17).

We also had festivals which were special holy days. Our most holy celebration was the "Day of Atonement," when the High Priest was to make sacrifices for the sins of all the people and sprinkle blood from the sacrificial animal on the ark of the covenant. These great festivals were intended to keep the people together and to help us all remember how God had set us free from slavery and brought us to our own land.

During these festivals we were never supposed to do any work. The same was true of every seventh day, which was called the "Sabbath." On this day we must rest because God rested on the seventh day after he had created the heavens and the earth.

I am grateful for all that God did for us in the desert. He made us into a nation and accepted us as his very own people. He gave us rules to help us survive as a free people. He appointed priests to be our spiritual leaders. He gave us a meeting place and showed us how to worship him and to make sacrifices for our sins. He assigned special times for us to come and worship him. Through all of these things God helped us to see that we are a special people.

A SAD AND A HAPPY ENDING

The end of my story is both sad and happy. The sad part is that when we got to the border of the promised land, the people refused to enter. They received reports that it would be too difficult to conquer the land, and they refused to believe that God, who had been with us all through the desert, would also bring us into the land. Because the people refused to believe God, he said that we must all stay out in the desert for forty years, until all the people over twenty years of age had died, except for two men who tried to persuade the people to enter. A few days after my father died, I brought a special sacrifice to the priest, who offered it for me. Then I made a promise that I would keep the covenant and prayed that I would be worthy to enter the promised land. The happy ending of my story is that I was one of those who was permitted to come all the way from Egypt and to enter the land God had promised to Abraham long ago.

Check Yourself

1. Why do you think it was so hard for the people to trust God after he had done so much for them?

2. What were the three main festivals and what did they celebrate?

3. Compare and contrast the worship of the Israelites with our worship today.

In Class

After thinking about the situations described by your teacher, write your response to the following question: What difference does God make in your life?

_____

_____

_____

_____

_____

_____

_____

_____

Rules that Make Us Free

BIBLE READING: Exodus 20:1-17
Other suggested Bible reading: Exodus 31:18-34:17

ASSIGNMENT: Memorize the Ten Commandments, either as they are written in this chapter or as they are written in the version of the Bible which your teacher suggests.

Have you noticed how quickly and freely a basketball player moves? Muscles seem to respond naturally in order to give the greatest strength and speed. The player got that way by following the training rules. The hands of the pianist move freely over the keyboard as though it were the most natural thing to do. The pianist can do this only by hours of practice and by following the rules of music. In the same way, the space ship that flies free from the earth's gravitation follows the rules of space flight. It seems strange, but we follow laws in order to be free.

When the Israelites were camped at Mt. Sinai, God gave Moses some laws to give the people. The most important of these were the Ten Commandments. These were laws to make them free. God said,

I am the LORD your God, who brought you out of Egypt, out of the land of slavery (Exodus 20:2, NIV).

Since he had brought his people out of slavery, he was giving them rules that would make it possible for them to live as free people.

Following are the Ten Commandments, together with some ideas of what they mean to us as Christians. They are quoted from Exodus 20:1-17 in the New International Version. (In the second and fourth commandments, only parts are included.)

1) I am the LORD your God, who brought you out of Egypt, out of the land of slavery. You shall have no other gods before me.

The first difference between the worship of the God of Israel and the worship of the gods of other nations was that the Israelites were to worship only one God.

We make gods of other things or people when they are more important to us than God is. He wants us to love and respect him as our heavenly Father.

2) You shall not make for yourselves an idol in the form of anything in heaven above or on the earth beneath or in the waters below.

You shall not bow down to them or worship them.

God is a Spirit, and we cannot see him. Many of the things, such as truth, faith and love, which are important to God, cannot be seen either. We break this commandment when we become more interested in things we can see than in God.

3) You shall not misuse the name of the LORD your God, for the LORD will not hold anyone guiltless who misuses his name.

If we were to make a solemn promise and say, "Yes, by God," or, "No, by God," we would be using God's name to emphasize that we were telling the truth. Then, if we did not keep that promise, we would be misusing God's name. We really do not need to use God's name at all in making a promise. If we are honest, all we need to say is, "Yes," or "No," and if we are dishonest, we only increase our sin by using God's name dishonestly. Using "swear" words which include God's name merely as an expression is also a misuse of his name.

4) Remember the Sabbath day by keeping it holy.

The word, "Sabbath," means, "rest." When we take time to rest and give thanks to God, and when we are faithful in meeting with other Christians regularly for worship and the study of his Word, we are obeying this commandment. The New Testament teaches us that we receive God's gift of "rest" when we have peace in our hearts because we trust in God and obey him. Therefore, the Sabbath for Christians is not just one certain day in the week. We obey this commandment by trusting God every day and worshiping him regularly with other Christians.

5) Honor your father and your mother, so that you may live long in the land the LORD your God is giving you.

We honor our parents by respecting them and by recognizing that they are responsible for us. This commandment is

obeyed in the best way when all the members of the family respect one another even when they disagree.

6) You shall not murder.

Murder begins with hatred, and we break this commandment not only by killing, but also by having hateful feelings toward someone.

7) You shall not commit adultery.

This commandment teaches us that God considers marriage to be very important. He wants us to respect marriage, and his people can be happy and free only when their marriages are honored by faithfulness. Sexual relations are proper between husbands and wives who respect their relationship and love one another. Sexual relations under other circumstances are against God's law. He will help his people to keep sexual desire under control by other satisfying relationships.

8) You shall not steal.

Stealing is condemned throughout the whole Bible. We steal from others not only by taking things that belong to them, but also by denying them their rights. Stealing is sinful even when we take small things that will never be missed because stealing destroys our own self-respect while it hurts other people.

9) You shall not give false testimony against your neighbor.
The Bible emphasizes the importance of being honest in everything we say and do. In addition to lying, this commandment can be broken without saying a word, by just failing to correct a false impression.

10) You shall not covet your neighbor's house. You shall not covet your neighbor's wife, or his manservant or maidservant, his ox or donkey, or anything that belongs to your neighbor.
To covet is to have a strong desire for something we have no right to have. This commandment teaches us that we should be content and not let ourselves become jealous of people who have things we do not have.

JESUS AND THE TEN COMMANDMENTS

Once, when Jesus was asked which was the greatest commandment, he answered, " 'Love the Lord your God with all your heart, with all your soul, and with all your mind.' This is the greatest and most important commandment. The second most important commandment is like it: 'Love your neighbor as you love yourself.' The whole Law of Moses and the teachings of the prophets depend on these two commandments" (Matthew 22:37-40, TEV).

Jesus taught us that God is our loving Father. He has brought God's love to us and made it possible for us to love God and other people in return. Through love we fulfill the commandments in all our relationships. We need the commandments to show us how to express God's love, and the love we express is his gift to us. This is good news to us about the commandments because it means that they are not rules that make slaves of us. With God's love in our hearts and with Jesus to help us and to forgive us when we fail, they are really rules that make us free.

Discuss the picture. What does or is it supposed to say?

Check Yourself

1. What was the basic difference between the worship of the God of Israel and the worship in other nations?

2. Which of the Ten Commandments have to do with our relationship to God, and which have to do with our relationship to other people?

3. What did Jesus teach about the commandments?

In Class

Select one of the Ten Commandments that is hard for you to obey and write a prayer asking for God's help in that area of your life. You may write it either in the space below or on a separate paper if you prefer:

_____

_____

_____

_____

_____

_____

_____

REVIEW OF UNIT FOUR

God called Moses and gave him strength to set his people free from slavery in Egypt. The way God set them free is called the "Passover." God was faithful to his people while they passed through the desert even though they complained to him. He showed them how to make an altar, which was to be used for worship in a special meeting place, and he told them to gather at certain times for "festivals." In this way he taught them how to receive forgiveness and worship him. God also gave them rules by which to live as free people. For us, the most important of these rules are known as "the Ten Commandments." When Jesus came, many centuries later, he helped us to understand more clearly what it means to obey these rules.

Settling in
the New Land

CHAPTER 15
Joshua: the Promise Kept

God kept his promise and brought his people he had promised to Abraham and his descendants. Joshua was their leader when they entered the land.

CHAPTER 16
Getting Started in the New Land

After the people entered the land, they were ruled by judges for about two hundred years. They faced many problems as they struggled with the people who had lived in the land, and they often gave in to the temptation to disobey God and become like these other people.

CHAPTER 17
The Rule of the Judges

Lessons from a few of the judges show us how God taught his people by being faithful to bless them when they obeyed him and by being faithful to punish them when they disobeyed.

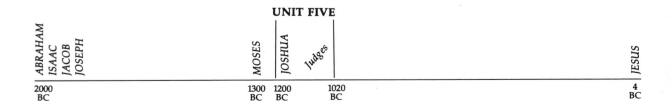

UNIT FIVE

ABRAHAM
ISAAC
JACOB
JOSEPH

MOSES

JOSHUA

Judges

JESUS

2000
BC

1300
BC

1200
BC

1020
BC

Joshua: the Promise Kept

BIBLE READING: Joshua 1-6
Other suggested Bible readings: Deuteronomy 31, 34

MOSES, THE GREAT LEADER, DIES
(Joshua 1:1)

God would not let Moses enter the land because he had disobeyed him in a fit of anger. Before he died, however, God took him to the top of a mountain where he could see the promised land.

Moses had been a great leader, and when he died the people felt a great loss, but God was faithful and promised to be with them even though they would now have a new leader.

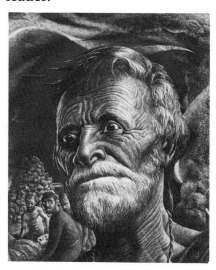

A NEW LEADER TAKES OVER
(Joshua 1:2-4)

Before Moses died, he trained his assistant, Joshua, to be the next leader. Through this new, young leader, God was now going to bring his people into the land he had promised them.

GOD PROMISES STRENGTH
FOR HIS WORK
(Joshua 1:5-9)

Before Joshua took over his new work, God repeated the promise he had made to Moses. He told Joshua that he would be with him and give him strength to lead the people into the land.

THE PEOPLE GET READY
(Joshua 1:10, 11)

The people could not just sit and wait for God to do everything for them. They had to gather supplies and prepare themselves to enter the land. If they expected God to do his part, they had to do their part.

RAHAB TRUSTS IN GOD
(Joshua 2:1-14)

There was a woman named Rahab, who lived in Jericho, which was the first city the Israelites were to destroy. She protected the spies that the Israelites had sent into Jericho because she trusted in God. Because she acted in faith, the spies promised her that she would be saved, and she believed their promise.

THE PEOPLE FOLLOW
THE ARK OF THE COVENANT
(Joshua 3:1-6)

We have already learned about the golden chest which was known as "the Ark of the Covenant." Now, as they began crossing the Jordan River, which separated them from the promised land, some of the priests carried it ahead of them. Since God was always present with the Ark of the Covenant, this emphasized that he was still their leader, and they were his followers.

THEY MARCH THROUGH THE JORDAN RIVER
(Joshua 3:14-17)

It was a miracle! As soon as the priests who carried the Ark of the Covenant stepped into the river, the water moved back and let them through! Here they learned the lesson that they must trust God by making a start. As they stepped into the water, God moved it back so they could cross.

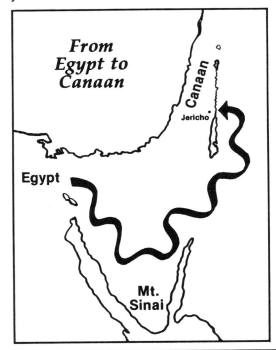

From Egypt to Canaan

THEY BUILD A MONUMENT
(Joshua 4:1-10)

The people took twelve stones out of the bottom of the river and used them to build a monument. God commanded them to do this because he wanted them to have something to help them remember the time when he had led them across the Jordan River.

THEY WORSHIP GOD (Joshua 5:10-12)

Now they no longer received any more "manna," the food which God had given them in the desert. At last they had fresh food to eat, and they took the time to thank him for all he had done for them. They celebrated their escape from Egypt and their entrance into the promised land by eating the same kind of food they had eaten the night they left Egypt. This was called "eating the Passover." God commanded them to "eat the Passover" once every year.

THEY MARCH AROUND JERICHO
(Joshua 6:1-15)

God commanded them to march around Jericho every day for six days, with the priests marching ahead and blowing trumpets. On the seventh day they were to march around the city seven times and to shout loudly. This may have seemed silly to them, but God was teaching them that they must do things his way rather than their way. They must obey him and trust him to win their battles.

68

city. When the Israelites finally shouted as God had told them to do, the walls "came tumbling down," and they captured the city.

RAHAB IS RESCUED (Joshua 6:22, 23)

When the city was captured, Rahab and her family were spared because she had believed the promise the spies had given her and had trusted in God.

GOD KEEPS HIS PROMISE

God had kept his promise! At last they were entering the land he had promised to Abraham, Isaac, and Jacob long ago! They were no longer slaves in Egypt, and their wanderings in the desert were over. They were free people, and this was the beginning of a new chapter in their lives.

"THE WALLS CAME TUMBLING DOWN" (Joshua 6:16-21)

The people did as God had commanded. There was no fighting because the people of Jericho had locked themselves inside the walls which were around the

Check Yourself

1. To what promise does the title of this chapter refer?

2. Why did the people build a monument after crossing the Jordan River?

3. Describe in one or two words the feeling of the people of each of the following events:

a. When Joshua became the leader.

b. As they walked through the river into the promised land.

c. When told to march around the city of Jericho.

d. When the walls of Jericho fell down.

In Class

Imagine that we are a group of the descendants of the people who entered the land of promise. But first take a few moments to practice pronouncing the word, "Ar-a-me-an." (This is another name for the nationality of Jacob.)

We have come to the place of worship with a sample of the crops. God has made it possible for us to grow them and we are bringing them to him as an offering. After giving the offering to the priest, we recite the following, which we shall now read in unison: "My ancestor was a wandering Aramean, who took his family to Egypt to live. They were few in number when they went there, but they became a large and powerful nation. The Egyptians treated us harshly and forced us to work as slaves. Then we cried out for help to the LORD, the God of our ancestors. He heard us and saw our suffering, hardship and misery. By his great power and strength he rescued us from Egypt. He worked miracles and wonders, and caused terrifying things to happen. He brought us here and gave us this rich and fertile land. So now I bring to the LORD this first part of the harvest that he has given me" (Deuteronomy 26:5-10, TEV).

Now try to think of something special that God has done for you or for your parents or grandparents for which you are thankful.

Getting Started in the New Land

16

BIBLE READING: Judges 2:11-23
Other suggested Bible reading: Judges 3:11-30

CATECHISM: WHAT IS SALVATION?

Salvation is the work of God through Christ which liberates people from sin and restores them to a right relationship with God.

Salvation is to be found through him alone; in all the world there is no one else whom God has given who can save us.

Acts 4:12, TEV

The Promised Land, which the Israelites had now entered, was called "Canaan," and the people who lived there were known as "Canaanites." Actually, the Canaanites only occupied a small part of the land. It was shared with several different small nations with strange names, like Jebusites, Ammonites, Hivites, Midianites, and Philistines. The Israelites were supposed to wipe out every trace of these people and to destroy everything they owned. The battles were violent and cruel.

To enter a land and drive out the people who were already settled there, and to do it in such a bloody way, seems entirely wrong for us Christians. We must remember, however, that those times were much different, and some of the rules by which the people of Israel lived were different from ours.

One reason for the severe treatment of the people of the land was their great wickedness and the danger that they would lead the Israelites away from God. These other people worshiped animals and other natural objects, and they engaged in forbidden sexual acts and other immoral practices, including the sacrificing of human beings to their gods. Distasteful as some of these practices were, they were also very tempting. The Israelites never succeeded in driving these other people from the land. The Canaanites continued to lead the Israelites away from God for many centuries.

THE LAW OF RETRIBUTION, OR "PAYING BACK"

Another reason for the violence was the Law of Retribution, which required that any harm done was to be "paid back" to the person who did it, "a life for a life, an eye for an eye, a tooth for a tooth."

According to the standards of the Israelites, the people of the land had lived so violently that they had lost all rights to live any longer and deserved to die as violently as they had lived. Therefore, the Israelites were to destroy them.

Jesus replaced the Law of Retribution with a law that requires us to forgive our enemies and to try to help them do better. Christians believe in discipline and punishment for crime, but we do not believe in cruel punishment or in "paying back" one evil by another.

The Law of Retribution is found in Deuteronomy 19:19-21. Here is the new law Jesus gave us to follow:
"You have heard that it was said, 'An eye for an eye and a tooth for a tooth.' But I

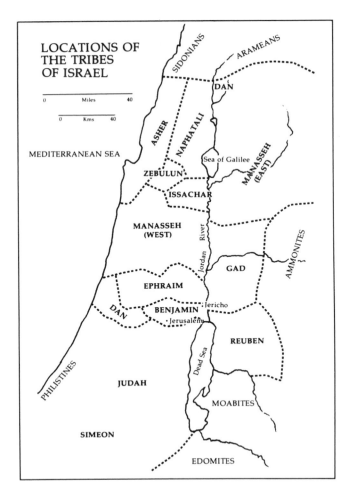

LOCATIONS OF THE TRIBES OF ISRAEL

SIDONIANS
ARAMEANS
DAN
ASHER
NAPHTALI
MEDITERRANEAN SEA
Sea of Galilee
ZEBULUN
MANASSEH (EAST)
ISSACHAR
MANASSEH (WEST)
Jordan River
AMMONITES
GAD
EPHRAIM
DAN
BENJAMIN
Jericho
Jerusalem
REUBEN
PHILISTINES
Dead Sea
JUDAH
MOABITES
SIMEON
EDOMITES

ed. It also shows the location of some of the people who already lived in the land when the Israelites came.

THE JUDGES

The leaders of the people for about two hundred years after they entered the land were known as "judges." They were not kings; God was the King. The judges received God's messages and gave them to the people. They handled complaints, settled arguments, and punished criminals. Most of them were military leaders who gained the respect of the people by leading them to victory over their enemies.

say to you, Do not resist one who is evil. But if anyone strikes you on the right cheek, turn to him the other also; and if anyone would sue you and take your coat, let him have your cloak as well; and if anyone forces you to go one mile, go with him two miles" (Matthew 5:38-41).

THE TWELVE TRIBES

The people were divided into twelve large families, called "tribes." Each tribe descended from one of the twelve sons of Jacob. Each of them was given a certain part of the land of Canaan, except the tribe of Levi, who served as priests and religious leaders. There still were twelve divisions in the land because the descendants of Joseph were divided into two tribes, named after Joseph's two sons, Ephraim and Manasseh. The map just above shows where the tribes were locat-

THE VICIOUS CIRCLE

After all the wonderful experiences through which God had taken the people and the way he had protected them and shown his love for them, it would seem that they would have obeyed his commands and followed him. This, however, was not the case. They were not even settled in the land before they turned away from God and began to take part in all the evil practices of the idol worshipers around them. When this happened, God deserted them to their enemies, and they were reduced to slavery and poverty. Then, when they realized what had happened and that God had deserted them, they cried out to him, and he led them to victory over their enemies again. Then they soon turned away from God once more, and the whole cycle was repeated. This is the way the story went, over and over:

1. The people turned away from God and sinned.
2. They were defeated by their enemies.
3. They were sorry and cried out to God for help.
4. God heard them and rescued them from their enemies.

THE FIRST JUDGES

The vicious circle began as soon as Joshua died. The people immediately turned away from God, and God let them become slaves of the king of Mesopotamia, one of the nations nearby. When they cried out to God he raised up the first judge, Othniel, who led them to victory, and they were free again. As soon as Othniel died, the people fell into sin and disobeyed God once more. This time he allowed Eglon, the king of the Moabites, to rule over them for eighteen years. Then the people cried out to the Lord for help, and he raised up Ehud to be their judge. Ehud was the person who took the money to Eglon which the Israelites were required to pay the Moabites. Ehud killed King Eglon with a homemade sword when he brought the money to him. Then Ehud blew a trumpet and called all the Israelites together, and they defeated the Moabites and had freedom and peace for eighty years. After Ehud died another judge, named Shamgar, ruled for a short time, but the people turned away from God again. This time God allowed them to become slaves of the Canaanites, and the vicious circle was repeated.

SALVATION

It is from this vicious circle during the days of the judges that we learn the meaning of the word "salvation." Here we discover that it was God who saved the people from their enemies. But we also discover that it was their sins that got them into trouble with their enemies in the first place. If they had not sinned they would not have been in trouble, and when they did sin, they needed God's forgiveness and help to get them out of trouble. Therefore, they learned that salvation really meant salvation from their sins.

The catechism for this chapter tells us that God, through Christ, sets us free from sin. This is something the judges could not do. All that any judge could do was to save the people from their enemies. Then, when that judge died, the people went right back to sinning again, and their enemies again made slaves of them. God sent Jesus to "save his people from their sins" (Matthew 1:21). This is far better news than the news of a new judge, who could never save the people from this vicious circle.

Check Yourself

1. How did Jesus change the Law of Retribution?

2. What are some differences between the salvation which the judges brought their people from God and the salvation which Jesus brings?

3. What are the four parts of the Vicious Circle?

In Class

After working on the story of Ehud, create a simple diagram describing the conditions that existed before, during, and after Ehud. You may draw the diagram in the space below:

The Rule of the Judges

17

BIBLE READING:

    About Deborah—Judges 4
    About Gideon—Judges 6, 7
    About Samson—Judges 14-16

During the time of the judges, God was letting his people learn through their own unhappy experiences that wrongdoing does not pay. By deserting them to their enemies when they sinned, he taught them that sin leads to slavery. Then, by rescuing them from their enemies when they repented and cried out to him, he taught them that he was their Savior, and that obedience to him led to freedom and victory.

They were not able to learn these lessons very well at the time, but they would look back to these experiences and tell these stories for centuries to come in order to remind themselves and their children that the way to be free from sin and its consequences is to trust God and obey him. In fact, this is the reason we repeat these stories in Confirmation, for it is just as important for us, in our time, to remember that sin always leads to slavery and that the only way to freedom is through repentance and obedience to God.

In this chapter we shall describe the life and work of three of the judges; Deborah, Gideon, and Samson.

DEBORAH

"The people of Israel again did what was evil in the sight of the LORD, after Ehud died" (Judges 4:1). This time God allowed them to become captives of the Canaanites, whose king was Jabin and whose commander-in-chief was a man named Sisera. The Israelites were powerless against the Canaanite army, which included nine hundred iron chariots. When they cried out to the Lord, he chose a prophetess named Deborah to deliver them. She called on Barak, one of the Israelites' battle leaders, to gather an army of 10,000 men. Barak agreed to go to battle if Deborah would go with him. Together they were successful in defeating the Canaanites, and Sisera was killed by a woman who posed as his friend. The Song of Deborah and Barak, which is recorded in Judges 5, celebrates their victory. Following the defeat of the Canaanites, the land was at peace for forty years.

GIDEON

"The people of Israel did what was evil in the sight of the LORD; and the LORD gave them into the hand of Midian for seven years" (Judges 6:1). Again the same vicious circle was being repeated. The people had to hide in caves and dens in

the mountains to protect themselves from the Midianites. When the people again cried out to the Lord, he chose Gideon to lead them to freedom.

The special lesson from the victory of Gideon is in the tiny army he used to fight the great Midianite army. God told Gideon that the thirty-two thousand men he had gathered was too large an army, and Gideon reduced it to ten thousand. God said that this was still too many, and Gideon reduced it to a mere three hundred persons. How could three hundred men defeat the Midianite army? It could be done only with God's help. By this means, God wanted to teach Israel that they must depend on him for victory and that without him they were powerless. With a larger army they would have boasted that they defeated the Midianites by their own strength. With only three hundred men, however, it was obvious that they would never have been victorious without God's help.

Gideon's message for us is that we must depend on God to overcome the evil forces that would make slaves of us and destroy us. The way to victory over our spiritual enemies is to recognize our weakness and seek God's help. We must fight, as Gideon did, but the strength comes from the Lord.

SAMSON

We read in Judges 13:1, "The people of Israel again did what was evil in the sight of the LORD; and the LORD gave

them into the hand of the Philistines for forty years." This time a man named Samson became their leader. Samson was dedicated by his parents to become a special servant of God. His gift for fighting the Philistines was his great strength, and he kept this gift as long as he obeyed God's command never to cut his hair. He was attracted to Philistine women, and this attraction finally led to his fall. One of these women, Delilah, persuaded him to tell her the secret of his strength. She cut off his hair while he was asleep, and the Philistines captured him, put his eyes out, and imprisoned him. In prison his hair grew long again, and he turned to the Lord, who heard his prayer. His last act of valor was to pull down the pillars of a banquet hall filled with the leaders of the Philistines, who had brought him there to entertain them. Samson died together with hundreds of Philistines when the building caved in.

Samson must have been one of the strangest of all God's special friends. His own life left much to be desired morally. He worked alone, and there are few if any signs of his influence for good among his people. He seems to be as much a part of their problems as a solution. We can learn as much from his mistakes, and the importance of avoiding them, as we can from his accomplishments.

A TIME OF MORAL DECLINE

Samson seems to be a part of a general moral decline that was affecting the whole nation. Following the story of his life, the Book of Judges describes some of the most wicked practices of which human beings are capable. In fact, it is a mark of the honesty of the Bible that it does not try to cover up this wickedness. Meanwhile, God continued patiently to teach his people by allowing them to learn from their mistakes. He always remained faithful to them. When they sinned he was faithful in turning them over to their enemies, and when they cried out to him, he was faithful in saving them from these same enemies. In either case, he never gave up on his people.

THE BOOK OF RUTH

In the middle of all this corruption and violence, we find the Book of Ruth. Here is a beautiful story of a Moabite woman, the widow of an Israelite, who found peace, friendship, care, and love among the Israelite people. The Book of Ruth is important because it tells us that life in Israel under the judges had another side. There were many good people who wanted nothing more than to live in peace with their neighbors, to do their daily work, to obey the law, and to serve their God

faithfully. To read the Book of Ruth is to discover that God really had some very fine friends during those days.

THE MESSAGE OF THIS CHAPTER: GOD'S FAITHFULNESS

The most important thing we learn from this chapter is that God is faithful both when we do wrong and when we do right. When we do wrong he is faithful in punishing us, so that wrongdoing leads us into trouble. This teaches us that wrongdoing does not pay, but God is always waiting, ready to forgive us when we are sorry for what we have done wrong and cry out for forgiveness.

Check Yourself

1. Why did God want Gideon to have such a small army? What lesson does this have for us?

2. What does the story of Ruth tell us about life in Israel during the time of the Judges?

3. How do you suppose God felt when his people kept turning against him over and over again? Why did he not give up on them?

In Class

In the following space draw a diagram to describe the repeating vicious circle of 1) sin, 2) judgment, 3) crying out to God, 4) God's forgiveness and salvation from enemies. How does this diagram compare with the diagram of Ehud's life in the last chapter?

After completing the diagram, write your answer to the following question in the space below: "How does this diagram apply to today?"

_____

_____

_____

_____

_____

_____

_____

_____

_____

_____

REVIEW OF UNIT FIVE

After Moses died, God chose another leader, Joshua, to lead his people into the land he had promised them. For about two hundred years they were ruled by judges. During this time the people kept going through a "vicious circle" which included 1) disobedience to God, 2) defeat by their enemies, 3) crying out to God for help, 4) victory over their enemies with God's help. In this way God taught them that he was faithful, both in punishing them when they did wrong and in blessing them when they returned to him.

The First Kings

CHAPTER 18
Saul, Israel's First King

Saul, the first king, failed because he would rather go his own way than God's way.

CHAPTER 19
David, the Shepherd King

Israel's greatest king was David. Although he committed sins, he kept a good relationship with God by being truly sorry for his sins and turning to God for forgiveness.

CHAPTER 20
Solomon: a Wise King, but Not Wise Enough

Solomon's wrong choices caused him and his people many problems.

CHAPTER 21
The Psalms: the Songs of God's People

The Psalms are a form of poetry through which God's people may express their faith and their feelings. From them we learn how important singing is in our worship.

CHAPTER 22
Wisdom for God's People

From the Wisdom Literature we learn that it is not only bad to disobey God, but it is also stupid. Wise people obey God and do what is right.

UNIT SIX

ABRAHAM ISAAC JACOB JOSEPH		MOSES	JOSHUA	Judges	SAUL	DAVID	SOLOMON		JESUS
2000 BC		1300 BC	1200 BC		1020 BC	1000 BC	961 BC		4 BC

Saul, Israel's First King

18

BIBLE READINGS: 1 Samuel 3, 8-10, 15

A NEW CHAPTER IN ISRAEL'S HISTORY

The period of the rule of the judges is about to come to an end, and the history of God's people, Israel, is about to enter a new chapter. From the beginning the people of Israel had recognized God as their king; they needed no other king. Government was simple and inexpensive. All it required was a system of judges, who led the people in battle, interpreted the law, and held court. However, there were signs that the people were growing weary of this simple kind of government. Judges may have been good enough when the people first came off the desert, but now they wanted to have a king like other nations.

SAMUEL

Samuel, the last judge, had been an honest and wise man and the people respected him, but when they discovered that his sons were corrupt and godless, they demanded that Samuel appoint a king "to govern us like all the nations." Samuel warned them that a king would not eliminate corruption. He would levy heavy taxes to make himself rich. He would expect contributions of farm produce and animals. He would take the best of the land and he would demand that the people work for him. When the people still insisted, God told Samuel to do as they asked. They were really rejecting the rule of God by choosing the rule of a king. However, they had already rejected God's rule by disobeying him time after time. Therefore, God said, they may as well have their wish. So, this was to be the beginning of a new chapter for Israel—the rule of the kings.

SAUL

Samuel anointed a man named Saul, who was installed as Israel's first king. Saul was a humble man, who could hardly believe that this great honor had been bestowed on him. Since he came from a wealthy family, he was well prepared for royal life. He was strong, tall and hand-

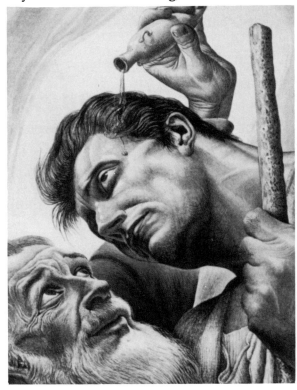

some, and he soon proved himself to be a successful military leader. Everyone was happy about the decision that was made, especially when Saul began to win battles. However, Saul had one problem—he could not remember that even though he was a king he must submit to God and obey him. He disobeyed God and as a result God rejected him as king over Israel. The words which Samuel spoke to Saul when he discovered what Saul had done are worth remembering:

"Has the Lord as much pleasure in your burnt offerings and sacrifices as in your obedience? Obedience is far better than sacrifice. He is much more interested in your listening to him than in your offering the fat of rams to him" (1 Samuel 15:22, LB).

What this means for us is that it is more important to obey God than to go through the forms of worshiping him. Worship is important, but it is of no value to us unless we also seek to do God's will.

God told Samuel to anoint another king to take Saul's place, and he led him to a shepherd boy named David, the youngest son of a man named Jesse. Saul could just as well have given up when he learned that God had rejected him and chosen someone else to rule in his place. However, he was too stubborn to do that. He was jealous of David and kept fighting him and trying to kill him. Saul's life became more and more of a tragedy, and finally he committed suicide.

SAUL'S WAY—OR GOD'S WAY

Saul is an example of a person who made the wrong choices. When he was faced with a decision, he chose to do what seemed best for him even though it was against God's will. Saul had every reason to be a winner, but he turned out to be a loser, merely because he chose to do things his way rather than God's way.

Check Yourself

1. Why did the people want a king?

2. What was Samuel's warning concerning a king?

3. What might be some reasons why a person like Saul would disobey God after God had honored him by making him a king?

In Class

We cannot always follow the example of others in making choices because so many people have made the wrong choices:

- Adam and Eve made the wrong choice.
- Cain made the wrong choice.
- Everyone on earth except Noah and his family made the wrong choice.
- Moses made the wrong choice when he tried to rescue his people by killing an Egyptian.
- The people of Israel made the wrong choice when they refused to enter the promised land.

- Many people made the wrong choice during the time of the judges.
- Now here is King Saul, with the opportunity to become a great leader and spoiling it all by making the wrong choice.
- Many of the problems in the world today are caused by people making the wrong choices.

In the Ten Commandments and in other parts of the Bible which we shall study, God tells us what his will is. Before making a choice we should:

1. Try to find out what God's will is in this choice.
2. Listen to our conscience.
3. Pray to God to help us.
4. Follow the example of people who are seeking to do God's will.
5. Always ask the question, when making a choice, "Is this God's way or is it my way?"

What are some choices that seem difficult to make according to God's will?

_____

_____

_____

_____

_____

_____

David, the Shepherd King

BIBLE READING: 1 Samuel 16:1-13 (Where David was anointed to be king)
2 Samuel 5:1-10 (Where David was made king)
2 Samuel 7:18-29 (David's prayer)
Other suggested Bible readings: 1 Samuel 17:1-50 (Where David killed the giant)
2 Samuel 11:1-12:15 (David and Bathsheba)

ASSIGNMENT: Memorize Psalm 139:1-12, 23, 24

David was the king whom Israel remembered as its greatest. There was something about his colorful personality that caused people to admire him. When the prophets predicted the coming of Jesus, whom they called "the Messiah," they spoke of him as a descendant of David, and when Jesus finally came, he was called "the Son of David." David's life can be an example to us in many ways, but it is also a warning, for he was far from perfect.

One of the reasons David was so popular was that he was a common person. He lived simply, and the costs of government were comparatively low during his reign. His closest friends were the people who had been with him long before he became king, and he never removed himself from the common people. We shall think of David's life by describing his relationships with those whom he knew.

DAVID AND SAMUEL

Samuel would remember David as the son of Jesse, as the shepherd boy who seemed the least suited of all Jesse's sons to become king. The Lord reminded Samuel, at the time when Samuel anointed David to be king:

"The LORD sees not as man sees; man looks on the outward appearance, but the LORD looks on the heart" (1 Samuel 16:7).

DAVID AND SAUL

David played the harp for Saul when he was troubled. Later, when it became obvious that David would replace him as king, Saul became so jealous that he tried to kill him. However, David always respected Saul as the man whom God had chosen to be king, and he refused to harm him.

DAVID AND GOLIATH

David's fame began when he entered into a one-to-one battle with the Philistine giant, Goliath. Goliath was covered with his armor and he ridiculed David as he came running toward him with only a slingshot, but David killed the giant with one stone. Goliath has become a symbol of the great evils that stand in our way when we seek to do God's will. The words of David as he approached Goliath are worth remembering when we meet such evils: "You come to me with a sword and with a spear and with a javelin; but I come to you in the name of the LORD . . . . The LORD saves not with sword and spear; for the battle is the LORD'S" (1 Samuel 17:45, 47).

DAVID AND JONATHAN

Jonathan was the son of King Saul. Yet the friendship between David and Jonathan was so deep that they remained loyal to one another even though Saul was David's enemy. Jonathan saved David from Saul, his father, and David grieved deeply when he heard of the death of Jonathan on the battlefield.

DAVID AND THE NATION

Immediately after the death of Saul, David was made king of the tribe of Judah. After seven years the other tribes also accepted him as king. This division between the tribe of Judah and the other tribes of Israel was never fully healed. The tribe of Judah became known as "Judah," and the other tribes became known as "Israel." Judah eventually became "the Southern Kingdom," and Israel became "the Northern Kingdom."

David united the nation and kept all the tribes loyal to himself during his reign of thirty-three years. He captured the city of Jerusalem from the Jebusites and made it the capital of the United Kingdom. This was a wise move because Jerusalem was on the border between the two parts of the kingdom. David instructed his son, Solomon, to build a temple in Jerusalem where the entire nation could worship the Lord. The map of Jerusalem at the end of this chapter shows the part of the city where the an-

David, by Michelangelo

cient Jebusite City of David once stood. This was also known as the city of Zion.

DAVID AND BATHSHEBA

One of the shadows over David's life was his immoral relationship with Bathsheba, the wife of one of his loyal warriors, named Uriah. David arranged to have Uriah killed, and then he married Bathsheba. He was punished for this sin, and he never fully recovered from the shame of what he had done. Psalm 51 is believed to have been written by David as an expression of his repentance.

DAVID AND ABSALOM

David's children did not always behave well. His son, Absalom, led a revolution against him, and David had to leave Jerusalem and flee for his life. After Absalom was killed the revolution ended, but David grieved so much for his son that he could hardly take up his responsibilities as king again.

DAVID AND GOD

David should be remembered for his great respect for God. He always took God and his commands seriously. David was quick to repent of sins when they were called to his attention, and he had a great appreciation for the sacredness of God. This respect for God is what we should take as an example from David's life.

DAVID AND THE PSALMS

Although he lived in violent times, David was a gentle person, and he appreciated music and singing. A great many of the psalms were written by him, and we recognize and remember him whenever we read or sing one of these psalms.

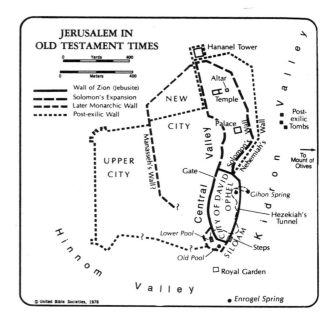

JERUSALEM IN
OLD TESTAMENT TIMES

Wall of Zion (Jebusite)
Solomon's Expansion
Later Monarchic Wall
Post-exilic Wall

NEW CITY

UPPER CITY

Manasseh's Wall?

Central Valley

Palace

Gate

Lower Pool

Old Pool

Hinnom Valley

Hananel Tower

Altar

Temple

Post-exilic Tombs

To Mount of Olives

Gihon Spring

Hezekiah's Tunnel

CITY OF DAVID

OPHEL

Nehemiah's Wall

Kidron Valley

SILOAM

Steps

Royal Garden

Enrogel Spring

© United Bible Societies, 1976

Check Yourself

1. Describe, in three or four words, the relationship between David and
   a) Samuel

   b) Jonathan

   c) Absalom

2. What city did David choose as a capital? Why?

3. In what way was David's relationship with God an example to us?

In Class

Since we have been thinking about David and his relationship with God, this is a good time to think about ourselves and to ask, "What is my relationship with God, and how can I be better friends with him?"

From Psalm 139:1-12 and verses 23 and 24, which you have memorized for this class, we learn that God knows everything about us. If we really want to be friends of God, we do not have to be afraid to invite him to examine our hearts and to "see if there be any wicked way in me, and lead me in the way everlasting!" He loves us and is willing to accept us just as we are, and he helps us overcome our temptations to do evil.

The life of David teaches us that God will forgive our sins if we respect and trust him and if we are serious about our desire to be his friends. These are the things that will help us to continue to be God's friends when we have done wrong:

1. From our study of the Bible we know what is right and wrong.

2. Therefore, when we have sinned by making a wrong choice, we know that we have done wrong.

3. God helps us to admit that we have sinned and to recognize how serious our sin is. "I recognize my faults; I am always conscious of my sins. I have sinned against you—only against you—and done what you consider evil. So you are right in judging me; you are justified in condemning me" (Psalm 51:3, 4, TEV).

4. We pray for forgiveness and ask God to remove our sin. "Remove my sin, and I will be clean; wash me, and I will be whiter than snow. Let me hear the sounds of joy and gladness; and though you have crushed me and broken me, I will be happy once again. Close your eyes to my sins and wipe out all my evil" (Psalm 51:7-9, TEV).

5. God forgives our sins when we come humbly to him. "My sacrifice is a humble spirit, O God; you will not reject a humble and repentant heart" (Psalm 51:17, TEV).

6. We then praise God for his forgiveness and for making us happy again. " . . . I will gladly proclaim your righteousness. Help me to speak, Lord, and I will praise you" (Psalm 51:14, 15, TEV).

God always wants to be our friend, but we are often tempted to turn away from him by making the wrong choices. When this happens we become sad and cannot enjoy his friendship. It does not help to try to excuse ourselves because God knows everything about us, as we learned from Psalm 139. Even so, he still wants us for his friends. He wants us to repent of our sins and ask forgiveness so we can have a happy relationship with him again.

Solomon: a Wise King, but Not Wise Enough   20

BIBLE READINGS: 1 Kings 8:1-13 (Solomon dedicates the new temple)
1 Kings 9:1-9 (God renews the covenant)
1 Kings 11:1-8 (Solomon's big mistake)
Other suggested Bible readings:
1 Kings 3:1-28, 4:29 (About Solomon's wisdom)
1 Kings 4:22-28 (About how rich Solomon was)
1 Kings 8:14-53 (Solomon's prayer of dedication)

When David was old and feeble, his son, Adonijah, gathered together a few followers and proclaimed himself king. When David was told what Adonijah had done, he immediately arranged to have his son, Solomon, made king. He planned such a big celebration and gathered so much support that Adonijah gave up, and Solomon became king of the United Kingdom.

SOLOMON ASKS FOR WISDOM

When he was just beginning his reign, Solomon had a dream that God had invited him to ask for anything he wished. Solomon asked for an understanding mind to govern the people. God was pleased with this request, and Solomon became famous for his great wisdom. Actually, he did not always use the wisdom God had given him. One foolish mistake that Solomon made was to follow the common practice of those days for kings to marry several women who were daughters of the kings of other nations. Solomon married many women who were idol worshipers, and even joined in their worship. Solomon's actions displeased God and caused many problems for the kings who followed.

SOLOMON'S WEALTH AND WISDOM

There was peace in Solomon's time. The nation was secure, and Solomon carried on trade with surrounding nations. Israel was on the trade route between great nations on either side, and Solomon taxed the traders as they passed through. He made favorable trade agreements and became immensely wealthy. He was respected in other nations, and many people came to learn from his great wisdom.

"You're not as smart as you think, young man!"

THE BUILDING AND DEDICATION OF THE TEMPLE

One of Solomon's great accomplishments was the building of the Temple in Jerusalem. He bought cedar and cypress wood from Hiram, king of Tyre, who had been a close friend of David's, and Hiram also provided Solomon with some skilled labor. Solomon required the people to donate a great deal of time to the building of the temple. When, after seven years of construction, it was finished, Solomon arranged a great celebration of dedication.

This celebration helps us to understand how dramatic and joyous the worship of the people of Israel was. There was a large choir and orchestra. The orchestra consisted of 120 trumpeters, and others who played cymbals, harps, and other instruments (2 Chronicles 5:12, 13). The sacrificing of animals was an important part of the worship of Israel. The forgiveness of sins was dependent on the shedding of the blood of an animal, which meant that the animal had given up its life for the person who had sinned. The real meaning of sacrifice was fulfilled in Jesus, who was called "the lamb of God, who takes away the sin of the world" (John 1:29). We shall never understand the mystery of Jesus' sacrifice, but every time we take part in the Lord's supper we confess our faith that he gave his life for us, and that through his sacrifice we have the forgiveness of sins. Part of our worship is to confess our sins and receive the assurance of forgiveness through Jesus.

Solomon also sacrificed a great many oxen and sheep at the dedication of the temple. The making of these sacrifices represented gratefulness to God for his blessings and the desire to be faithful to the covenant. Sacrifice is also an important part of our worship. We do not sacrifice animals, and because Jesus arose from the dead, we stress living sacrifices. God asks us to "present your bodies as a living sacrifice, holy and acceptable to God, which is your spiritual worship" (Romans 12:1). Part of all true worship is to give ourselves to God as living sacrifices, to be his servants.

RENEWAL OF THE COVENANT

After Solomon had dedicated the temple, God renewed his covenant with him. God promised Solomon that if he would be true to him he would bless him and all his descendants. However, God warned him that if he became untrue to him, God would allow this beautiful temple to become a pile of rubbish.

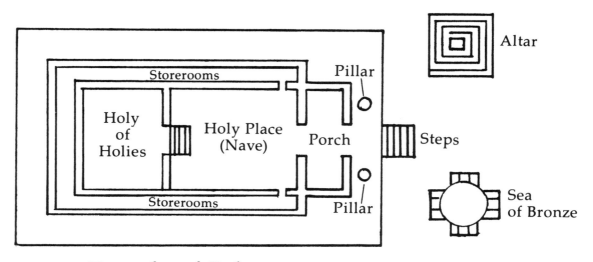

Temple of Solomon

SOLOMON IS UNFAITHFUL TO THE COVENANT

By marrying the daughters of many foreign kings, Solomon thought he would be better able to keep on friendly terms with these kings. This was against God's command. As a courtesy to these women, Solomon provided places for them to worship their own gods. This worship included immoral practices which often degraded human beings and even, in some cases, included the offering of human sacrifices. Eventually Solomon himself became interested in these gods and broke the covenant with the true God. So, wise as Solomon was, he was not wise enough.

THE KINGDOM DIVIDED

After the death of Solomon, his son, Rehoboam, came to the throne. When he was to be installed as king, the people from the northern tribes asked him to lighten the burdens of taxation and forced labor. Rehoboam stupidly refused and said that the burdens were to be made even heavier. At that time a revolutionary leader named Jeroboam, who had been driven out of the country by Solomon, came home to lead a revolt. The northern tribes rejected Rehoboam as king and set up their own kingdom under Jeroboam. Only the tribe of Judah remained loyal to Rehoboam. Thus the kingdom which had begun with such high expectations was now hopelessly divided, never to be united again.

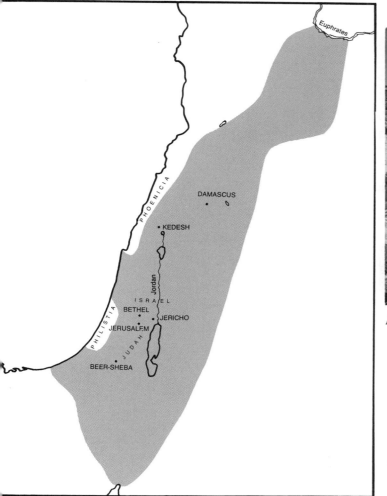

Solomon's kingdom

Mosque of Omar built on the site of the Temple.

Check Yourself

1. What was Solomon's wish at the beginning of his reign?

2. Why were animals sacrificed at the temple?

3. In what way was Solomon unfaithful to the covenant?

In Class

After building the temple and dedicating it to the true God, Solomon himself led the people into worshiping false gods.

What are some of the false gods that tempt us today?

_____

_____

_____

What problems are created when we worship them?

_____

_____

_____

What will happen if we continue to worship them?

_____

_____

_____

BIBLE READING: Psalms 32, 91, 96
Other suggested Bible Readings: Psalms 22, 104, 126, 130, 150

ASSIGNMENT: Memorize Psalm 23 in your favorite version of the Bible.

Can you imagine a world where there is no singing? Wherever we go, it seems, people have songs to sing. Through songs we are able to express our feelings.

SONGS OF WORSHIP

Singing is particularly important for worship. Songs used in worship are called "hymns." When we sing hymns we express our faith as well as our feelings. Much of the singing we hear every day on the radio expresses people's lack of faith and their hopelessness. Therefore it is important to pay attention to the hymns we sing, for they bring us hope and encourage us to trust God.

SINGING WITH ATTENTION

To benefit from hymns, we must pay attention to what we are singing. Hymns can change our attitude from discourage-ment to hope. We may begin a hymn feeling very blah, but if we pay attention to what we are singing life will often seem exciting and worthwhile when we come to the end of the hymn.

THE PSALMS: THE HYMNS OF ISRAEL

The songs of worship which the people of Israel used were the psalms we find in our Bible today. Many of these psalms were sung long before they were assembled into a book. By a long process they were put together into what is now the Book of Psalms. Singing was so important in Israel that special persons were appointed by the king to serve as musicians. According to 1 Chronicles 25:7, David appointed 288 persons for "singing to the Lord." This included many who played musical instruments.

WHO WROTE THE PSALMS?

We have already learned that David was a musician, and many Psalms were written by him. Some translations of the Bible include headings which tell the name of the writer. These headings were added long after the psalms were written, and they are not a part of God's message to us. We cannot be sure that they are correct in all cases, but they do give us an idea of the variety of persons who wrote the psalms. Perhaps you can borrow a copy of a translation that has these headings. According to these headings, David wrote a great many psalms, including 51, 61, 63, 64, and 65. The headings of Psalms 73-83 give the name of Asaph as their author. Asaph was one of the directors of the 288 musicians whom David appointed (see 1 Chronicles 25:6, 7).

According to the headings of Psalms 44-49, they are written by "the sons of Korah." These psalm writers may have formed an organization of musicians who descended from Korah. Though we cannot be sure about many of the writers, we do know that the psalms are the product of many authors over a long period of time, and through them God has taught us some valuable lessons about worshiping him.

THE POETRY OF THE PSALMS

The poetry of the people of Israel was formed by stating an idea on one line and then dealing in different ways with the same idea on one or more lines that follow. For instance, Psalm 126:2 says:
"Then our mouth was filled with laughter,
and our tongue with shouts of joy."
Here the second line repeats the idea of the first line, using different words.

In Psalm 7:9 the idea of the second line is the opposite of that of the first line:
"O let the evil of the wicked come to an end,
but establish thou the righteous."
In Psalm 118:1-4, you will see that the first line states an idea, and the lines that follow keep adding to that idea.
"Give thanks to the LORD, because he is
good,

and his love is eternal.
Let the people of Israel say,
'His love is eternal.'
Let the priests of God say,
'His love is eternal.'
Let all who worship him say,
'His love is eternal.' " (TEV)
These are illustrations of how the poetry consists of dealing in different ways with the same idea.

DIFFERENT KINDS OF PSALMS

There is a psalm that fits almost every feeling a person can have. For instance:
• Psalms 96 and 104 are songs of praise to God.
• The last five psalms, Psalm 146 through Psalm 150, all begin with "Praise the Lord," and Psalm 150 ends the Book of Psalms with a list of many instruments with which God may be praised. Finally, it brings the whole Book of Psalms to a climax with the words,
"Let everything that breathes praise the
    LORD!
Praise the LORD!"
• Psalms 32 and 130, on the other hand, describe a person with a great need to be forgiven. They are part of a group of psalms known as "penitential psalms."
• Psalm 109 is one of several psalms that express great anger against wicked people.
• Psalm 23 is a psalm of comfort that speaks of how God cares for us at all times.
• Psalm 22 describes a person in great suffering. This psalm was quoted by Jesus when he was on the cross. These are just a few of the feelings which dif-

ferent psalms describe.

The psalms express the faith and the feelings of their writers, and they also express the faith and the feelings of the people who use them in worship. They are part of God's Word, and he has given them to us to help us express how we really feel when we worship him. The Psalms help us to realize that it is okay to come to God with all kinds of differ- ent feelings. What God wants most of all is for us to come to him honestly, no matter what our feelings may be.

The Psalms are just as valuable for us as they were for the people of Israel. Whether we read or sing them in private or use them for public worship, we find them helpful for expressing our feelings as well as our faith.

Check Yourself

1. How were the Psalms used?

2. List three different feelings the Psalms express.

3. Compose two lines that illustrate one style of poetry used in the Psalms.

In Class

Since you may be writing your own psalm in class, I will include an example of a psalm that I wrote. Read it in class.

I want to praise God for all the times he has been with me.
   He was with me both when I was young and when I became older.
When I was a child he gave me parents who cared for me.
   He gave me teachers who helped me learn, and friends to enjoy.
   He gave me a church where I learned about him and his Son, Jesus.
When I became an adult, he was also with me.
   He taught me how to trust him and be his follower.
   He gave me worthwhile work to do.
   He gave me a loving wife and caring children, whom I love dearly.
There was a time when I turned away from him and refused to follow him.
   Yet, he was patient with me and led me back to himself.
Things have not always been pleasant in my life.
   There were times when I was poor, and there were times of sickness.
   There were many disappointments and discouragements.
During these times God was with me and comforted me.
   He showed me that he cared, and he taught me many valuable lessons.
As I grow older there are many things that worry me and make me anxious.
   Yet, I know that God will be with me as he was in the past.
I do not know whether my life will be easy or hard.
   In either case, God will be with me during the years I have left.
I thank him for Jesus, who is my Lord.

I thank him for forgiving my sins.
I thank him for his promise that I shall live forever with him. Praise the Lord!

Since we are all different, your psalm will be different from mine. Don't try to copy my style. Don't be afraid to be honest. If you are happy, write a happy psalm. If you are sad or worried or angry, write a psalm that fits your feelings. You may write it in the space below:

_____

_____

_____

_____

_____

_____

_____

_____

_____

_____

_____

_____

_____

_____

_____

_____

_____

_____

_____

_____

_____

_____

Wisdom for God's People

22

BIBLE READING: Proverbs 1:1-6, Proverbs 17

Other suggested Bible readings: Proverbs 1:20-33 18-20

Once, when some of my friends and I were tobogganing in the mountains, I noticed a slope that was much steeper than the one we were using. As I headed for it, they shouted a warning to me, but I paid no attention to them. All I could think of was showing them how brave I was. What I did not know was that near the bottom of that slope there was nothing but white gravel that looked like snow. When the toboggan hit the gravel, it stopped suddenly, and I slid off. Fortunately I was not seriously hurt, but the skin was rubbed off my nose and one side of my face, and one of my hands was bleeding. Painful as the injuries were, what hurt even more was to know that my friends would be thinking of me as a stupid fool.

If I had acted wisely, I would have paid attention to the advice of my friends. It was stupid of me not to listen to them, and I suffered the consequences of my stupidity. I was a living example of the words, "Stupid people always think they are right. Wise people listen to advice." I didn't know, at that time, that there were words like these in the Bible, but they are there, in some practical teaching about wisdom in daily living. (Proverbs 12:15, TEV)

This teaching about wisdom is known as "Wisdom Literature," and it is found, mostly, in the books of Job, Proverbs and Ecclesiastes. It is also found in some of the Psalms and in the Song of Solomon. In this chapter, we shall concentrate on the Book of Proverbs, and our quotations will be from Today's English Version—*The Good News Bible.*

THE MEANING OF "WISDOM"

The following passages will help us understand the meaning of "wisdom," as it is used in the Bible:

• *Someone who is sure of himself does not talk all the time. People who stay calm have real insight. After all, even a fool may be thought wise and intelligent if he stays quiet and keeps his mouth shut* (Proverbs 17:27-28).

• *If you brag all the time, you are asking for trouble* (Proverbs 17:19).

• *A fool does not care whether he understands a thing or not; all he wants to do is show how smart he is* (Proverbs 18:2).

• *Some people ruin themselves by their own stupid actions and then blame the Lord* (Proverbs 19:3).

To be a "wise" person means to have good sense and to use good judgment. To have knowledge is a sign of wisdom, and therefore, wise people desire to learn. *Stupid people have no respect for wisdom and refuse to learn* (Proverbs 1:7). *It does a fool no good to spend money on an education, because he has no common sense* (Proverbs 17:16). Wise people are industrious, make good use of their time and develop skills so they can do good work and be successful. *Do yourself a favor and learn all you can; then remember what you learn and you will prosper* (Proverbs 19:8).

WISDOM AND RIGHT LIVING

Wisdom is pictured in the Book of Proverbs as a lady calling to people to pay attention to her and become wise. *Listen! Wisdom is calling out in the streets and marketplaces, calling loudly at the city gates and wherever people come together. "Foolish people! How long do you want to be foolish? How long will you enjoy making fun of knowledge? Will you never learn? Listen when I reprimand you; I will give you good advice and share my knowledge with you"* (Proverbs 1:20-23).

Those who listen to wisdom will not only become wise, but they will also learn to do what is right and avoid doing evil because it is wise to do right and foolish to do wrong. *If you listen to me, you will know what is right, just and fair. You will know what you should do. You will become wise, and your knowledge will give you pleasure. Your insight and understanding will protect you and prevent you from doing the wrong thing* (Proverbs 2:9-12).

Most of us have known people who seem to think it is smart to be lazy and irresponsible, to take risks while driving, to boast about their immorality and to participate in things, like drugs, that can destroy them. The Wisdom literature in the Bible teaches us that this is not only bad; it is also stupid. It will get us into trouble and make us unhappy. It might even cause us to suffer for the rest of our lives. On the other hand, it is smart to be honest and responsible, to have respect for God and to live according to his will. A wise person will understand this, but a stupid person will pay no attention to it.

THE REWARDS OF WISDOM AND RIGHT LIVING

Wisdom and right living bring their own rewards. Wise people prosper and are successful. *Ask the LORD to bless your plans, and you will be successful in carrying them out* (Proverbs 16:3). *Have reverence for the LORD, be humble, and you will get riches, honor and a long life* (Proverbs 22:4).

However, all good people do not become rich, and riches are not everything. *"It is better to be poor but honest than to be a lying fool* (Proverbs 19:1). *It is better to have a little, honestly earned, than to have a large income, dishonestly gained* (Proverbs 16:8). It is generally true that good people who tend to their business and live responsibly will be more prosperous than lazy, irresponsible, and evil people, but this does not necessarily mean that wise and good people will always become rich or that poverty and suffering are signs of wrongdoing.

The Book of Job deals with the problem of why suffering comes to good people. Job was a righteous and wealthy man who suddenly lost all he owned, as well as his family and his health. While he was bemoaning these disasters, three of his friends, Eliphaz, Bildad and Zophar, came to comfort him. Unfortunately, these friends all believed that prosperity and health were signs of right living and that disaster and suffering were signs of wrongdoing. Therefore, they accused Job of having done something wrong to bring on all this suffering. When Job did not admit to any sins that might have caused his suffering, they accused him of being unrepentant and stubborn. What these men did not know, and what Job did not know, was that God was demonstrating to Satan that Job was not being a good man just because of the rewards that God had given him. The message of Job to us is that no one can look behind the scenes to discover what God's purposes are. The truly wise people realize that hardships and disasters may come even to those who are good. The values of self-respect, a good conscience, and a good name are rewards in themselves.

SOME PRACTICAL APPLICATIONS OF WISE LIVING

There are many ways in which wisdom may be applied to our daily living, but we shall list only three of them.

1. Family Relationships

Most of us know, from experience, that

it takes a great deal of wisdom to maintain good relationships within one's family. Tensions and hard feelings exist in some homes simply because members of the family are unwise. The relationships are pleasant in other homes because the family knows how to apply the principles of wisdom. Good family relationships are more important, even than fine food. *Better to eat a dry crust of bread with peace of mind than to have a banquet in a house full of trouble* (Proverbs 17:1). If you glance through the Book of Proverbs, you will be able to find other words of wisdom about family relationships.

2. Anger and Temper

Hot tempers cause arguments, but patience brings peace (Proverbs 15:18). Proverbs 19:19 has another message of wisdom about hot tempers. You may wish to see if you can find other proverbs about anger and temper.

3. Getting Along

If you look through the Book of Proverbs, you will find many wise sayings about getting along with other people. They have to do with such things as:

• Being self-centered: *People who do not get along with others are interested only in themselves* (Proverbs 18:1).

• Arguments: *The start of an argument is like the first break in a dam; stop it before it goes any further* (Proverbs 17:14).

• Gossip: *Gossip is spread by wicked people; they stir up trouble and break up friendships* (Proverbs 16:28).

• Forgiveness: *If you want people to like you, forgive them when they wrong you. Remembering wrongs can break up a friendship* (Proverbs 17:9).

God has given us these and other teachings about wisdom as part of his message to us because he wants his friends to enjoy the benefits of wisdom. This part of the Bible can be very helpful to us as we seek to apply it to our daily living.

Check Yourself

1. Define wisdom as it is used in this part of the Bible.

2. With what problem does the Book of Job deal?

3. List three situations in daily living that are addressed in the Book of Proverbs.

In Class

From this chapter on wisdom literature I learned

_____

_____

_____

_____

_____

_____

_____

_____

_____

_____

_____

_____

REVIEW OF UNIT SIX

Israel's first king, Saul, disobeyed God, and God took the kingdom away from him and gave it to David. David became Israel's greatest king. He was a humble person, and when he made mistakes he repented with great sorrow, and God forgave him. David's son, Solomon, received great wisdom, but he still disobeyed God. The Psalms were the songs of God's ancient people, and they are God's gift to us. They are useful both for reading privately and for public worship. "Wisdom Literature" is found mostly in Job, Proverbs, and Ecclesiastes. These books teach us that it is stupid to disobey God and do wrong. Wise people live as God wants them to live.

The Kingdom Divides and Falls

CHAPTER 23
The Divided Kingdom

The kingdom of Israel divided when Solomon's son, Rehoboam, became king. The northern kingdom of Israel fell to the Assyrians in 721 BC, and the southern kingdom of Judah fell to the Babylonians in 587 BC. The prophets called the people back to God, but few people paid any attention.

CHAPTER 24
The Prophets Speak for God

From prophets like Elijah, Elisha, and Amos we learn how the prophets spoke God's message and called the people to repent.

CHAPTER 25
The Prophets Stand Alone for God

The messages and lives of Hosea, Isaiah, Micah, and Jeremiah illustrate how the prophets often stood alone for God.

UNIT SEVEN

ABRAHAM ISAAC JACOB JOSEPH	MOSES	JOSHUA	Judges	SAUL	DAVID	SOLOMON	Kingdom divided	Fall of Northern Kingdom	Fall of Southern Kingdom	JESUS
2000 BC	1300 BC	1200 BC		1020 BC	1000 BC	922 BC		721 BC	587 BC	4 BC

The
Divided Kingdom 23

BIBLE READING: 2 Kings 17:1-20

Other suggested Bible readings: 2 Kings 12:1-20; 2 Kings 18:13-19:37

It is hard for us, who live in large and powerful countries like Canada or the United States, to imagine what it would be like to be citizens of a small kingdom, like Israel, entirely at the mercy of the great nations around it. From the map below we see that Israel was located in the narrow space between the Mediterranean Sea and the Arabian Desert. This space separated Egypt from the Assyrian and the Babylonian Empires. Any one of these great powers was strong enough to overthrow the tiny nation of Israel and make it part of its empire whenever it wished. Israel's only hope was to depend on God. He had made a covenant with his people and had promised to protect them if they would remain true to him. They had agreed to worship only him and to refrain from taking part in the immoral and cruel practices of the idol worshipers around them. They had also agreed to depend on God for protection and had promised to make no alliances with other nations.

Under the leadership of Jeroboam, ten of the twelve tribes had rebelled against Rehoboam, David's grandson, who had

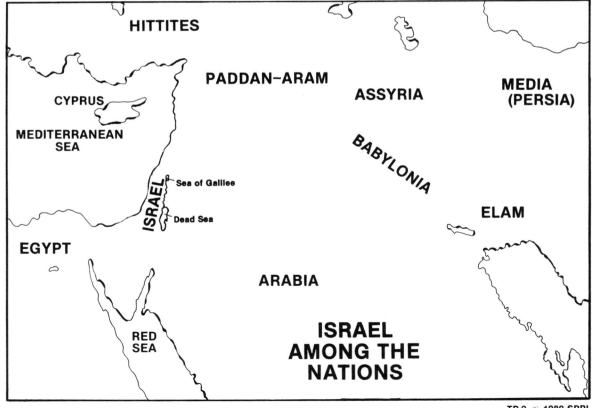

ISRAEL AMONG THE NATIONS

just become king. From now on there were two nations instead of one. Both nations found it hard to keep their covenant with God and they soon began to worship idols. Their unfaithfulness to God led them to a kind of life that was just the opposite of what God had taught them. Cruel and immoral practices were part of this idol worship.

They even burned their own children as sacrifices to the idols. They also kept taking sides in the struggles the great empires had with each other.

All this finally led to their downfall. The Northern Kingdom, now known as "Israel," was overrun by the Assyrians, and its people were taken captive to Assyria. Later the Babylonians captured Jerusalem and they brought many of the people of the Southern Kingdom, known as "Judah," as captives to Babylon. Therefore, the people of the Divided Kingdom learned by hard experience that continual disobedience leads to judgment and destruction.

THE PROPHETS

During the time of the Divided Kingdom, God chose some special servants known as "prophets" to call the people back to himself. We usually think of prophets as persons who predict what will happen in the future. However, these prophets did much more than that. Their most important work was to tell the people to repent and turn back to God and to warn them that they would be destroyed if they continued to disobey him.

SOME OF THE KINGS AND PROPHETS OF THE DIVIDED KINGDOM

Rehoboam and Jeroboam

> *A date to remember is 922 BC, when the kingdom was divided and both Rehoboam and Jeroboam began to rule.*

Jeroboam was the first of nineteen kings to rule over the Northern Kingdom of Israel, and Rehoboam was the first of twenty kings to rule over the Southern

Divine guardian of the god Nabu, from the Neo-Assyrian period in the reign of Sargon II (721-105 B.C.).

Kingdom of Judah. Both began to rule in 922 BC, when the kingdom was divided.

Jeroboam recognized that if the people of the Northern Kingdom would go to Jerusalem to worship, they would be tempted to go back to Rehoboam, who ruled in Jerusalem. Therefore he placed golden calves for them to worship in Dan and Bethel, two of the towns of the Northern Kingdom.

Meanwhile Rehoboam, king of the Southern Kingdom, encouraged the people to follow the evil customs of the nations around them. He had trouble with the Egyptians, who came up and took away the golden ornaments from the temple, and he was forced to replace them with bronze ornaments.

Ahab and Jehoshaphat

Ahab, another king of the Northern Kingdom, married a woman named Jezebel, whose father was king of Sidon. Under her influence, Ahab introduced the worship of Baal, a religion which included things like sexual immorality and the sacrificing of children, which God had forbidden. Because of this, the prophet

105

Elijah condemned Ahab and Jezebel. Jehoshaphat, who was now king of the Southern Kingdom, was more faithful to God than Ahab was. He stopped much of the idol worship and the immoral practices associated with it. Jehoshaphat and Ahab joined forces against Syria, a nation to the north of Israel, and Ahab was killed during this war with the Syrians.

Jehu and Joash

Jehu was anointed by the prophet, Elisha, to be king of Israel. He killed the whole family of Ahab and ordered the wicked queen, Jezebel, thrown down through a window in the tower where she was hiding. Jehu stopped the worship of Baal during his reign, but he did not remove the golden calves, and he disobeyed God in other ways.

During the reign of Jehu in Israel, Joash became king in Judah. He was only seven years old when he came to the throne, but the high priest instructed him how to follow God faithfully. He removed the idols and raised money for repairing the temple in Jerusalem. However, he took most of the treasures in the temple to pay the king of Syria not to attack Jerusalem.

Jeroboam II and Uzziah

Jeroboam II had a long and peaceful reign in the Northern Kingdom, and the people enjoyed many luxuries. The prophet, Amos, warned them that this luxurious living would soon come to an end if they did not turn to God. Meanwhile, Uzziah, who was now king in Judah, was a good king, and he tried to be faithful to God.

THE END OF THE NORTHERN KINGDOM OF ISRAEL

After the death of Jeroboam II the kingdom of Israel declined rapidly, and in 721 BC the Assyrian armies came in and took many of the people captive to Assyria.

> *721 BC is another date to remember, the date when the Northern Kingdom of Israel fell to the Assyrians.*

The reasons why God let the Northern Kingdom be destroyed are listed in 2 Kings 17:7-18. Some of these reasons are:
• They turned from the true God and worshiped idols.
• They followed the leading of their kings and adopted practices that were against God's commands.
• They paid no attention to the warnings of the prophets.
• They were unfaithful to the Covenant God had made with them.
• They worshipped Baal and the golden calves; and they even sacrificed their own sons and daughters in their worship of these idols.

KINGS AND PROPHETS OF THE SOUTHERN KINGDOM OF JUDAH AFTER THE FALL OF ISRAEL

Hezekiah

> *701 BC is another date to remember, the date when God protected Jerusalem from the Assyrian army.*

Hezekiah was king in Judah when the Northern Kingdom of Israel fell to the Assyrians. In 701 BC Sennacherib, king of Assyria, invaded Judah. He took most of the cities of Judah, and Hezekiah was quite sure he would capture Jerusalem. However, Isaiah, the prophet, told Hezekiah not to give in to the Assyrians. God had promised to protect the city. For some reason the Assyrians suddenly withdrew from Jerusalem without shooting a single arrow into it.

Josiah and the discovery of the Book of the Law

Josiah was only eight years old when he began to rule, but he had wise advisors. He turned the people back to God, repaired the temple and ordered the people to observe the Passover Festival, which had been neglected. During the repair of the temple, the Book of the Law, which had been lost, was discovered. This book explained how God wanted his people to worship and serve him. They used this book to guide them to restoring worship in the temple.

Jehoichim and the decline
of the Southern Kingdom

Jehoichim seemed to delight in rejecting all the good things his father, King Josiah, had done, and he turned away from the Lord. During his reign the Babylonians were becoming a threat to Jerusalem, but even this did not cause him to turn to God. He listened to false prophets who told him that God would protect the city from the Babylonians. The prophet, Jeremiah, warned him that God would punish the nation by letting the Babylonians capture Jerusalem, but Jehoichim paid no attention.

THE SOUTHERN KINGDOM FALLS TO THE BABYLONIANS

In 597 BC, the city of Jerusalem was captured by the Babylonians, and Jehoichin, the son of Jehoichim, was deported to Babylon, along with other leaders of the government.

> *587 is another date to remember, the date when the temple was destroyed and the Southern Kingdom was brought to an end by the Babylonians.*

In 587 BC the Babylonians came again and destroyed the temple and took a great many captives to Babylon.

Thus ended more than three centuries of history that could have been much different if the people had obeyed God and kept his covenant. However, this was not to be the end for the people whom God had chosen to be his special friends. He was not going to desert them even though they were now to be strangers in a foreign land. He had lessons to teach them there that would help them to understand his purposes better.

DATES TO REMEMBER

• 922 BC, when the United Kingdom was divided into the Northern and Southern Kingdoms, and both Jeroboam and Rehoboam began to rule.
• 721 BC, when the Northern Kingdom of Israel fell to the Assyrians.
• 701 BC, when God protected Jerusalem from the Assyrian army.
• 587 BC, when the temple in Jerusalem was destroyed and the Southern Kingdom was brought to an end by the Babylonians.

ISRAEL—The Northern Kingdom

KINGS OF ISRAEL
1. Jeroboam I
2. Nadab
3. Baasha
4. Elah
5. Zimri
6. Omri
7. Ahab
8. Ahaziah
9. Joram
10. Jehu
11. Jehoahaz
12. Jehoash
13. Jeroboam II
14. Zechariah
15. Shallum
16. Menahem
17. Pekahiah
18. Pekah
19. Hoshea

The Northern Kingdom (Israel) was defeated and taken captive by the Assyrians in 722 B.C.

JUDAH—The Southern Kingdom

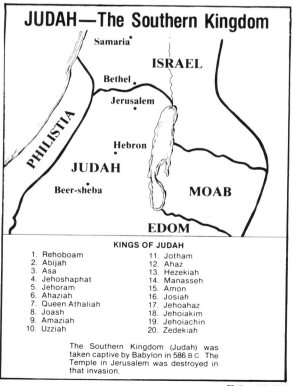

KINGS OF JUDAH

1. Rehoboam
2. Abijah
3. Asa
4. Jehoshaphat
5. Jehoram
6. Ahaziah
7. Queen Athaliah
8. Joash
9. Amaziah
10. Uzziah
11. Jotham
12. Ahaz
13. Hezekiah
14. Manasseh
15. Amon
16. Josiah
17. Jehoahaz
18. Jehoiakim
19. Jehoiachin
20. Zedekiah

The Southern Kingdom (Judah) was taken captive by Babylon in 586 B.C. The Temple in Jerusalem was destroyed in that invasion.

KINGS AND PROPHETS OF THE DIVIDED KINGDOM

	IMPORTANT EVENTS	KINGS OF THE NORTHERN KINGDOM	SOME PROPHETS OF THE NORTHERN KINGDOM	OF THE SOUTHERN KINGDOM	KINGS OF THE SOUTHERN KINGDOM	
925 BC						925 BC
	922—The Kingdom is divided	JEROBOAM 922-901			REHOBOAM 922-915 (Abijam, Asa 915-873)	
900 BC						900 BC
		(Nadab, Baasha, Elah, Zimri, Omri 901-869)				
875 BC						875 BC
		AHAB 869-850	ELIJAH (About 870-845)		JEHOSHAPHAT 873-849	
850 BC						850 BC
		(Azariah, Joram 850-842) JEHU 842-815	ELISHA (About 845-800)		(Jehoram, Ahaziah, Athaliah 849-837) JOASH 837-800	
825 BC						825 BC
		(Jehoahaz, Jehoash 815-786)				
800 BC						800 BC
		JEROBOAM II 786-746			(Amaziah 800-783) UZZIAH 783-742	
775 BC						775 BC
			AMOS (About 760-750)			
750 BC						750 BC
		(Zechariah, Shallum, Menahem, Pekahiah, Pekah 746-732) HOSHEA 732-724	HOSEA (About 750-730)	ISAIAH (About 742-700) MICAH (About 740-700)	(Jotham 742-735) AHAZ 735-715	
725 BC						725 BC
	721—Fall of Northern Kingdom to Assyria				HEZEKIAH 715-687	
700 BC						700 BC
	701—Assyrians fail to capture Jerusalem				MANASSEH 687-642	
675 BC						675 BC
650 BC						650 BC
					(Amon 642-640) JOSIAH 640-609	
625 BC						625 BC
				JEREMIAH (About 620-580)	(Jehoahaz 609) JEHOIACHIM 609-598	
600 BC						600 BC
	597—Jerusalem falls to the Babylonians				JEHOIACHIN 598-597 ZEDEKIAH 597-587	
575 BC	587—Temple destroyed; many Jews taken captive to Babylon					575 BC
550 BC						550 BC
	539—Cyrus conquers Babylon; he permits some Jews to return in 537					
525 BC						525 BC
	About 517—Temple rebuilt; more Jews return					
500 BC						500 BC

Check Yourself

1. Name four important events listed in this chapter and give the date of each event.

2. What lessons does the tragic ending of Israel and Judah have for us today?

In Class

1. What would have happened if Israel and Judah had put God first?

_____

_____

_____

_____

2. What would happen in my country if it put God first?

_____

_____

_____

_____

3. What would happen in my life if I would put God first?

_____

_____

_____

_____

_____

The Prophets Speak for God

BIBLE READING: Amos 5:21-24—God's message about meaningless worship
Amos 7:10-17—God's message about punishment for evil
Amos 8:4-8—God's message about caring for poor people
Amos 9:13-15—God's message of hope

Other suggested Bible readings: 1 Kings, 18, 19, and 21, Amos 2:6-16

CATECHISM: WHO ARE THE PROPHETS?

Prophets are chosen by God to show nations and individuals their sin, to call them to obedience, and to present the hope of the Messiah.

The Sovereign Lord has filled me with his spirit. He has chosen me and sent me to bring good news to the poor, to heal the broken-hearted, to announce release to captives and freedom to those in prison. He has sent me to proclaim that the time has come when the Lord will save his people and defeat their enemies.

Isaiah 61:1, 2a, TEV

"What would the prophets say today?"

Let's go back to the story of the two friends who became separated. One of the friends represents God and the other represents human beings. Human beings turned their backs on God way back in the beginning, but God still loves them very much, and he has always had some special people to help him draw them back to himself. He has even chosen a special nation, Israel, to help bring the world back to himself.

But even this special nation became unfaithful to him. Now it had divided into two parts, and God needed someone to call both parts of this nation to return to himself. For this purpose he chose the prophets. They brought God's message to the people and warned them that if they continued to disobey him, they would be destroyed.

The prophets did not say, "It seems to me," or, "I think this is the way things are." They lived so close to God that they were absolutely certain of what God wanted them to say. When they spoke, they said, "Thus says the Lord." They were independent people, and they spoke fearlessly against the sins of both the common people and their rulers. They suffered for God, and many of them lost their lives, but God spoke to his people through them.

These prophets, who spoke to the people of the divided kingdom, brought messages from God that fit our time as well as the time, over 2500 years ago, when they spoke. What God said through them is timeless.

THE MESSAGE OF THE PROPHETS

The prophets:
1. Condemned wasteful luxury and injustice.
2. Told the people to be concerned about the poor.
3. Condemned immorality.
4. Called the people to be obedient to God's commands.
5. Condemned insincere worship.
6. Called the people to live consistently with their worship.
7. Warned of God's judgment.
8. Promised hope for those who returned to God.

The message of the prophets is summarized in Isaiah 61:1, 2a, which is part of the Catechism for this chapter.

ELIJAH AND ELISHA SPEAK FOR GOD

The first great prophet of this time was Elijah, who prophesied in the Northern Kingdom during the reign of Ahab and his wicked queen Jezebel. Elijah opposed the worship of Baal, and he challenged the prophets of Baal to prove that their religion was true by having their god send down fire from heaven. They prayed all day in vain, even cutting themselves with their swords until the blood gushed out, but their god did not answer. Then Elijah offered a simple prayer, and God immediately sent down fire on the altar he had built. After this victory four hundred prophets of Baal were killed. This made Jezebel very angry, and Elijah had

to run and hide in a cave. Here God met him and encouraged him and gave him strength to continue his work.

The story of Naboth's vineyard helps us to understand the difference between the worship of idols like Baal and the worship of the God of Israel. Naboth owned a vineyard right next to the palace where Ahab and Jezebel lived. Ahab wanted to buy Naboth's vineyard, but Naboth would not sell it. This upset Ahab, but it gave Jezebel no problem at all. She arranged to have two people falsely accuse Naboth of cursing God and the king. There was a trial and Naboth was condemned to die. Then Jezebel invited Ahab to go out and take possession of the vineyard. Her religion allowed her to mistreat innocent people and even to have them put to death in order to get what she wanted. But God required even the kings to respect the rights of common citizens. Elijah condemned Ahab and Jezebel for this cruel act, and he told Ahab that he would lose the throne of Israel and all his descendants would die. Elijah had enough courage to speak for God even to the king, and to demand that justice be shown to everyone.

Elisha was Elijah's student and became his successor. He also opposed the wor-

ship of Baal. He anointed Jehu to be king, and Jehu wiped out the worship of Baal in Israel.

AMOS SPEAKS FOR GOD

"Get out of here," said the priest to Amos. "Go back to your own country and tell the people how to live. We don't want a foreigner like you up here telling us how bad we are."

Amos came up to Bethel in the northern kingdom of Israel during the prosperous reign of Jeroboam II. He had been a shepherd in Judah, the southern kingdom, but God had now called him to be a prophet to Israel. He began giving God's

message in Bethel, where the people came to worship. The priest did not like what Amos was saying and told him to go back home, but Amos refused to leave, because God had sent him to speak to the people there.

These are some of the things God told the people of Israel through Amos:

1. God would punish all the nations for their sins, but especially Israel.

2. It was wrong to live in luxury and cheat the poor, as they were doing.

3. Their worship was of no value as long as they lived as wickedly as they did.

4. There were wonderful days ahead for them if they would only return to God.

Just imagine what might happen if someone came from another country and went to some of our churches and to our government offices and started telling us to change our way of living. What do you suppose he would say to us? How do you think we would respond? Yet, this is the way the prophets worked; they gave God's message so clearly that we still listen to them, even though many of the people of their time paid no attention to them.

Check Yourself

1. List four concerns addressed by the prophets.

2. What difference between the worship of God and the worship of Baal is illustrated by the story of Naboth and his vineyard?

3. Amos said that the future of Israel would be _____ if the people would _____.

In Class

Discuss the following questions:

1. Is there a need for an Amos today?

_____

_____

_____

2. Would the things he talked about be the same?

_____

_____

_____

_____

_____

3. What issues would be different?

_____

_____

_____

_____

_____

4. How do you think your church would respond if Amos came to speak?

_____

_____

_____

_____

_____

5. How would you respond?

_____

_____

_____

_____

_____

_____

The Prophets Stand Alone for God

BIBLE READING: Hosea 2:2-20

Other suggested Bible readings: Isaiah 1:1-20; Micah 6:6-8; Jeremiah 11:9-17

Think how hard it would be to know that your country was about to be destroyed by its enemies and you were the one God had called to speak for him and tell the people that they would be saved from their enemies if they would repent and turn to him. It would be even harder and more discouraging to discover that very few people paid any attention to you when you gave them God's message.

This is what the prophets did. During the days of the Divided Kingdom there were many great prophets who warned the people that their enemies would invade their country and take them captive if they did not turn to God. This warning did not make the prophets very popular, but they were courageous people. They brought God's message faithfully even though they often had to stand alone for him.

In this chapter we shall become acquainted with four prophets: Hosea, Isaiah, Micah, and Jeremiah. We shall learn a little about who they were and the message they brought the people from God.

Three of these prophets—Hosea, Isaiah and Micah—lived and prophesied before and during the time the Northern Kingdom was captured by the Assyrians. Hosea prophesied in the Northern Kingdom before it was destroyed. He warned the people what would happen if they did not return to God. Isaiah and Micah prophesied in the Southern Kingdom during the time the Northern Kingdom

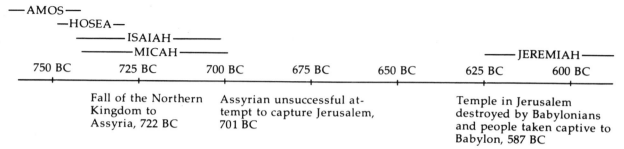

—AMOS—
—HOSEA—
————ISAIAH————
————MICAH————
———— JEREMIAH————

750 BC	725 BC	700 BC	675 BC	650 BC	625 BC	600 BC

Fall of the Northern
Kingdom to
Assyria, 722 BC

Assyrian unsuccessful at-
tempt to capture Jerusalem,
701 BC

Temple in Jerusalem
destroyed by Babylonians
and people taken captive to
Babylon, 587 BC

TIME LINE FOR THE PROPHETS: AMOS, HOSEA, ISAIAH, MICAH, JEREMIAH
(See full chart on page 108)

was destroyed. They warned the people of the Southern Kingdom that the same thing would happen to them if they did not repent and return to God.

Jeremiah prophesied about a century later, just before and during the time Jerusalem was being destroyed by the Babylonians. He warned the people that it was too late to repent and expect God to save the city. He told them to give in to the Babylonians, who would destroy the city and take them captive to Babylon. He said that God would be with them in Babylon and bring them back to their own land again.

All of these prophets lived in times when God was about to punish their people for their sins by letting them be captured by great foreign empires. Therefore, since their message was a warning of destruction which was coming, it was a hard and unpopular message, but they gave it with great courage even though they often had to suffer for it.

As we now look at a summary of the message of each of these four prophets, notice how each message is like the others and how it is different.

THE MESSAGE OF HOSEA

God says:

1. I have been like a husband to you, but I cannot be your husband any more because you have committed adultery against me. You have chased after other gods as an unfaithful wife chases after other lovers (Hosea 2:2-6).
2. You think these false gods that have become like lovers to you are the ones that have cared for you. You have forgotten that I am the one who brought you

out of Egypt and gave you all these things which you have now used to sacrifice to Baal (Hosea 2:7, 8).

3. Therefore, I am going to punish you and take all these things away from you (Hosea 2:9-13).
4. But I am going to win you back to myself again, and you will say that I, not Baal, am your husband (Hosea 2:14-17).

THE MESSAGE OF ISAIAH

God says:

1. The people of Jerusalem and all of Judah are like sons whom I have brought up, who have rebelled against their own father. They are like an ox or a donkey who doesn't know its own master (Isaiah 1:2-4).
2. You are so sinful that you are like a person who is sick from the bottom of your feet up to your head (Isaiah 1:4-6).
3. Therefore, your whole country will be destroyed, and there will only be a few survivors (Isaiah 1:7-9).
4. I will not accept your offerings or hear your prayers because you have bloody hands (Isaiah 1:11-15).
5. If you will turn away from your evil, I will forgive you and bless you again

115

(Isaiah 1:16-20).
6. But there is hope for the future. A descendant of Jesse (who was the father of King David) will come, and under his rule there will be peace and prosperity (Isaiah 11:1-9).

THE MESSAGE OF MICAH

God says:
1. Woe to the wealthy people who are so greedy that they figure out ways to grab the fields and houses of poor people. (Micah 2:1-2).

2. Woe to those who oppress the weak, the women and the children. (Micah 2:8, 9)
3. Woe to the rulers who hate good and love evil and use their power to destroy people (Micah 3:1-3).
4. Woe to all those who accept bribes (Micah 3:11).
5. It is because of sins like these that Jerusalem will be destroyed (Micah 3:12).
6. But there is hope. The mountain on which the house of the Lord stands will become the center of worship, and there will be justice and peace and prosperity (Micah 4:2-4).
7. From the little town of Bethlehem will come a great ruler (Micah 5:2).

THE MESSAGE OF JEREMIAH

God says:
1. You have rebelled against me and broken my covenant and turned to idols (Jeremiah 11:9, 10).
2. Therefore Jerusalem will suffer, and all Judah will be destroyed (Jeremiah 11:11-13).
3. It is of no use to pray for the salvation of the city. I have determined to let it be destroyed (Jeremiah 11:14-17).
4. The false prophets promise peace, but they are lying, and they will be punished (Jeremiah 14:13-16).

116

5. You are going to be taken captive to Babylon (Jeremiah 20:4, 5).

6. But this is not the end. You will return to your own land after seventy years, and you will live in prosperity and peace (Jeremiah 29:10-14).
7. One day I will make a new covenant with my people, not like the old covenant which you kept breaking. I will write this new covenant in your hearts so you will be true to me (Jeremiah 31:31-34).

THE PROPHETS STAND ALONE FOR GOD

Because the prophets had an unpopular message to bring, they often had to stand alone. Hosea prophesied during the time of Jeroboam II, which was a time of prosperity. Everything seemed to be going so well that the people could not believe their whole country would be destroyed in a few years. This made it very difficult for Hosea, and he often had to stand alone.

God called Isaiah by a vision when he was in the temple in the year when good King Uzziah died. Following Uzziah came Jotham and Ahaz. Ahaz almost bankrupted the country by asking the

A modern day prophet, Martin Luther King, Jr., 1929-1968.

Assyrians to come and help him resist an attack by Israel and Syria. For this he had to pay the Assyrians so much that he brought the nation to poverty. He paid no attention to Isaiah's warnings, and Isaiah stood very much alone (see 2 Kings 16:5-8, and Isaiah 7:3-9).

Hezekiah, who ruled after Ahaz, refused to pay the Assyrians what they demanded, and in 701 BC they came against Jerusalem with a huge army. King Hezekiah was so frightened that he was ready to give in to the demands of the Assyrians, but again, Isaiah stood alone when he gave him God's promise that the Assyrians would not even shoot an arrow into the city. Something happened to the Assyrian army and they returned to Assyria without even beginning the siege against Jerusalem. By being willing to stand alone, Isaiah proved that God was faithful.

We do not know much about the personal life of Micah, but his strong message against the powerful rulers and the corrupt prophets must have left him very much alone many times.

Because Jeremiah advised the people to give in to the Babylonians, he was accused of being a traitor to his country. During his time the false prophets were saying that God would save the city of Jerusalem, and he alone warned the people of its destruction. When he sent a message to King Jehoiachim he had to hide, and Jehoiachim cut up the message with a knife and threw it into a fireplace. Once Jeremiah was put in an empty water storage tank and left to die. Fortunately he was rescued by a friend, but from then on he had to spend much of his life in prison. He saw his own nation destroyed and his own people taken captive. Few of God's servants have had as difficult a life as Jeremiah, and sometimes we find him complaining to God. Yet, he remained faithful through it all.

The prophets were really some of God's best friends. They were loyal and courageous people, and they still continue to be examples to us when we find it necessary to stand alone for God.

Check Yourself

1. List the four prophets discussed in this chapter, the kingdom in which they prophesied, and one danger that kingdom faced during the time they spoke.

Prophet	Kingdom	Danger
a) _____	_____	_____
b) _____	_____	_____
c) _____	_____	_____
d) _____	_____	_____

2. In what ways might you, as a Christian, be called to stand alone for God?

117

In Class

Study one of the prophets we have discussed in this chapter and write a statement about the prophet's concerns as if the prophet were speaking to you. The material and the Bible passages that are suggested will help you make this study.

_____

_____

_____

_____

_____

_____

_____

_____

_____

_____

_____

REVIEW OF UNIT SEVEN

After Solomon's death, God's nation was divided, with Israel on the north and Judah on the south. Many of the kings of both nations were unfaithful to God, and the prophets warned the people of what would happen if they did not repent. Because many of the people paid no attention to the prophets, both nations were destroyed, and the people went into captivity.

A New Beginning

CHAPTER 26
Lessons Learned in Captivity

During their captivity in Babylon, God's people came to realize that their God really is the God of all nations.

CHAPTER 27
Coming Home Again

When the people were permitted to return, they rebuilt Jerusalem and the temple and restored their worship under leaders such as Nehemiah and Ezra.

CHAPTER 28
The Prophets and the Messiah

The prophets told the people to look forward to the coming of one who was known as "the Messiah," which is another name for "the Christ."

CHAPTER 29
The World into Which Jesus Came

Jesus came at just "the right time" to a world that had been prepared for his coming. At the time of Jesus' coming, conditions were right for his message to be accepted by many people and preached to all the nations.

CHAPTER 30
Looking Back

UNIT EIGHT

ABRAHAM ISAAC JACOB JOSEPH	MOSES	JOSHUA	Judges	SAUL	DAVID	SOLOMON	Kingdom divided	Fall of Northern Kingdom	Fall of Southern Kingdom	Jews begin to return	Temple rebuilt	Maccabean revolt	Romans control Jerusalem	Herod becomes king	JESUS
2000 BC	1300 BC	1200 BC		1020 BC	1000 BC	922 BC		721 BC	587 BC	537 BC	515 BC	167 BC	63 BC	37 BC	4 BC

Lessons Learned in Captivity

26

BIBLE READING: Ezekiel 37:1-14

Other suggested Bible Readings: Psalm 137; Isaiah 40; Isaiah 46:1-9

Can you imagine what it would be like to be forced to leave your home and your country and to have to go to a strange land where you knew no one? Can you imagine becoming separated from most of your friends and seeing only strangers who thought of you as a foreign captive?

As a young person, you would see other young people looking at you and laughing and talking about you in a language you could not understand. You could not get the food you liked, and you had to live in temporary shacks that were uncomfortable. Because you came as a captive you had to leave behind most of the things you enjoyed having. If you

went to school, you could not understand what people were saying, and there was no one to help you learn. While you had been in your own country, you had gone to the temple in Jerusalem, where you and your parents worshiped. Now there was nowhere to go to worship, and you did not even know if God could hear your prayers this far away from home. You longed for the places you loved at home and for the people who cared for you, and you were very homesick.

This is what happened to the people of Judah. The Babylonians first took King Jehoiachin and some of the government leaders to Babylon and put a man named Zedekiah on the throne in Jerusalem. However, Zedekiah also rebelled against the Babylonians, and they took him and large numbers of the people captive and destroyed the temple.

When the people got to Babylon they found a large and wonderful city that made Jerusalem seem like a small town. The marvelous Ishtar Gate and the hanging gardens of Babylon must have seemed frightening to them. Psalm 137 tells how homesick, discouraged and bitter they were. The Babylonians tried to get the people from Judah to entertain them with some of their native songs, but they said it was impossible for them to sing about the Lord in a foreign land. They wanted only to think about Jerusalem and weep. However, the Babylonians were generally kind to their captives, and the people from Judah found work, entered into business, and made new friends.

The Ishtar Gate and the Hanging Gardens

THE GREAT GODS OF THE BABYLONIANS

Many of the people of Judah soon began to be attracted to the gods of the Babylonians. After all, it seemed to them, these gods must have great power to make Babylon become such a splendid city.

Others, however, remained faithful to their God and longed for the day when they could return to Jerusalem and rebuild the temple. They soon learned that the gods of the Babylonians were no greater than the idols of the people back home. When the Persians captured the city, the gods of the Babylonians did not seem to be able to help defend it. In Isaiah 46:1-9, the prophet ridicules two great Babylonian gods, Bel and Nebo, who could not even defend themselves from being taken prisoners.

"THE EXILE"

The time which the people of Judah spent in Babylon is known as "the Exile." As prophesied by Jeremiah, there were about 70 years from the time the temple in Jerusalem was destroyed and they were taken to Babylon until they finally

returned and rebuilt the temple and the city of Jerusalem. (587 BC—517 BC; see chart on page 108). During the Exile, the people of Judah became known as "Jews," which is the name by which they are known today. Their history is divided by the Exile so that what happened before the Exile is known as "pre-exilic," and what happened after the Exile is known as "post-exilic."

LESSONS LEARNED IN CAPTIVITY

Up to this time many of the people of Judah had thought of their God as being concerned only about their own land. During the Exile, God taught them that he was the Lord of all the earth. They learned that the gods of the great empires were only idols just like the gods of the people around their homeland. They also learned that they could worship God anywhere they were, even in a foreign land. They learned that they could still believe in God and that they belonged to him. He would hear their prayers in Babylon as well as at home. When they got back to their own land they had a much better understanding of how great God really is and how much he cares.

God had a purpose in allowing them to become captives for a while. This was his way of helping them to understand that he was concerned about the people of all nations. They were being prepared for the day, still many centuries away, when Jesus would choose some disciples from among them and command these disciples to bring his message to all peoples everywhere (see Matthew 28:19).

Whose god is the strongest?

Check Yourself

1. Who were Bel and Nebo?

2. What new name for God's people developed during the exile?

3. What was one important lesson that God's people learned while they were in exile in Babylon?

In Class

Think for a moment how lonely the people must have felt during the Exile. In the space below write the answers to the following questions: As a young person today, what is there in your life that makes you sad and lonely like a person in exile?

_____

_____

_____

_____

_____

_____

_____

_____

_____

_____

What cheers you up and lets you know that God cares for you?

_____

_____

_____

_____

_____

Coming Home Again

27

BIBLE READING: Psalm 126

Other suggested Bible readings: Nehemiah 1:1-11, 4:1-14, 6:15-7:3; Ezra 1, 8:31-10:17

"You may return to your homes!" At last the word came from the Emperor Cyrus that the captives were free to return. The Persians had defeated the Babylonians and were now the rulers of Babylon. The policy of this government was to let the captives who had been brought to Babylon return to their homes to take care of their land, conduct their business and pay their taxes.

At first only a few of the Jewish captives wanted to return to their own homeland. Only the older people remembered Jerusalem; the young people had never seen it. They had settled down in Babylon where they worked and conducted their businesses, and where they had made friends. So, at first, only a few of them began to trickle back to Judah. They managed to begin building the temple and to carry on worship at the altar, but they were desperately poor, and they met with a great deal of opposition. Therefore, the temple was not finished until several years had passed.

NEHEMIAH

One of the servants of the Persian emperor, Artaxerxes, was a Jew named Nehemiah. He was greatly troubled by the news that Jerusalem was still in ruins. He received permission to lead an expedition back to Jerusalem to rebuild the city. Some people who had been living in the land during the years of the exile did not want Nehemiah to succeed. The opposition was so great that he had to divide the workers so that only half of them worked, and the others protected the workers. Nehemiah's enthusiasm caught on, however, and the walls of the city were rebuilt in spite of opposition.

EZRA

Ezra was a priest and also a scribe. "Scribes" were people who copied the Law of God and other sacred papers. Ezra received permission from Emperor Artaxerxes to lead an expedition to Jerusalem. He also received a large grant of money which was a welcome help because the people who had already come to Jerusalem were still suffering from great poverty.

Ezra made the people familiar with the Law of God. Many of them did not even know that the Law existed and many others had no idea what it said because they had never read it. Ezra gathered the people together and read the Law to them. When they realized how far they had drifted from God's commands, many of them repented and returned to God.

A young student reads the Hebrew scriptures.

ligion of Jesus as he grew up. For others, however, it was a religion of many rules rather than a faith that lived in their hearts. Judaism is still the religion of most Jews, but it has undergone many changes since the time of Jesus.

BACK IN THE LAND

Gradually the people came back to the land of Judah and to Jerusalem. They were loyal and faithful, and they formed a strong body of serious believers who struggled for their freedom and for their faith. Yet they knew that something was still missing. Psalm 126 speaks of the excitement they felt when they came back to Jerusalem, but it also contains a prayer for God to do something more for them. They still were not satisfied. They longed very much for the promised King, or "Messiah," to come. The prophets had told them that he would be a descendant of David and that he would bring them peace and freedom. Unfortunately, many of them thought only of being free from the great empires around them. They did not yet realize that what they really needed was to be free from their sins. Therefore, they were not prepared for a lowly person like Jesus. There were some, however, who understood that they needed to be saved from their sins by a New Covenant that would change their hearts, as Jeremiah had promised.

Archaeological excavations along the west corner of the wall surrounding the Temple Mount in Jerusalem.

JUDAISM

Through the influence of Ezra and some of the prophets of that time, the faith of the Jewish people became an organized religion, which has become known as "Judaism." This religion brought the people back to the commands of God and helped them to be faithful to him. It produced some very devout and godly people. It was the re-

125

Check Yourself

1. Why were the Jewish captives in Babylon so slow in accepting the invitation to return to their own homeland?

2. Why do we remember Nehemiah?

3. Through the influence of Ezra and some of the prophets the faith of the Jewish people became an organized religion, known as _____

In Class

When I was growing up there came a time when I was between childhood and adulthood. I resented that my parents treated me as a child, and I wanted to be an adult. I wanted to live my own life as an adult and to have no one tell me what I must and what I must not do. I looked forward to becoming an adult just as the exiles looked forward to coming back to their own land where they would be free.

Yet, the adult world was so different from the world of my childhood that it frightened me, and as I became an adult I did not feel comfortable. There seemed to be enemies in the adult world who did not want me to have a job or to accept me as an adult. Now that I have been an adult for many years, I feel comfortable as an adult, but that is not the way I felt when I was growing up.

1. What do you look forward to as you become an adult?

_____

_____

_____

_____

_____

_____

2. What frightens you about becoming an adult?

_____

_____

_____

_____

_____

The Prophets and the Messiah 28

BIBLE READING: Isaiah 35:5, 6; Matthew 11:2-6

Other suggested Bible readings: Isaiah 53, 61:1, 2; Luke 4:16-21

CATECHISM: WHO IS JESUS CHRIST?

Jesus Christ is the Messiah, God's son, promised through the prophets. He came into the world to free people from sin and establish his kingdom on earth.

"Who do you say that I am?" Simon Peter answered, "You are the Christ, the Son of the Living God."

Matthew 16:15b, 16, NIV

THE IMPORTANCE OF HOPE

Hope is what makes life worth living. When things go wrong, we need to have hope for better things to come. When we lose a game we need to have hope that we will win the next one. When we are sick we need to have hope for getting well again. If we lose our job we need hope for getting another one. No matter what happens, we must have hope or we will give up in despair.

Hope is a gift from God, and we who believe in him have hope. The prophets of whom we have studied gave the people hope by telling them that God was faithful and would not give up on them.

The greatest hope the prophets gave was for a time when there would be no more sorrow, no more suffering, no more war and violence. A time was coming, they said, when God would bring peace and security to the whole earth. The prophets promised that a time would come when:

"They shall beat their swords
   into plowshares,
and their spears into pruning
   hooks;

nation shall not lift up sword
   against nation,
neither shall they learn war any
   more" (Isaiah 2:4)
"The wolf shall dwell with the
   lamb,
and the leopard shall lie down
   with the kid,
and the calf and the lion and
   the fatling together,
and a little child shall lead
   them . . . .
They shall not hurt or destroy in
all my holy mountain;
for the earth shall be full of the
   knowledge of the Lord as the
   waters cover the sea."
(Isaiah 11:6, 9)

All of this, the prophets said, would come to pass through the coming of a great and good Ruler who would be a descendant of David:

"Of the increase of his government and of peace there will be
   no end, upon the throne of David, and over his kingdom, to
   establish it, and to uphold it
   with justice and righteousness
   from this time forth and
   forevermore." (Isaiah 9:7)

"THE MESSIAH"

This person who was to come was called "the Messiah." The word "messiah" came from the practice of putting oil on the head of a person when he was declared to be king. "Messiah" means, "A person who has been anointed." God would bless that person with wisdom and strength to be a good and successful ruler. Therefore, a king was "an anointed person," or "a messiah." As the prophets spoke of the great King whom God would send some day, they applied the word "messiah" to him. He was God's promised "Messiah" or "Anointed King" who would some day come to fulfill the hopes of the people.

JESUS, THE MESSIAH

We Christians believe that Jesus is the Messiah. The word "Christ" is the Greek word for "messiah," and when we say, "Jesus Christ," we mean, "Jesus, the Messiah." We believe that he fulfilled what the prophets said the Messiah would be and do. As the Catechism for this chapter says, he was the one who was promised "through the prophets."

The Messiah as King

Over and over the prophets said that a descendant of David would rule forever. For instance, we read in Psalms 89:35, 36, "Once for all I have sworn by my holiness; I will not lie to David. His line shall endure forever, his throne as long as the sun before me."

From the time Jesus was born, those who considered him to be the Messiah thought of him as a king. When the wise men came looking for him, they asked "Where is he who has been born king of the Jews?" Jesus never denied that he was a king, and he always spoke with authority, but he said, "My kingdom is not of this world." By this he meant that he was not a competitor of earthly kings and authorities. He had power over illness, storms, evil spirits, and death, but most of all he came to rule in the hearts of people. He did not even fight to defend his kingdom when he was being crucified. Yet for many centuries he has been able to claim the loyalty of more subjects than any other king has ever had.

The Messiah As A Bringer of Good News

As part of the answer to the catechism question, "Who are the prophets?" we quoted Isaiah 61:1, 2a, which describes a prophet as a bringer of good news to poor

and needy people. Now, in Luke 4:18, 19, we find Jesus speaking these same words about himself. He brought good news to poor and needy people. He healed broken hearts and set people free who were captive to sin and fear. He was always on the side of the poor and the oppressed. Through the centuries Jesus has brought good news to millions of people.

The Messiah As Healer

The prophets promised a time when blind people would see, deaf people would hear, lame people would run, and people who could not speak would sing for joy (see Isaiah 35:5, 6).

Once when Jesus was asked if he really was the Messiah, he performed some miracles, and then he said, "The blind receive their sight and the lame walk, lepers are cleansed and the deaf hear, the dead are raised up and the poor have good news preached to them" (Matthew 11:2-6). By this, Jesus was pointing out that the very things he was doing were the things the prophets had promised.

The Messiah as Savior

One message of the prophets that was very hard for the people to understand was a description of a servant of the Lord who suffered for other people. Isaiah 53 says, "He was despised and rejected by men; a man of sorrows, and acquainted with grief." "He was wounded for our transgressions, he was bruised for our iniquities." "Like a lamb that is led to the slaughter, and like a sheep that before his shearers is dumb, so he opened not his mouth." This chapter speaks of this person as dying for the sins of the people and then rising again.

Few, if any, of the people in Jesus' time recognized that his crucifixion had any-

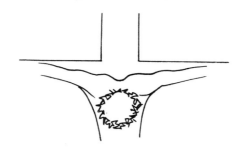

thing to do with these words from Isaiah 53. Everyone was looking for a person who would start a revolution and set up a kingdom by force. When Jesus allowed himself to be crucified and when he died on the cross, even his disciples were confused and disappointed. Then, finally, God helped them to see that the very things that were spoken about the servant who suffered were fulfilled in Jesus' death and resurrection. Then they used this message from Isaiah 53 more than any other words from the prophets to prove that Jesus was the Savior, who died for the sins of the people and rose again.

THE PROMISE OF THE MESSIAH BROUGHT HOPE

As the prophets spoke of a better time to come, and as they told of the great and good Son of David who would rule forever, they brought hope. Whenever God's people were forced to suffer, especially after they returned from the Exile in Babylon, they were kept from despair by the hope that the Messiah would come some day.

Check Yourself

1. For what kind of Messiah were the people of Jesus' day looking?

2. List four ways in which Jesus fulfilled the role of Messiah.

3. List four things that Jesus did to remove suffering that showed him to be the Messiah.

4. What is the meaning of the word "messiah?"

In Class

You will try to find some of the different words or phrases used in the Bible to describe the Messiah. Here are some of the references in which you will find these different descriptions. Look up the reference and write the descriptive word or phrase.

Old Testament

New Testament

Micah 5:2-4 _____ Matthew 2:6 _____

Isaiah 35:5, 6 _____ Matthew 11:2-6 _____

Isaiah 61:1, 2 _____ Luke 4:16-21 _____

Isaiah 40:9-11 _____ John 10:11-16 _____

Isaiah 53:4-6 _____ Matthew 17:1-13 _____

Isaiah 9:6, 7 _____ Mark 2:1-12 _____

Jeremiah 31:31-34 _____ Luke 9:22-27 _____

John 10:22-32 _____

BIBLE READING: Galatians 4:4

There is a "right time" for everything that is important. There is a "right time" to begin school. There is a "right time" to begin driving a car. There is a "right time," when we are old enough to get a job. We keep growing up until we reach the "right time" for different things.

The world also had to grow up to the "right time" for Jesus to be born. "When the right time came, the time God decided on, he sent his Son." (Galatians 4:4, LB) Up to that time God had spoken through prophets, but when the "right time" came, he sent Jesus, his Son.

THE WORLD AT THE "RIGHT TIME" FOR JESUS TO COME

The message of Jesus was to be preached to all people. The nations had always been in conflict with one another, especially around Palestine, which formed a natural bridge between the east and the west (see map on page 104). But finally, for the first time in the history of the world, all of the land from what is now England, on the west, to the border of what is now Iraq on the east, was united under the Roman Empire. The existence of the Roman Empire created four conditions that made this the "right time" for God to send his Son into the world. These conditions were:

1. The Roman armies were strong enough to keep peace, so the message could go out through the great Roman Empire without being hindered by nations at war.

2. The Romans had built roads which made it possible to travel to all parts of the empire with the message.

3. Greek had become a common language, so the earliest missionaries could be understood wherever they went. When the books of the New Testament were

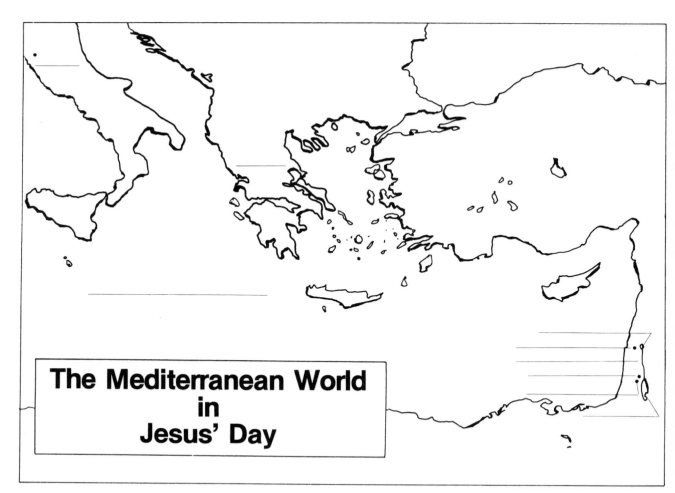

written in Greek, they, too, could be read all over the Roman Empire.

4. The Roman gods did not satisfy the spiritual needs of the people. Even though the Greeks had a high degree of civilization, their society was full of corruption and immorality. The gods they worshiped were as bad as the people were, and there was a great longing for a message that would offer them something more worthwhile. The message of Jesus met that need.

EVENTS WHICH LED UP TO THE COMING OF JESUS

While the Jews had been in exile they had learned really to believe in their God as the God of the whole earth. During the seventy years they had spent in Babylon they lost all interest in the golden calves and the worship of Baal. They had discovered that their God was greater even than the idols of Babylon. Now, as the time approached for Jesus to be born, they were brought face-to-face with a world that was entirely different from the world in which they had lived before. During this time they faced different problems and new temptations. These are the main events of this period:

1. 538 BC—333 BC

THE JEWS UNDER PERSIAN RULE
During this time the Jews returned from Babylon, and the temple was rebuilt by 517 B.C. The city was restored, and worship was renewed under the leadership of people like Ezra and some of the prophets.

2. 333 BC—323 BC

THE JEWS UNDER ALEXANDER THE GREAT

132

The great general Alexander brought all the nations from Greece to India under his control in ten years. During this time Palestine, the homeland of the Jews, became part of his empire. Alexander brought Greek culture wherever he went, and the Jewish people were now introduced to a new way of thinking. The Greek religion, with its many gods, was opposed by the faithful Jews. Other Jews who were not as faithful were attracted to the Greek ideas, and these differences produced conflicts for many years to come.

3. 323 BC—199 BC

THE JEWS UNDER EGYPTIAN CONTROL
When Alexander died and his empire broke up, Palestine came under the control of Egypt. The Egyptians gave little trouble to the Jews, who were permitted to worship in peace.

4. 199 BC—167 BC

THE JEWS UNDER SYRIAN CONTROL
By this time the Syrian part of Alexander's former empire was growing stronger, and Palestine came under Syrian control. The Syrian emperors were enthusiastic for Greek culture and religion, and they tried, without success, to introduce it into Palestine. Antiochus Epiphanes, who became emperor of Syria in 175 BC, was particularly distressed with the Jews' unwillingness to cooperate, and his army marched into Jerusalem in an attempt to force the Greek way of life on the people. He turned the temple into a place for the worship of Greek gods, and he offered sacrifices to them on the altar that had been dedicated to the worship of the God of Israel. He even sacrificed a pig as an insult to the Jewish people. The Jews who remained true to their faith suffered great persecution, and many of them were killed.

5. 167 BC—63 BC

THE MACCABEAN REVOLT
A man named Mattathias was so enraged at this desecration of God's house that he and his sons took the name of "Maccabee" (which means "hammer") and formed a guerrilla band. Mattathias' son Judas became the leader of a revolt that won freedom for the Jewish people.

The Hasidim
During this time a movement developed for the purpose of interpreting and keeping the Law of God in the new kind of world which was being influenced so much by Greek ideas. Its followers were known as "the Hasidim." It is believed that the Pharisees came from this movement. The Pharisees accepted many traditions that were not part of the written Law of God. The Sadducees were opponents of the Pharisees. They accepted only what was written in the Law. Both the Pharisees and the Sadducees were active in Jesus' time.

An Orthodox scribe of today working on a Torah scroll for use in a synogogue. The scrolls are hand-copied, using a quill pen.

The Synagogues
During the days of the Kingdom the people had been expected to come to Jerusalem to worship. Now, however, when many Jews were far away from Jerusalem, there devel-

oped a need for places of worship in their own communities. These were called "synagogues." We do not know just when they began to appear, but they were common during the time of Jesus.

Synagogue ruins at Capernaum

6. 63 BC

ROMAN OCCUPATION BEGINS
The Roman general Pompey captured Jerusalem after a bloody siege of three months. The Jewish people now lost their independence and surrendered to the supervision of Rome.

In 37 BC Herod the Great was appointed by the Romans to be king in Jerusalem. He was a cruel man who thought nothing of murdering anyone whom he even suspected of becoming his enemy. Therefore, when some men from the east came to him asking, "Where is he who is born king of the Jews?" Herod became afraid that if this baby for whom they were looking was allowed to grow up, he would become a competitor for his throne. When Herod learned that the Messiah was to be born in Bethlehem he immediately had all the baby boys in Bethlehem killed. However, he would not have needed to be afraid. This baby was born to be King of another kind of Kingdom. God warned his parents to get him out of Bethlehem before Herod's soldiers arrived. He was the One for whom the world had now been made ready. This, finally, was the "right time," for Jesus to be born in Bethlehem.

Check Yourself

1. List the four situations in the world at the time of Jesus that made this the right time for him to be born.

2. What was the Maccabean revolt?

3. a. At the beginning of the period covered by this chapter, the Jews were under the control of what great empire?

   b. At the end of the period they were under the control of what great empire?

In Class

On the map of the Mediterranean world in Jesus' day, on page 132, you will be asked to mark certain places. To find these places you will look at maps in your Bible (For finding places in Palestine, use the map of Palestine, which shows greater detail than the map of the Roman Empire. Some places will be very close together.). Using the maps in your Bible, you will then be asked to estimate the distances between some of these places and to compare them with distances between places from where you live.

• Read silently 1 John 1:5-7 and then write the message that God would have you share with your world today.

_____

_____

_____

_____

What hinders and helps you to share this message with your friends? _____

_____

_____

_____

_____

_____

_____

_____

_____

_____

_____

_____

Looking Back

ASSIGNMENT: Review all memory work assigned during the year.

This chapter contains some reminders to help you prepare for the review which you will have in class. Go back through the book to find answers you do not know. Your teacher may suggest other things to include in this review.

Many of the dates in this chapter are only approximate. They are included to help you know the order of the events and the times when some of the persons lived.

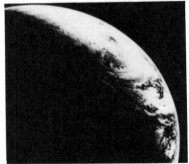

1. "We believe in the Holy Scriptures, the Old and New Testaments, as the Word of God and the only perfect rule for faith, doctrine and conduct." What person is also called "The Word"? Why is he called "The Word"?

2. God created the heavens and the earth and all its creatures. What does it mean that human beings were created in God's likeness? What are some things we can do to live as good friends of the earth?

3. Adam and Eve made the wrong choice. Since then we have all made wrong choices, and God is seeking to bring us back to himself. What were the steps that led to Adam and Eve's wrong choice? What has God done to make it possible for us to have a relationship with him?

4. God had no friends left on earth except Noah and his family. Sin had spread like an epidemic over the whole earth. What does the story of Noah teach us?

5. God chose Abraham to be one of his special friends and told him to go to a land which God would show him. He led him to the land of Canaan, which is now the land of Palestine. God made a covenant with Abraham.
What is meant by a covenant between God and his people? What is an example from the life of Abraham of "faithful obedience?"

6. Abraham's son, Isaac, and his grandson, Jacob, inherit the Covenant.
What was the frightening experience Isaac had when he was a boy? Compare the characters of Isaac and Jacob.

7. Joseph brought his father, Jacob, and his brothers down to Egypt.
What happened to cause Joseph to bring his family to Egypt?
What did Joseph's brothers do that was intended for evil that turned out for good?

8. The number of Jacob's descendants increased while they lived in Egypt, and this continued for several generations.
How did the Egyptians like the way the descendants of Jacob increased in numbers and what did the Egyptians do about it?

To
about
1300 BC

About
1300 BC

9. Moses was another of God's special friends. He brought the Israelites out of Egypt and formed them into a nation.
How did Moses get the people of God out of Egypt?
Why did the Israelites have to stay in the desert for forty years?

10. While the Israelites were in the desert, God gave them some laws, including the Ten Commandments.
What did Jesus say were the two greatest commandments and how do these commandments relate to the Ten Commandments?

11. Joshua followed Moses as the leader of the Israelites.
What did Joshua do?

About
1200 BC

About
1200 BC

12. After the people got into the land which God had promised them they were ruled by judges.
Name some of these judges.
What was the "vicious circle"?

1020 BC

1020 BC
1000 BC

13. Saul was Israel's first king.
Why did Saul fail?

1000 BC

14. God chose David to be the next king. Tell about David's relationships with two or three different persons.
What are two or three other things you remember about David?

961 BC

961 BC	15. Solomon followed David as king. Though he was a wise king, he made one big mistake.
922 BC	What was Solomon's big mistake?

922 BC	16. After Solomon the kingdom divided. Israel was to the north, and Judah was to the south.
	Over which of the two kingdoms did each of the following kings rule:
	Jeroboam?
	Ahab?
	Rehoboam?
	Hezekiah?
	Jeohoiachim?
	Tell one other thing about each of the above kings.
	What did the prophets do?
	Name as many of the prophets as you can and tell one thing about each
721 BC	prophet you name.

721 BC	17. The Assyrians captured the Northern Kingdom of Israel and took many of the people captive to Assyria.
	Why did God let the Northern Kingdom of
701 BC	Israel be destroyed?

701 BC	18. The Assyrians invaded the Southern Kingdom of Judah.
	What happened when the Assyrians came to
587 BC	Jerusalem?

587 BC	19. The Babylonians destroyed the temple and much of the city of Jerusalem, and they took many of the people captive to Babylon.
	What special lesson did the people of Judah learn while they were captives in Babylon?
537 BC	What word is used to describe the captivity in Babylon?

537 BC	20. The people of Judah were permitted to return to their own land.
	What was the name of the emperor who permit-
517 BC	ted them to return?

517 BC	21. The temple was rebuilt by 517 BC and the rebuilding of the city continued for many years.
	What person gave leadership in rebuilding the city of Jerusalem?
	What person do we remember for restoring the worship of the people?
	Two persons who influenced the life of the Jewish people between the time of their return from captivity in Babylon and the coming of Jesus were Antiochus Epiphanes and Judas Maccabee.
	What did each of these persons do to influence the life of these people?
4 BC	The birth of Jesus. ★

★ Note: The calendar in use during Jesus' time counted the years from the year Rome was founded. This was replaced about five hundred years later by the calendar which was intended to count the years from the year Jesus was born. Because the people who established this calendar did not have exact information about the date of Jesus' birth, they made an error of about four years. This is the reason the birth of Jesus comes at about 4 BC.

Some general questions:

22. We saw how the Psalms express both the faith and the feelings of God's people.

    How were the Psalms originally used?

23. The Book of Proverbs is one of several books of the Bible known as "Wisdom Literature."

    What is the main emphasis of Wisdom Literature?

24. Jesus was born at a time when conditions in the world were right for him to come.

    What four conditions at the time when Jesus was born made this appear to be the right time for him to be born?

Class Picture

Autographs

Time Line

2000 BC	ABRAHAM ISAAC JACOB JOSEPH
1300 BC	MOSES
1200 BC	JOSHUA
	Judges
1020 BC	SAUL
1000 BC	DAVID
922 BC	SOLOMON
	Kingdom divided
721 BC	Fall of Northern Kingdom
587 BC	Fall of Southern Kingdom
537 BC	Jews begin to return
515 BC	Temple rebuilt
167 BC	Maccabean revolt
63 BC	Romans control Jerusalem
37 BC	Herod becomes king
4 BC	JESUS

30 AD	Life of Jesus
325 AD	Council of Nicaea
397 AD	Council of Carthage
410 AD	Fall of Rome
622 AD	GREGORY THE GREAT Beginning of Moslem faith
732 AD	Battle of Tours
800 AD	Holy Roman Empire begins
1054 AD	The Church divides
1096 AD	Crusades begin
	ST. DOMINIC ST. FRANCIS OF ASSISI
	The Inquisition
	JOHN WYCLIFF JOHN HUS

1517 AD	Reformation begins
	    LUTHER
	    ZWINGLI
	    CALVIN
	    JOHN WESLEY
	    JONATHAN EDWARDS
	    GEORGE WHITFIELD
	    CHARLES G. FINNEY

1800 AD	Covenant Churches organized:

1900 AD	Sweden—1878
	    United States—1885
	    Canada—1904

Part Two

Jesus Has Come!

UNIT ONE

CHAPTER 1
Getting Started

Welcome, especially to any new members! We begin the second part of our course by renewing our relationships and reviewing Part One.

CHAPTER 2
The Coming of Jesus

Jesus has come! We learn about him through the four Gospels, Matthew, Mark, Luke and John. They are really one message of the good news of Jesus, as told by four people.

CHAPTER 3
Jesus Begins His Work

Jesus began his work by receiving God's Holy Spirit and power at his baptism and by overcoming the temptation to use this power for his own benefit.

CHAPTER 4
Jesus Chooses Some Friends to Be On His "Team"

Jesus chose twelve disciples to be with him, to learn from him and to work with him in what is known as a "community." Jesus' disciples include all who believe in him and belong to him. He wants us all to learn to love each other and enjoy happy relationships and to carry on his ministry as his representatives.

CHAPTER 5
Some of Jesus' Other Friends

Jesus had many friends who were "outsiders" and not acceptable to some people. Jesus wants to take away the separation between "outsiders" and "insiders."

Birth of Jesus

Jesus baptized, tempted, begins ministry

Writing of the four gospels during last half of first century

| 4 BC | 27 AD | 50 AD | 100 AD |

Getting Started 1

In Class

Welcome to Confirmation! This chapter is in three sections: Section I is for those who are just beginning confirmation study. Section II is for those who have already finished Part One. Section III is for both those who are just beginning and for those who have already finished Part One.

SECTION I
FOR THOSE WHO ARE
JUST BEGINNING CONFIRMATION

Members of the class who have finished Part One welcome you as you join them. You may have mixed feelings because you don't know what to expect. One of the things we learned as we studied Part One was that it is okay to have mixed feelings. As you become more familiar with the class you will no doubt feel much more comfortable. First, I would like to have you get to know me a little better. I hope that knowing me better will make it more interesting for you to read this book. Please turn to Part One, Chapter 1, page 5, and read what I have written about myself. Then, after you have finished you may write something about yourself in the spaces that follow. If you wish, you may share this information with other members of the class.

SECTION II
FOR THOSE WHO HAVE ALREADY FINISHED PART ONE
A REVIEW OF PART ONE

How much do you remember from Part One? Your teacher will pass out cards with some words that complete the following statements:

1. In the beginning God created all things. _humans beings_ are God's special creation. They are created in _Gods form_. They are able to _respond to God's love_, and to _be creative_.

2. The first persons to disobey God were _Adam_ and _Eve_. They were tempted by _Satan_ in the form of a _snake_. The reason sin is so tempting is that it seems so _attractive_. Sometimes it even seems _good_.

3. After the first people had sinned, sin became an epidemic and spread to all people. Sin always brings _judgement_, and God sent a great _flood_. The only people to escape were _Noah_ and his family.

4. God called a certain man to leave his own country and go to another country, which God promised to show him. This man had to live by _faith_, and God made a _covenant_ with him, promising to be faithful to him. The name of this man was _Abraham_.

5. One man was sold by his eleven brothers to be a slave in _Egypt_. When his brothers came to buy bread, he forgave them and gave them what they needed. This man's name was _Joseph_. The descendants of these twelve brothers became known as the Children of _Israel_.

This story helps us to understand that God keeps his _promise_ and continues to be _faithful_ even when everything seems to go wrong.

6. God set his people free from slavery in _Egypt_ and brought them to a country he had _promised_. On their way to this country they had to pass through the _Red Sea_. Here their leader learned that God gives strength for whatever he has commanded us to do. The name of their leader was _Moses_. During this time God taught them how to _worship_ him and gave them the _ten comandments_.

7. God's people were led into the Promised Land by _Joshua_. After they arrived, they were first ruled by _judges_. During this time they kept going through sin circles. Each circle had four parts. The parts were: 1) They _disobeyed_ God. 2) their enemies _conquered_ them, 3) they _cried_ _out_ to God, 4) God _saved_ them from their enemies.

8. After the time of the judges, Israel was ruled by kings. The first king made the wrong choice and disobeyed God. The name of this king was _Saul_. God rejected him and chose another, who was a _sheperd_ and a _musician_. He became Israel's greatest king. His relationships with God and with other people are both a _example_ and an _warning_ to us. His name was _David_.

9. The next king was very wise, but he also made some wrong choices. He encouraged the people to worship other gods beside the true God. After him, the kingdom was divided into two parts. The northern part was called _Isrial_ and the southern part was called _Judah_. The name of this king was _Salomen_.

10. The Psalms were the _hyms_ of Israel. The Psalms have several values to us. One value is that they give us an opportunity to express our _Feelings_ and our _beleifs_.

11. Books like Job, Proverbs and Ecclesiastes are known as _Wisdom literature_. They teach us that wrong living is not only bad, it is also _stupid_, and those who are _wise_ try to live righteously according to God's commandments.

12. During the rule of the kings, God sent some special persons to call the people back to himself and to warn them against disobeying him. They also told the people of a _Coming king_. From these special persons we learn that God speaks through _people_ and that those who remain true to God must sometimes _Stand alone_. These special persons were called _prophits_.

13. Because God's people kept _disobeying_ him, he allowed their enemies to take them away from their own country. The people of the Northern Kingdom were taken to _Assyria_. The people of the Southern Kingdom were taken to _Babylon_ and returned after seventy years. While they were captives, they learned that God would _take care_ of them even while they were far from their own

country.

14. There were four conditions during the time of Jesus that made the world ready for his message. They were made possible by the Roman empire. These four conditions were 1) _Good roads_ 2) _peace one language_ 3) _____ 4) the people were tired of their _False Gods_.

SECTION III
FOR THOSE WHO ARE JUST BEGINNING AND FOR THOSE WHO HAVE ALREADY FINISHED PART ONE

One purpose of the confirmation class is to be what is known as a "community." For Christians this word has a special meaning. Read John 15:1-17 and, with the help of your teacher, list some of the things in this passage that are found in a Christian community. After you have listed as many things as you can find, write, in the space below, your answer to the question, "What are some things I should do to be a member of the Confirmation Class community?" Write your answer in the form of a sentence.

_____

_____

_____

_____

_____

_____

_____

How We Learn About Jesus

2

BIBLE READING: Matthew 2:1-12; Luke 1:26-38; 2:1-14
Other suggested Bible readings: Mark 1:1-11; John 1:1-14

ASSIGNMENT: Memorize the books of the New Testament, as you find them listed in the front of your Bible.

JESUS HAS COME!

The prophets of Israel had promised his coming, and for hundreds of years, people had been waiting for him. Now, at last, he has come. This is the greatest moment of all in God's plan to win people back to himself, to be his friends.

HOW WE LEARN ABOUT THE COMING OF JESUS

From the first four books of the New Testament we learn about Jesus' birth, who he was, what he said and what he did. These books are "The Gospel According to Matthew," "The Gospel According to Mark," "The Gospel According to Luke," and "The Gospel According to John." The word "gospel" means "good news," and these four books are really the "Good News about Jesus" according to these four persons. They tell us the Good News about his coming and what he means to us.

FOUR GOSPELS BUT ONLY ONE MESSAGE

These four books are often called "the Four Gospels," but they bring only one message. They tell us that:
• Jesus is the Messiah, or the Christ, the Son of God; but he is also truly human.
• Jesus has brought God's Kingdom to us. He is the King, and he has shown us how to enter that Kingdom.
• Jesus is our Savior, who died for us and arose again, and we may believe in him and receive eternal life.
• Jesus gave us many valuable teachings and he did many wonderful things.
• Jesus has great authority, and he deserves to be followed and obeyed, but he is also humble and forgiving, and he cares tenderly for us.

FOUR GOSPELS WITH DIFFERENT EMPHASES

Why should there be four Gospels? Would not one be enough? While it is true that they all bring the same message of Jesus, each one places more emphasis on certain things than the others do, so we get a much more complete account of Jesus by reading all four of the Gospels than by reading only one.
1. *Matthew emphasizes Jesus as a person of great authority.*
• Matthew quotes more of the sayings of Jesus than the other Gospels do. To Mat-

Andrea Mantegna

Rembrandt

Neale Murray

Warner Sallman

Lars-Birger Sponberg

These four pictures illustrate other characteristics of the Gospels. What do they say to you?

thew Jesus was a teacher, and Matthew tells us that Jesus taught with authority (Matthew 7:28, 29).
• The Gospel of Matthew ends with Jesus having all authority in heaven and on earth (Matthew 28:18).
• Matthew was no doubt writing with Jewish people in mind because he emphasizes, more than the other Gospels, that Jesus fulfilled the Old Testament prophecies.
• Since Matthew emphasizes the authority of Jesus, he does not say anything about the humble circumstances of his birth. Instead, he tells of the Wise Men who came looking for a King, and who worshiped the baby Jesus and gave him expensive gifts (Matthew 2:1-11).

2. *Mark emphasizes Jesus as a person of action.*
• Mark also presents Jesus as the Son of God and a person of great authority, but Mark includes fewer of the sayings of Jesus and concentrates on what he did.
• Mark shows Jesus as doing many things in rapid succession. Before the end of the first chapter he has already recorded a dozen things Jesus had done.
• Since Mark emphasizes Jesus as a per-

son of action, he does not even mention his birth.

3. *Luke emphasizes Jesus as a human being.*
• Although Luke makes it clear that Jesus is God, he emphasizes the things in Jesus' life that show him to be fully human.
• Luke speaks more of prayer and home life than the other Gospels.
• Luke includes more human interest stories than the other Gospels.
Following are some stories that are found only in Luke:
- A story from Jesus' childhood (Luke 2:40-52).
- The parable of the Good Samaritan (Luke 10:25-37).
- The disagreement between two sisters, Martha and Mary (Luke 10:38-42).
- The parable of the father and his two sons (Luke 15:11-32).
• Since Luke emphasizes Jesus as a human being, he goes into great detail about his birth. Luke tells of the angel whom God sent to Mary, a young woman engaged to a man named Joseph, to tell her that she was going to have a baby who would become great and be called

the Son of God and rule on the throne of David over a kingdom that would never end. When Mary asked how she could be having a baby since she had never had sexual relations with any man, the angel explained to her that the Holy Spirit of God would make it possible for her to have this baby by a miracle, and that she should name him "Jesus." Luke tells how Mary traveled with Joseph from Nazareth to Bethlehem to register for a special tax just when her baby was due to be born. Because the hotel in Bethlehem was full, they had to stay in a barn. There the baby Jesus was born and laid in a manger from which the cattle were fed. The first persons to hear about his birth were some shepherds to whom angels appeared while they were watching their sheep at night.

From Luke we learn that, even though Jesus was the Son of God and was miraculously born of a virgin mother, he was born and grew up to become an adult as other human beings do.

4. *John emphasizes Jesus as God.*

• Although John also teaches that Jesus is human, he places more emphasis on Jesus as God.

• Many of the incidents that John uses

from the life of Jesus are different from those that are recorded by the other Gospels, and he emphasizes the spiritual meaning of these incidents.

• John tells how Jesus used words like "life," "light," "bread," "water," "the Good Shepherd," "the door" to illustrate spiritual truths and to help explain who Jesus really is.

• The word "light" appears twice as many times in John, and the word "life" appears nearly three times as often in John as in the other Gospels. John speaks of Jesus as the light of the world (John 8:12) and as the One who gives eternal life (John 1:4, 3:16).

• Much of the Gospel of John is a series of miraculous things Jesus did to prove that he really is the Son of God, and John states at the close that this Gospel was written so "that you may believe that Jesus is the Christ, the Son of God, and that believing you may have life in his name" (John 20:31).

• Since John emphasizes Jesus as being God, and since Jesus' life as God did not begin with his birth, John does not mention Jesus' birth at all. Instead, he begins by speaking of Jesus as "the Word of God" who was with God and was God from the very beginning and who now became a human being and lived with us on this earth (see John 1:1-14).

These are just a few of the ways the four Gospels differ because of their different emphases. When we include all of them, they give us a clearer and more complete picture of Jesus.

THE "SYNOPTIC" GOSPELS

The first three Gospels, Matthew, Mark and Luke, are called "Synoptic Gospels." The word, "synoptic," means "to see alike." These three Gospels are called "synoptic" because they look at Jesus from very much the same viewpoint. They all contain many of the same events from Jesus' life, and sometimes they use exactly the same words. The Gospel of John, on the other hand, contains many events that are quite different from the other three. One example from the Synoptic Gospels is found in the following three passages. If you will compare these passages, you will find that they are exactly alike in some places, with just a few differences in other places:

Matthew 9:5-7
"For which is easier, to say, 'Your sins are forgiven,' or to say, 'Rise and walk'? But that you may know that the Son of man has authority on earth to forgive sins"—he then said to the paralytic—"Rise, take up your bed and go home." And he rose and went home.

Mark 2:9-12
"Which is easier, to say to the paralytic, 'Your sins are forgiven,' or to say, 'Rise, take up your pallet and walk'? But that you may know that the Son of man has authority on earth to forgive sins"—he said to the paralytic—"I say to you, rise, take up your pallet and go home." And he rose, and immediately took up the pallet and went out before them all.

Luke 5:23-25
"Which is easier, to say, 'Your sins are forgiven you,' or to say, 'Rise and walk'? But that you may know that the Son of man has authority on earth to forgive sins"—he said to the man who was paralyzed—"I say to you, rise, take up your bed and go home." And immediately he rose before them, and took up that on which he lay, and went home, glorifying God.

From the four Gospels we learn about the coming of Jesus, his life and work, and what it means to believe in him and belong to him.

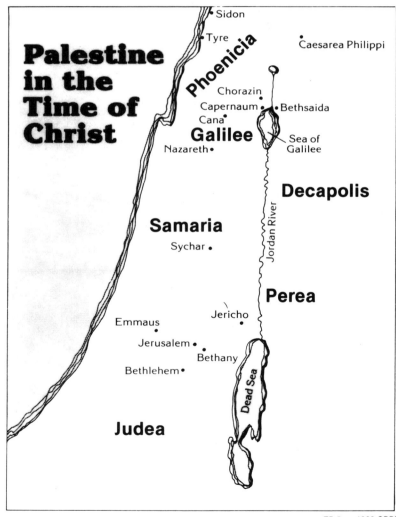

Palestine in the Time of Christ

Sidon
Tyre
Phoenicia
Caesarea Philippi
Chorazin
Capernaum • Bethsaida
Cana
Galilee
Sea of Galilee
Nazareth
Decapolis
Jordan River
Samaria
Sychar
Perea
Jericho
Emmaus
Jerusalem • Bethany
Bethlehem
Dead Sea
Judea

TP-5   1980 SPPI

Check Yourself

1. What does the word "gospel" mean?

The good news about Jesus.

2. Explain the value of having four "Gospels" instead of only one.

They all give the same messages, but in different ways.

3. What does the word "synoptic" mean, and why are the first three Gospels called "Synoptics"?

Very much alike, and they all look at Jesus in the same way.

4. From your understanding of Jesus, what do you believe are some of the reasons for his coming?

To forgive all sins, tell people about God, and offer salvation.

In Class

After comparing what Jesus meant to Matthew, Mark, Luke and John, think about what Jesus means to you. Then complete the following sentence in the space below: "To me, Jesus is . . .

_____

_____

_____

_____

Jesus Begins His Work

3

BIBLE READING: Matthew 3:1—4:11
Other suggested Bible readings: Mark 1:1-13; Luke 3:21, 22; Luke 4:1-13

Memorize the Second Article of the Apostles' Creed and Luther's explanation of it, as stated in the answers to the two following questions:
1. What is the Second Article of the Apostles' Creed?
I believe in Jesus Christ his only Son, our Lord; who was conceived by the Holy Spirit, born of the Virgin Mary, suffered under Pontius Pilate, was crucified, dead and buried; he descended into hades; the third day he rose again from the dead; he ascended into heaven, and sitteth on the right hand of God, the Father Almighty; from thence he shall come to judge the quick and the dead.
2. What does this mean?
I believe that Jesus Christ—true God, son of the Father from eternity, and true man, born of the Virgin Mary—is my Lord.

He has redeemed me, a lost and condemned person, saved me at great cost from sin, death, and the power of the devil—not with silver or gold, but with his holy and precious suffering and death.

All this he has done that I may be his own, live under him in his kingdom, and serve him in everlasting righteousness, innocence and blessedness, just as he is risen from the dead and lives and rules eternally.

This is most certainly true.

ASSIGNMENT: Finish memorizing the books of the New Testament if you have not already done so.

I shall never forget the time when I first gave my life over to Jesus. I had just begun college, and I was looking forward both to having fun and to making a success out of my life. But nothing seemed to make any sense to me; there didn't seem to be any purpose for living. My conscience was troubling me about some of the things I was doing, and I became more and more unhappy. Even though I had learned about Jesus in Sunday school, I had never taken him seriously, and now I thought I was too old for Sunday school. It never really occurred to me that trusting in Jesus might make my life more satisfying because by this time I did not believe in Jesus, and I did not believe in God.

I kept trying to find ways to enjoy myself, but nothing seemed to work. The harder I tried the more troubled I became. I began to wonder if Jesus might be real after all. I prayed to him, even though at that time I had very little faith in him. I asked him to forgive me for the things I had been doing and to take control of my life.

This was the beginning of a great change for me. Everything did not happen at once. I struggled to understand what it really meant to believe in Jesus. During this time God helped me to realize that I belonged to him and that he would continue to help me. Gradually my faith became stronger. Life was becoming more and more worthwhile, and trusting in Jesus was giving me a purpose for living.

Then I realized that thousands of other people had learned to trust in Jesus and to follow him just as I had done, and that they could also tell what he had done for them. What is there about Jesus that makes him so important to so many people from all over the world? In some of the chapters which follow I plan to tell you what makes Jesus so important to me and to all these other people. In this chapter we shall see how Jesus began his work of giving people a new hope and a new kind of life to live.

JESUS IS BAPTIZED AND CALLED TO BEGIN HIS WORK

When it was time for Jesus to begin his work, he came to John the Baptist to be baptized. John the Baptist was a prophet whom God had called to prepare the way for the soon coming of the Messiah. He was telling the people they must repent of their sins in order to be ready for his coming. When people said they were sorry for their sins and wanted to turn back to God, John baptized them.

What a great moment it must have been for John when he saw Jesus! He recognized him as the Messiah he had been speaking about. Here the Messiah was asking John to baptize him! John objected because he did not feel worthy to baptize Jesus. Jesus explained that he wanted to do everything that was expected of other people. Even though Jesus had not committed any sins, he did not want to put himself above other people; he wanted to show people that he was one of them. Then John baptized Jesus.

As Jesus was being baptized a wonderful thing happened. The Spirit of God came down on him like a dove, and God spoke from heaven, saying, "This is my beloved Son, with whom I am well pleased." The coming of the Spirit of God on Jesus meant that God had given him the power to do his work and that God was now calling him to begin this work.

Jesus was led by the spirit into the wilderness to be tempted by the devil (Matthew 4:1, RSV).

JESUS IS TEMPTED

Before Jesus began his work, however, he was led by God's Spirit out into the desert to be tested. After he had fasted forty days, the Devil tempted him to prove that he was the Son of God by turning stones into food. Like many other temptations, this might seem like something good to do. God had provided manna for his people when they had been out in the desert on their way to the Promised Land. Now Jesus could prove that he was the Son of God by providing food for himself out in the desert also.

But Jesus recognized this as a temptation of the Devil. The power he had received when the Spirit came down on him at his baptism was to be used to help other people. Now the Devil was tempting him to use it for his own benefit. Jesus resisted the temptation by quoting from the Bible, "Man shall not live by bread alone, but by every word that proceeds from the mouth of God." Jesus knew that he could not prove anything unless he followed God's Word.

Then the Devil tempted Jesus to prove that he was the Son of God by jumping off the highest tower of the temple in Jerusalem. The Devil pointed out that God had promised to have his angels protect him. This also seemed like a good thing. Certainly many people would believe in him if they saw him do a trick like that. But Jesus recognized this also to be a temptation. He resisted it by again quoting from the Bible, "Again it is written, 'You shall not tempt the Lord your God.' " Jesus knew that it was wrong to use God's promises just for doing some magic tricks. He also knew that if people were persuaded to turn to him just because he could jump off a high place without getting hurt, their hearts would not really be changed, and their faith would always require new tricks.

Finally the Devil gave Jesus a vision of all the wonderful things in all the nations of the world and promised to give them to him if he would only bow down and worship him. What an exciting thing it would be to have all these things! Jesus could even use them to accomplish his purpose and do his work, and then he could turn back to God and stop worshiping the Devil. Jesus also resisted this temptation by quoting from the Bible. He said, "Get away, Satan! For it is written, 'You shall worship the Lord your God and him only shall you serve.' " Jesus knew, of course, that it is never right to surrender to Satan for anything, no matter how great and how good the reward seems to be.

WHAT JESUS' TEMPTATION MEANS TO US

As we struggle with temptations, we can learn from Jesus' temptation and the way he overcame it:

JESUS' TEMPTATION

1. Jesus was tempted after a wonderful experience at his baptism, when he received God's Spirit and God's power.
2. The Devil tried to make Jesus' temptation seem attractive and good.
3. Jesus was tempted to do something to satisfy himself without considering God's will.

4. Jesus overcame temptation by using the Bible.

5. Jesus was alone when he won the battle with temptation. He was being tested when he had no one to help him resist.

6. Jesus knew that the Devil was trying to keep him from doing the work God had given him to do.

7. Because Jesus passed the test, he could begin his work of bringing new life to people and helping them overcome temptation.

OUR TEMPTATIONS

1. Our worst temptations often come after God has done something great for us.
2. Temptation will often fool us into thinking it is something good.
3. We are usually tempted to do something that will make us comfortable and popular without considering what God wants.
4. The Bible can help us overcome temptation if we learn to understand it and if we desire to follow it. A helpful verse when we are tempted is 1 Corinthians 10:13.
5. Temptation is hardest when we have to fight it alone. Whenever possible, ask some Christian friends to pray for you. They can also encourage you to resist.
6. When we are tempted to do something wrong, it helps to concentrate on doing something we know God wants us to do.
7. Jesus will help us overcome our temptations. He will be patient with us when we fail and help us do better next time. We can win over temptation because Jesus is a winner, and he is on our side!

Martin Luther, whose explanation of the Apostles' Creed we are learning, has also written the following words, which are part of a song we often sing in church:

Did we in our own strength confide, Our striving would be losing,
Were not the right man on our side, the man of God's own choosing.
Dost ask who that might be? Christ Jesus, it is he—Lord Sabaoth ★ his name,
From age to age the same, And he must win the battle.

("A Mighty Fortress Is Our God," stanza 2, *The Covenant Hymnal*, No. 377)

★ *Commander in Chief*

159

The Second Article of the Apostles' Creed and Luther's explanation of it help us to understand more clearly who Jesus was and what he did for us. We are grateful that he won the battle with temptation, and with his help we can be winners over temptation also.

Check Yourself

1. What wonderful thing happened when Jesus was baptized, and what did it mean?

The spirit of God came down like a dove, he was ready to begin his work.

2. In what three ways did the Devil tempt Jesus, and what did all three temptations have in common? *Turn stone into food, jumping of the highest tower on the temple in Jerusalem, to have all the wonderful things on earth if Jesus would worship the devil.*

3. What are some things you might do to seek Jesus' help to overcome some temptation? *Pray to him to help me.*

In Class

As your teacher rereads the stories of the events we have been studying for this session, close your eyes and imagine that you are there. After the reading of each story write your response to the following question:

If you had seen this baptism, what would you be thinking about this man Jesus?

Is he really the messaiah?

If you had seen the temptations, what would you be thinking of this man Jesus?

Why won't he do those things to prove that he is really

Jesus Chooses Some Friends to Be on His "Team"   4

BIBLE READING: John 1:35-51; Luke 6:12-16
Other suggested Bible readings: Matthew 10:1-4; Mark 3:13-19

Finish memorizing the Second Article of the Apostles' Creed and Luther's explanation of it.

Have you ever seen anyone trying to play baseball alone? I remember a boy who tried to organize a baseball team, but he thought he could do everything himself. He began as catcher, but he did not trust the pitcher, so he appointed himself pitcher. Then he became dissatisfied with the first baseman, so he traded with him. Finally all his friends quit and left him alone. All he could do was throw the ball against a brick wall and try to hit it with his bat when it bounced back. It was a sad experience for him because he liked to play baseball very much, but

he never learned that it is impossible to do certain things without trusting other people to do their part.

Even Jesus did not try to do all his work alone. He knew that he needed other people to help him and to carry on his ministry after he returned to heaven, so he chose twelve special friends to be on his "team."

FRIENDS, DISCIPLES, APOSTLES

As soon as Jesus began teaching and healing and helping other people, he made many friends. Some of these friends took his teachings seriously enough to become his followers. They were known as his "disciples" because "disciple" means "learner." They recognized Jesus as being the Messiah and accepted his teachings as being true, and they learned from him. The number of Jesus' disciples increased rapidly, especially after he returned to heaven. They later were called "Christians," which is the name by which Jesus' disciples are known today (see Acts 11:26).

From among his disciples, Jesus chose twelve to be on his "team." They left their work in order to be with him all the time. They lived with him, they ate together, talked together, laughed and sang and cried together. Wherever he went they also went. Sometimes they are called "the twelve disciples," and sometimes they are called "the twelve apos-

tles." An apostle is a person who has been sent out on a mission, so the disciples became "apostles" when Jesus sent them out.

The names of the Twelve Apostles, in the order in which they are listed in Luke 6:12-16, are:

Simon, whom Jesus named Peter,
Andrew, Simon Peter's brother,
James,
John, James' brother,
Philip,
Bartholomew,
Matthew,
Thomas,
James, the son of Alphaeus,
Simon, the Zealot,
Judas, son of James (also known as Thaedus)
Judas Iscariot (who became a traitor)

THE DISCIPLES WERE CHOSEN FOR MINISTRY

Jesus chose his "team," not to play baseball, but to help him in his ministry. They learned from him as they saw him heal the sick and heard him teach, and he gave them power to work miracles so they could act as his representatives. All except Judas Iscariot became leaders of the early Christians. They taught what Jesus had commanded, they helped to organize churches and solve problems, and they used their power to help other people. Since they had seen Jesus after he had risen from the dead, they were witnesses of his resurrection, and they traveled to many places to tell people about him. Peter and John, for instance, went to Samaria to take part in the beginning of the new church there (Acts 8:14-25). Peter was the first to preach the Good News about Jesus to Gentiles. We believe that John lived and taught in Ephesus for many years, and Thomas may have brought the message of Jesus as far as India. Most of them lost their lives because of their faithfulness. James, the brother of John, was the first of this group to die. He was put to death in Jerusalem by King Herod Antipas (Acts 12:1-3). Herod had Peter put in prison, but Peter escaped by a miracle. He was later crucified in Rome.

Of course, Jesus had many other disciples beside these twelve, who also helped to carry on his ministry. The names of some of them are found in the New Testament, but many thousands of other people have become his disciples since that time. Jesus is still calling people to believe in him, to become his friends and disciples and to engage in his ministry. Although pastors are sometimes called "ministers," it is incorrect to limit the work of ministry to pastors. Jesus wants all his friends to become disciples and help carry on his ministry.

THE TWELVE DISCIPLES BECOME A COMMUNITY

"What a wonderful thing it would be," we might think, "if we could have joined that group of dedicated and unselfish people whom Jesus chose for his team. What could be better than being with a group of people as spiritual as the twelve disciples." But that was not the way things were among them. These disciples were, in many ways, ordinary people, and they had much to learn. They quarreled with each other and even argued about who was going to be greatest in the revolutionary government they thought Jesus was going to set up. Matthew had been a tax collector, working for the Roman government and he must have had a hard time learning to love Simon the Zealot, who had been a member of a rebel terrorist group.

Simon Peter often spoke and acted without first thinking. Thomas was a pessimist who found it hard to believe Jesus. James and John must have lost their tempers easily, for they were called the "Sons of Thunder." It took a long time for these people to learn to understand each other.

It was hard for them, also, to learn what it meant to be true disciples of Jesus. They often found it hard to trust him when he told them how different their lives were to be from the lives of other people. James and John thought they should be calling down fire from heaven to destroy some people who would not welcome them into their city. Jesus' closest disciples went to sleep the night before he was crucified, even

though he had asked them to stay awake with him. This band of twelve men whom Jesus had chosen for ministry appeared to be interested only in themselves, and they had no idea of what it meant to give themselves in ministry to other people.

A group of people who care for each other and who work for the same cause is known as a "community." Even though it took a long time for Jesus' disciples to stop being jealous and quarreling with one another, they finally learned to love each other. As they were learning this, they were becoming more and more of a community.

We began this chapter with the story of the boy who could not enjoy baseball because he could not get along with others. This was the way Jesus' disciples began, but Jesus taught them patiently until they became a good "team," with each one doing his part.

YOUR CHURCH AS A COMMUNITY OF CHRISTIAN DISCIPLES

It is God's purpose for every church to be a "community" where all the Christians love one another, help one another and work together in Jesus' ministry. This relationship of love and trust is known as "fellowship" or "koinonia." Good fellowship among Christians helps us *personally,* and it also helps us in our *ministry.* Good fellowship among Christians helps us *personally* because we are not alone. Others can encourage us, and others can correct us and pray for us when we do wrong.

Good fellowship among Christians helps us in our *ministry* because we can share the different gifts and abilities God has given us, just as the players on a baseball team share their different skills. When we have good fellowship with other Christians we can also demonstrate the love of Jesus by the way we care for each other, and we can work more easily when others share the responsibilities with us.

WE, TOO, ARE CALLED TO BE JESUS' DISCIPLES

From Jesus' first disciples we learn that Jesus accepts ordinary people, who may have many faults, to be his disciples. Maybe the Christian group to which you belong has some people who are far from being perfect. Maybe some of them are hard to love. Maybe few of them could ever meet your qualification for being your friends. Let us remember that this is the kind of people Jesus chooses to be his friends and disciples. We are all in training to be part of Jesus' larger "team." Through his Spirit, Jesus will help us to learn to live in fellowship with each other and to become a true Christian community in spite of our faults and differences.

Jesus also invites us to take part in his ministry even though we may think of ourselves as ordinary people with many faults. To be disciples of Jesus means that we are learning from him. He will teach us how to be faithful to him and how to use the gifts and abilities he has given us to serve him. Then, as members of his larger "team," we shall have the satisfaction of knowing that we are ministering to others as he is ministering to us.

Check Yourself

1. What does each of the following words mean to us as Christians:

disciple?

community?

fellowship?

koinonia?

ministry?

2. What is another name for Jesus' twelve disciples, and why did Jesus choose them?

3. Explain how good fellowship in a Christian community helps us personally and in our ministry as Jesus' disciples.

In Class

After discussing the two following questions in class, write your own answers to them in the spaces below:

1. In what ways are you called to be a disciple of Jesus? _____

_____

_____

_____

2. In what ways is our Confirmation class a community of disciples? _____

_____

_____

_____

Some of Jesus' Other Friends

BIBLE READING: Luke 5:12-32
Other suggested Bible readings: Luke 7:1-17; Luke 19:1-10

"INSIDERS" AND "OUTSIDERS"

Once I was invited to a big dinner party, and I was seated at a table where I was a stranger to everyone. All the people at the table knew each other, but none of them knew me. They talked with each other all evening about things of which I had never heard. No one talked with me, and I was never able to break into the conversation. When I tried asking a question, they answered, "Yes," or "No," and went right back to talking with each other. About all I could say all evening was, "Please pass the sugar," and, "No, thanks, I don't care for any more potatoes."

I kept getting more and more uncomfortable, and I was so bored that I could hardly wait for the dinner to end. I realized that this was what it means to be an "outsider." I was the "outsider," and all the others at the table were "insiders."

Has anything like this ever happened to you? If so, can you remember how you felt? Have you ever been in a group where you were an "insider," but where someone else was an "outsider"?

"Outsiders" may be strangers or new people. They may be poor people who cannot afford the right kind of clothes or people of other races or nationalities. They may be disabled persons, or people who are just shy.

Sometimes even rich people can be outsiders. I can remember two people who never seemed to be "insiders." One was a boy who always had greasy spots on his clothes. We called him "flycatcher," because these greasy spots seemed to at-

tract flies. The other was a boy who came from a rich family, and his parents made him wear expensive clothes wherever he went. I realize now how cruel it was for us to torment those boys the way we did. I should have known better because I limped when I was a boy, and the other kids laughed at me and called me "Limpy." I was always the last one to be chosen for baseball or volleyball, and sometimes I would hear someone say, "do we *have* to have *him* on our team?"

JESUS AND "OUTSIDERS"

In Jesus' time there were certain people who were considered "outsiders." These included: poor people, people from Galilee, people from Samaria, people of other nationalities, sick or disabled people, and people who were not religious. Tax collectors were considered to be "outsiders" because they collected taxes from their own people for the Roman government, and they often were dishonest. Even women were often considered "outsiders." "Insiders" were the people of Judea, Pharisees, and other religious people who claimed to keep every detail of God's law. Wealthy people and healthy people were often considered to be "insiders."

Some "outsiders" who received Jesus' special attention were:
1. Levi, the tax collector. Even though Levi was a tax collector, Jesus invited him to become his follower. Before Levi left to follow Jesus, he arranged a dinner for Jesus and invited other "outsiders." The Pharisees, who were "insiders," criticized Jesus for having dinner with "outsiders," but Jesus said that they were the people who needed him most. He said, "I have not come to call the righteous, but sinners to repentance" (Luke 5:27-32).
2. A man who had leprosy (Luke 5:12-14).
3. A paralyzed man (Luke 5:18-26).

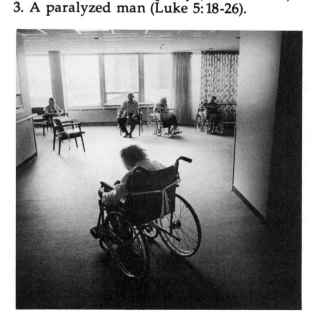

4. A slave of a Roman army officer (Luke 7:1-10).
5. A widow whose son had died (Luke 7:11-17).
6. A sinful woman (Luke 7:36-50).
7. Zacchaeus, a tax collector who was an "outsider" even though he was rich (Luke 19:1-10).

JESUS AND "INSIDERS"

We must not think that Jesus cared only for "outsiders." He was just as much concerned about "insiders." He went to dinner with Pharisees, and he taught that God loves all people equally. Many "insiders" repented of their sins and followed Jesus, and he accepted them. He wants to bring "insiders" and "outsiders" together into one group and to teach them to love and respect one another. He invites both to belong to him.

PROBLEMS OF "INSIDERS" AND "OUTSIDERS"

Both "insiders" and "outsiders" have problems. "Insiders" are in danger of thinking of themselves as being better than "outsiders," and of associating only with other "insiders." Sometimes they become proud of themselves for following strict rules so carefully. "Outsiders" are in danger of feeling sorry for themselves, of not taking their responsibilities seriously, of not following the rules of proper conduct, and of being critical of "insiders."

Some people are considered to be "outsiders" because they are not religious or they do not believe in Jesus, or they do not take him seriously. It is important for those who enjoy spiritual activities, like Bible study, not to consider themselves better or more spiritual than those who do not. We need to follow Jesus' example in caring for all people and in giving special attention to those who need it most. Jesus can help both "insiders" and "outsiders," and he wants both to have a part of his ministry. He wants to bring them together so there are no "insiders" or "outsiders" among his friends.

Check Yourself

1. Define "insiders" and "outsiders" in your own words.

2. What was there about the following groups of people that caused them to be thought of as "insiders" or "outsiders": tax collectors, Pharisees, slaves, slave owners, gentiles, members of the governing council, women, men?

3. What things can you remember that Jesus did to show that he cared for both "insiders" and "outsiders" equally?

In Class

Think about your school and define what it means to be an insider and an outsider. Complete the following: "In my school an 'insider' is a person who

_____

_____

_____

and an 'outsider' is a person who _____

_____

_____

_____

If Jesus came to your school, where would he fit in? _____

_____

_____

_____

REVIEW OF UNIT ONE

The good news about Jesus is found in the first four books of the New Testament, which are the Gospels of Matthew, Mark, Luke and John. From these Gospels we learn that Jesus received power to begin his work when he was baptized. After Jesus' baptism, he resisted three temptations to use his power and to make himself great and powerful. Many people became his friends, and some of these became his disciples. From his disciples, he chose twelve to be with him on his special "team." Many of Jesus' disciples were "outsiders," who were not acceptable to everyone else, but Jesus wants all his disciples to love each other and work together in what is known as a Christian "community."

The Kingdom of God Comes

UNIT TWO

CHAPTER 6
Jesus and the Kingdom of God

Jesus announced that the Kingdom of God had now come. He explained that we enter it by becoming like little children and by choosing to let God rule in our hearts and lives.

CHAPTER 7
Living in God's Kingdom

Jesus explained what it means to live in God's Kingdom. Jesus, the King, is also our gentle helper and patient teacher.

CHAPTER 8
Signs of the Kingdom

Two of the signs that the Kingdom is now here are 1) the miracles that Jesus performed and 2) his triumphal entry into Jerusalem. These and other signs show us what kind of King Jesus is. They also invite us to enter his Kingdom.

Birth of Jesus

Jesus' baptism and temptation

Jesus' ministry
Jesus' triumphal entry

Writing of the four gospels during last half of first century

4
BC

27
AD

30
AD

50
AD

100
AD

Jesus and the Kingdom of God 6

BIBLE READING: Mark 1:14; Mark 10:13-15; John 3:1-3
Other suggested Bible readings: Matthew 13:1-9, 18-23; John 3:16, 17

CATECHISM: *WHAT IS THE KINGDOM OF GOD?*

The kingdom of God is the reign of God expressed in the hearts and lives of his people both now and through eternity.

"The kingdom of God does not come visibly, nor will people say, 'Here it is,' or 'There it is,' because the kingdom of God is within you."

Luke 17:20b, 21, NIV

"The new world you've been waiting for has come! Stop running away from God. Turn around, tell him you are sorry, and he will forgive you. Trust me, and you may begin a new kind of life in this new world." Jesus began his work with an exciting announcement like this. As he preached in one place after another, he said, "The time has come, the Kingdom of God is near. Repent and believe the good news" (Mark 1:14, NIV).

"The Kingdom of God" (also called "the Kingdom of Heaven") is that new world God had promised his people. Now Jesus was telling them that it was here at last. Great crowds came to hear him preach, and many of the people wanted to become a part of this new Kingdom. But it was so different from other kingdoms that they could not understand what Jesus meant when he invited them to enter it. Most of them expected him to organize an army, overthrow the government and set up his Kingdom by force as other conquerors had done.

Jesus told them that no one can be forced into God's Kingdom. It can be entered only by those who choose to let God rule in their hearts and lives. Jesus urged the people to seek God's Kingdom above everything else in the world. Then, he said, all other worthwhile things would also be given to them. The cate-chism which you are learning for this chapter helps to make this clear. It tells us that the "Kingdom of God" is God's "reign" or "rule" in the hearts and lives of people and that his Kingdom will last forever. When anyone turns his or her life over to God, God rules in that person's heart. All those who make this choice belong to God's Kingdom, and he cares for them as his special friends.

"The Kingdom of God?"

172

JESUS TELLS US HOW TO ENTER THE KINGDOM OF GOD

Because it was hard for people to understand what the Kingdom of God was like, Jesus used many different ways to explain how to enter it. Once when his disciples told the people not to bother Jesus with little children, he told them to let the children come to him because the Kingdom of God belongs especially to them. He said the only way anyone can get into the Kingdom of God is to come as a little child. Children know they are not able to do everything by themselves. They know they have many things to learn and that they need someone else on whom they can depend. Jesus used little children as examples so the people would understand that no one can enter God's Kingdom by seeking to become great. Only those who are willing to start all over and who choose to admit that they need a leader to help and guide them through life are ready to enter the Kingdom of God (see Mark 10:13-15).

One night an important religious leader named Nicodemus came to see Jesus. Jesus told him that the only way to enter the Kingdom of God is to be "born again." This was confusing to Nicodemus, and he asked Jesus how it could be possible for a person to actually be born all over again. Jesus explained to him that to be "born again" meant to begin an entirely new kind of life. This new kind of life is a gift from God, which we receive when we believe in Jesus as God's own Son, and which will never end (see John 3:1-3; John 3:16, 17).

Jesus also told many stories about the Kingdom of God and how to enter it. These stories are called "parables." One of these stories was about a farmer who scattered seed on the ground, hoping it would take root and grow, but some of the seed was wasted because it fell on the path where people walked. Other seed fell on rocky ground where there was not enough soil to keep the new plants alive. Some of the seed fell into weeds that were so thick that they choked out the new plants. However, some of the seed fell into good ground, where they took root and grew and produced grain.

Jesus explained that the seed represents God's Word. Those who listen to what God has said and who pay attention to it are like good soil that receives the seed and produces grain. They are the people who choose to accept God's rule over their lives and to become his friends. When God's Word is planted in their hearts it produces the kind of life that will make them good citizens of his Kingdom.

THE KINGDOM OF GOD NOW AND IN THE FUTURE

God has not asked his friends to go off and live in a world of their own. They remain in the natural world of daily living which the Bible calls "this world." Since they are also in the Kingdom of God, they are living in two worlds, as illustrated by the diagram below:

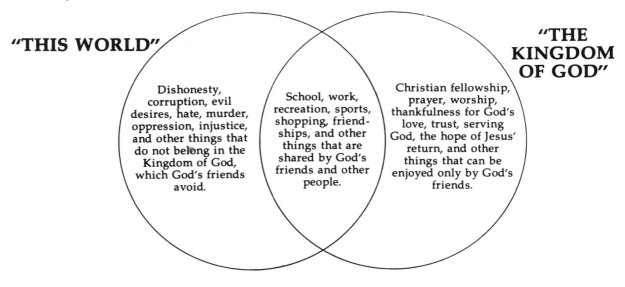

"THIS WORLD"

Dishonesty, corruption, evil desires, hate, murder, oppression, injustice, and other things that do not belong in the Kingdom of God, which God's friends avoid.

School, work, recreation, sports, shopping, friendships, and other things that are shared by God's friends and other people.

"THE KINGDOM OF GOD"

Christian fellowship, prayer, worship, thankfulness for God's love, trust, serving God, the hope of Jesus' return, and other things that can be enjoyed only by God's friends.

THE TWO WORLDS OF GOD'S FRIENDS

His grace . . . instructs us to give up ungodly living and worldly passions, and to live self-controlled, upright and godly lives in this world, as we wait for the blessed Day we hope for, when the glory of our great God and Savior Jesus Christ will appear (Titus 2:11-13, TEV).

The left circle represents "this world" and the right circle represents the Kingdom of God. The part where the two circles overlap represents all the things God's friends have in common with the people of "this world." They work, go to school, shop, enjoy sports and recreation, make friends and do many other things together with other people.

But God's friends are commanded to separate themselves from the evil of "this world." They refrain from dishonesty, pride, corruption, evil desires and all other ungodliness. These things are represented by the part of the left circle that is outside the "Kingdom of God" circle, to the far left.

God's friends enjoy some things that are not a part of "this world," which other people cannot enjoy. These include Christian fellowship, trust in God, prayer, worship, rejoicing in God's love, the hope of Jesus' coming, and other things that are only for those who belong

to the Kingdom of God. These are represented by the far right part of the right circle, which is outside the "this world" circle.

There will come a time in the future when "this world" will pass away. Then there will only be one circle, the Kingdom of God, in which his friends will live forever (see 1 John 2:17).

One of Jesus' parables, which is recorded in Matthew 13:47-50, is about fishermen who caught fish in their net and kept the good fish but threw the bad ones away. Jesus explained that, at the end of this age, those who do not belong to God's Kingdom will suffer his judgment. Then only God's Kingdom and those who belong to him will remain, and God's rule will extend to all peoples. Righteousness, justice, love and peace will then cover the whole earth. This Kingdom will last forever, as the catechism for this chapter tells us.

174

THE KINGDOM OF GOD IS FOR US

This exciting Kingdom of God is not just for great and special people. Jesus invites all of us to enter it. We must come like little children, willing to admit that we cannot live in God's Kingdom without God and his new life. We turn from our old life and ask Jesus to take charge and be our King. The good news is that this Kingdom is for everybody—it is for us!

Check Yourself

1. Jesus began his work with an announcement. Using your own words, tell what that announcement was.

2. Name one characteristic of children that helps us to understand why we must become like little children to enter God's Kingdom.

3. Name something: (1) that is practiced in "this world" that should not be practiced by people who belong to God's Kingdom, (2) that is practiced by both, (3) that can be enjoyed only by those who belong to God's Kingdom.

In Class

If the Kingdom of God is the rule of God in the lives of his people (or use the definition developed by your class), in what ways do you feel that God is in charge of your life? Write your response in the form of a sentence prayer.

_____

_____

_____

_____

Living in God's Kingdom

7

BIBLE READING: Matthew, Chapters 5, 6, 7

CATECHISM: WHAT DID JESUS TEACH US CONCERNING LIFE IN THE KINGDOM OF GOD?

Jesus taught us that life in the Kingdom of God means we are to live in a loving relationship with God, self and others.

And he said to him, "You shall love the Lord your God with all your heart, and with all your soul, and with all your mind . . . You shall love your neighbor as yourself."

Matthew 22:37, 39 RSV

"Silly boy! Silly boy!" Why was everyone calling me "Silly boy"? Wherever I went on the school grounds, someone would laugh at me and say, "Silly boy." What had I done to make everyone call me that stupid name? Finally someone pulled a sign off my back. It said, "SILLY BOY!" Everyone else had seen it, but I had not even known it was there. After school I went home as fast as I could and lay down on my bed and cried. I was so embarrassed and angry that I did not want to go back to school anymore.

I found out who put the sign on my back, and every time I saw him, for a long time after that, I got a sick feeling in my stomach. I am sure that he soon forgot what he had done to me, but I did not forget.

Should I forgive him? I couldn't do

that, no matter how hard I tried. I am sure I suffered more from my bad feelings toward him during the next year than I did from what he had done to me. I would have been a much happier person if I could have forgiven him, but I couldn't do it.

There really was no reason for me to be so angry with him, because I had done things that were just as bad to other people. I used to laugh at some of the kids in school who wore different kinds of clothes or ate different kinds of food or had customs that seemed strange to me. Sometimes my friends and I would make up funny names to call them. We knew this was wrong and that we had no right to judge them just because they were different from us, but we did it anyway.

I never used to think about how different I felt when I was tormenting someone else than the way I felt when someone else was tormenting me. I am sure that other people were hurt very much when my friends and I made jokes about them, but this never occurred to me when I was joking about other people.

My family had very little money, and I often worried about getting enough to eat or about not having some of the

DO UNTO OTHERS . . .

things other young people had. Sometimes I worried about what would happen to me when I grew up. I often wished that there would be someone to whom I could talk and who could assure me that I did not need to worry.

Then, one day, my Sunday school teacher asked me how I was feeling. I talked with him a long time, and he listened while I told him about my problems. He didn't give me any advice; he just stood there and listened for a whole hour! I have often remembered that talk and how helpful it was to have someone care enough to listen. My Sunday school teacher was the only person I ever dared to talk with about the things that bothered me.

I thought these problems would go away when I became an adult, but, as I grew older, they changed to other problems that troubled me just as much. I also discovered that others have problems like these.

JESUS UNDERSTANDS OUR PROBLEMS

Jesus knew that people who would come into God's Kingdom would have problems, and many of his teachings are about these problems and how to deal with them. Once, when great crowds were gathering around Jesus, he went up on a mountain with his disciples and taught them about life in the Kingdom of God. What he said then has been called "the Sermon on the Mount." It is found in Matthew, chapters five, six, and seven. Following are some of the problems Jesus dealt with in the Sermon on the Mount:

1. The problem of finding true satisfaction and happiness (Matthew 5:3-12).

Jesus knew that we humans are tempted to think that happiness and satisfaction come from being rich and popular and from having everything that can make us comfortable. He explained that true happiness among his disciples comes to those who mourn, who are meek, who hunger and thirst to be righteous. True happiness comes to those who are merciful, and pure in heart and who are peacemakers, and to those who are persecuted for their faithfulness to Jesus.

2. The problem of controlling our feelings and desires (Matthew 5:21-30).

Jesus understood how easy it is for us to let our feelings get control of us, but he also understood that we can never be truly happy unless we are in control of them. Murder, he says, begins when we have feelings of hatred toward someone, and we are guilty of adultery when we have allowed ourselves to enjoy uncontrolled sexual desire. In these cases, it is not just that murder and adultery are wrong, but it is also that we can never be free people as long as we are slaves to our desires and feelings.

3. The problem of forgiving and being forgiven (Matthew 6:14, 15).

It is hard for us to forgive people who hurt us, but Jesus tells us that it is impossible for us to be forgiven until we are willing to give up the bitter feelings we have toward other people and to forgive them.

4. The problem of worry (Matthew 6:25-33).

Jesus knew that we humans cannot be happy and satisfied when we are troubled by worry, so he told his disciples

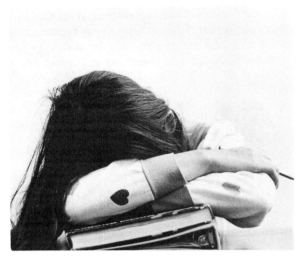

not to worry about the things they need. Since God cares for the birds and the flowers, he will care even more for us.

---

5. The problem of a critical spirit (Matthew 7:1-5).

It is easy to become critical of other people, and this critical spirit keeps us from being loving and helpful. Because of this, Jesus told his disciples to avoid being critical of others by giving attention to their own faults instead.

---

6. The problem of treating other people fairly (Matthew 7:12).

When we are saying or doing things that hurt other people, it is easy for us to forget how badly we feel when other people hurt us. Therefore, Jesus asks his disciples to think about how they would like to have other people treat them and use this as a guide in their relations with others. He said, "In everything, do to others what you would have them do to you." This has been called "the Golden Rule." Jesus said that it is a summary of everything God's law commands and his prophets have taught.

THE GOOD NEWS— JESUS WILL HELP US!

Just knowing about these problems and being told to do something about them is not enough. In fact, this might make life even harder. The good news is that Jesus did not just tell people about their problems and give them good advice. When he saw how tired the people had become from trying to do the things that were expected of them, he said,

"Come to me, all you who are weary and burdened, and I will give you rest. Take my yoke upon you and learn from me, for I am gentle and humble in heart, and you will find rest for your souls. For my yoke is easy and my burden is light" (Matthew 11:28-30, NIV).

What a wonderful invitation! Jesus is still with us in his Spirit. He invites us to make him our King and to follow him as our Leader. His Kingdom is different from all other kingdoms, and he is different from all other Kings. Can you imagine a king being gentle and humble, as Jesus is? When we invite him to be our King he will patiently teach us how to live in his Kingdom. With his help we can find satisfaction and happiness in living as he has commanded us. He will show us how to keep our feelings and desires under control, and he will help us forgive people who hurt us. When we believe that he is with us and that we belong to him, we are less worried about the things that trouble us. He will help

us to overcome a critical spirit and to treat other people as we would like to have them treat us. When we fail, he will be patient with us and forgive us. With Jesus as our King, this new life in the Kingdom of God becomes exciting to live.

A PRAYER TO JESUS, OUR KING

Read the following prayer slowly, stopping to think about the meaning of each sentence. Then, if you are ready to apply it to yourself, read it again as your own prayer to Jesus:

"Jesus, I accept your invitation to make you my King. I know that the only way to live in God's Kingdom is to love you and to love other people as I love myself. I know that I cannot do this without your help. How wonderful it is for me to know that you, who are my King, will also be my gentle and humble teacher. Thank you for inviting me to come to you. I am grateful for your promise to teach me how to live a loving, useful and happy life in God's Kingdom. Thank you, also, for your patience and your willingness to forgive me and help me when I fail. Amen."

Check Yourself

1. Where, in the New Testament, is the Sermon on the Mount found? Where was Jesus when he gave this "sermon" and to whom did he give it?

2. List at least three of the problems with which Jesus dealt in the Sermon on the Mount.

3. In what way does Jesus help us to keep his commandments?

Signs of the Kingdom

8

BIBLE READING: The sign of Jesus' miracles: Matthew 8:1-16; John 20:30-31
The sign of Jesus' Triumphal Entry into Jerusalem: Matthew 21:1-11
The meaning of signs: Matthew 12:28; Acts 2:22
Other suggested Bible readings: Matthew 9:18-33; Matthew 14:15-32; John 2:1-11

ASSIGNMENT: Memorize the Lord's Prayer

CATECHISM REVIEW: WHAT IS THE KINGDOM OF GOD?
WHAT DID JESUS TEACH US CONCERNING LIFE IN THE KINGDOM OF GOD?

Learn the Lord's Prayer and think of it as "the Prayer of the Kingdom." Your teacher will suggest which of the following versions to learn:

Our Father who art in heaven,
*   hallowed be thy Name,*
*   thy kingdom come,*
*   thy will be done,*
*   on earth as it is in heaven.*
Give us this day our daily bread.
And forgive us our debts
*   as we forgive our debtors.*
And lead us not into temptation,
*   but deliver us from evil.*
For thine is the kingdom, and the
*   power, and the glory forever.*
*   Amen.*

Our Father in heaven,
*   hallowed be your Name,*
*   your kingdom come,*
*   your will be done,*
*   on earth as in heaven.*
Give us today our daily bread.
Forgive us our sins
*   as we forgive those who sin*
*   against us.*
Save us from the time of trial
*   and deliver us from evil.*
For the kingdom, the power, and
the glory are yours now and
forever.
*   Amen.*

WHAT IS A "SIGN"?

We are all familiar with road signs. They tell us how fast we may drive and where we must stop. They tell us what is ahead and warn us of dangers.

There are many other signs, such as robins and warm weather, which are signs of spring, and a steady heartbeat and the right body temperature, which are signs of good health. The value of signs is that they tell us how to respond to what is happening.

Jesus gave us signs to tell us that the Kingdom of God is now here so that we may respond to his invitation to enter it. The miracles Jesus performed were one kind of sign. Another kind of sign was his entry into Jerusalem riding on a donkey.

MIRACLES

Miracles are things that happen that have no natural explanation. They are signs that God is doing something without using natural methods. Jesus performed at least four kinds of miracles:
1. He healed sick people (see Matthew 8:1-15).
2. He drove out demons and evil spirits from people (see Matthew 8:16). This is called "exorcism."
3. He raised people from the dead (see Matthew 9:18-26).

4. He performed natural wonders, like feeding thousands of people with only five small loaves of bread and two small fish or like walking on water to come to his disciples, who were struggling with their boat in a storm (Matthew 14:15-33).

Many of the wonderful things that Jesus did were the very things the prophets had said the Messiah would do. Once, when John the Baptist was in prison, he sent two of his disciples to ask Jesus if he really was the Messiah. Just as these men came to Jesus, he performed some miracles, and then Jesus said to them, "Go back and report to John what you have seen and heard: the blind receive their sight, the lame walk, those who have leprosy are cured, the deaf hear, the dead are raised, and the good news is preached to the poor" (Luke 7:18-22 NIV). Jesus was doing the very things the prophets had said the Messiah would do. Therefore Jesus must be the Messiah.

These miracles caused the people to be amazed, but they were more than amazing things. The miracles were never just magic tricks, and Jesus did not perform them to help himself. They proved that Jesus was a compassionate person and that he had the power to help those who were in need. This is what was expected of the Messiah. They were like road signs to tell the people that the Kingdom of God was now here and that Jesus was the King whom the prophets had promised.

SEVEN MIRACULOUS SIGNS IN THE GOSPEL OF JOHN

The Gospel of John records seven signs which Jesus performed. John tells us that Jesus performed many other signs, but that he recorded these signs so "that you may believe that Jesus is the Christ, the Son of God, and that believing you may have life in his name" (John 20:31). The seven miraculous signs are:
1. Changing water into wine (John 2:1-10)
2. Healing an officer's son (John 4:46-54)
3. Healing a man at the Pool of Bethesda (John 5:1-9).
4. Feeding a large crowd of people (John 6:1-14).

5. Stilling a storm on the Sea of Galilee (John 6:16-21).

6. Healing a blind man (John 9:1-7).

7. Raising Lazarus from the dead (John 11:1-45).

John hardly ever used the term "Kingdom of God." Instead, he described Jesus as the Son of God who gives eternal life to those who believe in him. John was no doubt writing to people who would understand him better if he described Jesus in this way rather than if he spoke of him as the King of the Kingdom of God. Most of us, also, find this description of Jesus easier to understand. Kingdoms do not have much meaning for people who live in a democracy, but we are very much interested in making life as full as we can and in extending it as long as possible. To think of Jesus as the Son of God, who offers a full and unending life, will probably mean more to us than to think of Jesus as the King of a Kingdom. Yet we also need to know about the Kingdom of God in order to understand how Jesus fulfilled the promises from the Old Testament about his coming. This is the value of having both the Gospel of John and the Synoptic Gospels.

JESUS' TRIUMPHAL ENTRY INTO JERUSALEM (Matthew 21:1-11)

Hundreds of years before the birth of Jesus, the Prophet Zechariah had said, "Rejoice greatly, O Daughter of Zion! Shout, Daughter of Jerusalem! See, your King comes to you, righteous and having salvation, gentle and riding on a donkey, on a colt, the foal of a donkey" (Zechariah 9:9, NIV). Matthew 21:4, 5 tells us that this prophecy was fulfilled by Jesus. This is the way it happened:

On the Sunday before Jesus was crucified, he came into Jerusalem. Before he entered the city, he asked two of his disciples to bring him a young donkey on which no one had yet ridden. Jesus rode into the city on this donkey.

Crowds of people were coming to Jerusalem at this time for the Passover, which was a celebration they held every year in memory of the time when God had set their forefathers free from slavery in Egypt. Among these people were many who were friends of Jesus. They formed a procession around Jesus and escorted him into the city while they sang praises to God.

This event has become known as "the Triumphal Entry." It was a sign of the Kingdom because it fulfilled the promise of the prophet Zechariah that the King would enter the city riding on a donkey. Other kings would have entered the city with chariots and great armies of soldiers, but Jesus was a different kind of King. The way he entered Jerusalem was a sign that he would rule with humility and love.

WHAT THE SIGNS OF THE KINGDOM MEAN TO US

Road signs do not force us to obey them. We have to choose whether or not to pay attention to what they tell us, and we must accept the responsibility for our choice. The signs of God's Kingdom also require a choice. They say, THE KINGDOM OF GOD—NOW OPEN—JESUS IS THE KING—ENTER HERE. They invite us to make our choice about believing in Jesus and belonging to God's Kingdom.

Check Yourself

1. What is the purpose of ordinary signs in our daily life, and what is the meaning of "signs" as they apply to the Kingdom of God?

2. Name four kinds of miracles Jesus performed.

3. In what way was Jesus' Triumphal Entry into Jerusalem a sign?

In Class

After discussing the meaning of the signs of the Kingdom, fill in the following chart, commenting on one of the miracles and Christ's triumphal entry.

THE MEANING OF THE SIGNS OF THE KINGDOM

	Meaning then	Meaning now
ONE OF THE MIRACLES		
THE TRIUMPHAL ENTRY		

In the space below write the answer to the question, "What do these signs tell me about Jesus, the King of the Kingdom?"

_____

_____

_____

_____

_____

_____

_____

_____

_____

_____

REVIEW OF UNIT TWO

Jesus announced that the Kingdom of God had come, and he explained how to enter it. He also explained how to live in God's Kingdom and promised to help his friends become good citizens of the Kingdom. He gave signs to tell that the Kingdom was now here, to show what the Kingdom was like and to invite people to enter it.

Jesus Gives Himself For Us

UNIT THREE

CHAPTER 9
Jesus Establishes the Lord's Supper

Jesus established the New Covenant at his Last Supper with his disciples on the night before he was crucified. He has commanded us to eat this supper, remembering him and what he did for us and looking forward to his coming again.

CHAPTER 10
Jesus Dies and Rises From the Dead

God has now made the greatest possible sacrifice so that we may be his friends. He gave his Son to die for our sins on the cross. But God also raised him from the dead! We learn the meaning of Jesus' death and resurrection.

CHAPTER 11
Jesus Prepares His Disciples to Do His Work

Jesus appeared many times to his disciples after his resurrection. He proved to them that he had risen from the dead, and he prepared them to be his witnesses. After forty days he ascended into heaven, but he still rules in the hearts and lives of his friends.

Birth of Jesus

Jesus' ministry

Jesus' death and resurrection
40 days with his disciples
Jesus' ascension into heaven

| 4 BC | 27 AD | 30 AD | 50 AD | 100 AD |

Jesus Establishes the Lord's Supper

BIBLE READING: Matthew 26:17—27:30; Luke 22:14-23

CATECHISM: WHAT IS THE SACRAMENT OF THE LORD'S SUPPER?

The Lord's Supper is the sacred use of bread and the cup as commanded by Jesus Christ. In communion with one another we remember his suffering for us, proclaim his death until he comes, and partake of him in faith.

For I received from the Lord what I also delivered to you, that the Lord Jesus on the night when he was betrayed took bread, and when he had given thanks, he broke it, and said, "This is my body which is for you. Do this in remembrance of me." In the same way also the cup, after supper, saying, "This cup is the new covenant in my blood. Do this, as often as you drink it, in remembrance of me. For as often as you eat this bread and drink the cup, you proclaim the Lord's death until he comes.

1 Corinthians 11:23-26, RSV

Jesus, the Son of God and the greatest person ever to live is now about to make the greatest sacrifice of love that it is possible to make. In this chapter and the next we shall see what it really means that God loved us so much that he sent his only Son to win people back to himself. Our whole Christian faith and life and our hope for the future depend on the events we shall describe.

JESUS' ENEMIES DETERMINE TO HAVE HIM KILLED

After Jesus' triumphal entry into Jerusalem, the religious leaders kept asking him hard questions to try to confuse and embarrass him, but Jesus answered them so well that it was they who were embarrassed. Finally they paid one of his disciples, Judas Iscariot, to lead them to Jesus. They planned to arrest him and to prove falsely that he had made statements that were against the law of God and to have him condemned to die.

JESUS ESTABLISHES THE LORD'S SUPPER

Meanwhile, Jesus and his disciples gathered to eat the Passover. This was the meal which the Jewish people ate to celebrate the time when God had set them free from slavery in Egypt.

Near the beginning of the meal Judas left to lead the authorities to the place where he knew Jesus would be going later. This left Jesus to celebrate the Passover with his eleven faithful disciples. Jesus followed the custom of the Passover by taking some bread, breaking and blessing it and giving it to them. But he did something new. He said, "This is my body which is given for you. Do this in remembrance of me" (Luke 22:19). At the end of the meal he took a cup of wine and asked them to drink from it. Here, also, he added something new when he said, "This cup which is poured out for you is the new covenant in my blood." (Luke 22:20).

In Chapter 25 of Part One of this book

Leonardo da Vinci

we learned how Jeremiah had prophesied of a New Covenant that God would make with his people, that would change their hearts so they would love God (see Jeremiah 31:31-34). Now Jesus was putting this New Covenant into effect.

This last meal which Jesus ate with his disciples is known as "the Lord's Supper." He told them to celebrate this supper until he comes again. Therefore, we Christians gather from time to time to eat bread and drink wine or grape juice and to repeat the words which he spoke when he ate this meal with his disciples.

THE MEANING OF THE LORD'S SUPPER

The Lord's Supper is a time to emphasize the three relationships of the Christian life. They are 1) our relationship with God, 2) our relationship with ourselves and 3) our relationship with

others.

Our Relationship with God

At the Lord's Supper we remember that God loved us enough to send Jesus as a gift to us. This is the reason the Lord's Supper is sometimes called, "the Eucharist," which means "the good gift." We also remember that God has made a New Covenant with us. In this covenant we let him rule in our lives because we love him and wish to obey him. This relationship with God is known as "communion," and this is the reason that the Lord's Supper is sometimes called "Holy Communion." Communion with God is possible because Jesus died for us, our sins are forgiven, and we know that God wants to be our friend. We can never explain just how the Holy Spirit makes Jesus so real to us when we take part in the Lord's Supper. It is one of our most sacred times of worship, and we always take part in it with great reverence.

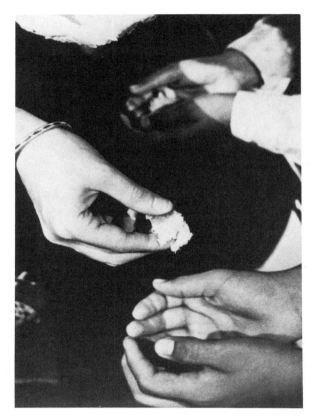

Our Relationship with Ourselves.

We prepare ourselves for the Lord's Supper by asking God to show us any sin that is in our hearts. As we confess our sins to God we also accept his forgiveness, and we pray for his help to be faithful to him in the future. Because we know that our sins are forgiven, our consciences do not trouble us, and we have peace with ourselves. We also have hope for the future because we know that Jesus has promised to come again to finish the establishing of his righteous Kingdom.

Our Relationship With Others.

"Communion" means to have good relationships with other people as well as with God. If we have sinned against other people, we determine to make it right with them as soon as we can. Immediately after the Lord's Supper is a good time to greet one another and to wish each other God's peace. If we have sinned against any of our Christian brothers and sisters, this is a good time to ask them for forgiveness. Some churches have a time during the service of the Lord's Supper when the people may greet one another. This is known as "passing the peace."

Every time we take part in the Lord's Supper we are reminded that Jesus died and arose again in order that we might have good relationships with God, with ourselves and with others. We end each time together with joy because we have again been assured that our sins are forgiven, because we know that God will help us to be faithful Christians, and because Jesus has promised to come again.

An ancient olive tree in the Garden of Gethsemane, outside of Jerusalem

THE END OF A DREAM

JERUSALEM (Friday) All hopes for the new kingdom, which the followers of Jesus, the Galilean, were singing about so enthusiastically last Sunday, now appear to be dead. Jesus was officially pronounced guilty of blasphemy early this morning, and Governor Pilate has just authorized his crucifixion.

It all began about three years ago with Jesus calling for people to join his movement. He insisted on simplicity of life, honesty and purity of heart, and his exposure of the hypocrisy and corruption of the Pharisees and other religious party officials angered them. There has been conflict ever since, until this week they decided to take action against him.

He had the power to heal the sick, he was interested in the poor and he appeared to have compassion for everyone. Even though he asked for a sacrificial commitment from those who wished to enter his kingdom, his followers appeared to be satisfied and loyal. His movement has fallen off recently, especially since the people who came along for a free ride discovered how much of a sacrifice he expected from them. Yet, this week he still had such a large following that the council was afraid of a riot if he were arrested publicly.

Then one of Jesus' disciples, Judas Iscariot, offered to turn traitor, and somebody paid him to lead the officials with some soldiers to Jesus during the night.

They found Jesus in Gethsemane Garden with three of his disciples. The other disciples appear to have been nearby, but when Jesus was arrested they all disappeared in the darkness.

It was reported that one of Jesus' followers was seen late last night in the courtyard of the home of the High Priest, where Jesus was being questioned. When he was confronted by persons in the crowd he denied any connection with Jesus. A reporter on the scene tried to interview him, but he had left. Bystanders said that he appeared to be startled by the crowing of a rooster.

The council found it difficult to place any charges against Jesus, but they finally discovered two people who said they had heard him misuse the name of God. Early this morning, the council met again and pronounced him guilty. Governor Pilate made a feeble attempt to save Jesus, but an angry crowd of Jesus' opponents had gathered. To avoid any further disturbance, he ordered the soldiers to crucify him.

Jesus' movement appears to have had possibilities, particularly since it seemed to fulfill the ancient prophecies. There was something about Jesus that made you believe that he could have been the person so many were waiting for. With these most recent developments, however, there can be no more hope. As this goes to press Jesus is being prepared for crucifixion. Eventually his disciples will go back to fishing, and in a few years both he and his kingdom will be forgotten. Nothing short of a resurrection could save him now.

Check Yourself

1. What three relationships do we emphasize in the Lord's Supper?

2. The Lord's Supper has also been called "Communion." What do we remember when we take part in the Lord's Supper that makes communion with God possible?

3. What three things should bring us joy after each time we celebrate the Lord's Supper?

In Class

After you have talked in class about the Lord's Supper, complete the following statement: "To me the Lord's Supper means...

_____

_____

_____

_____

_____

_____

Jesus Dies and Rises from the Dead 10

BIBLE READINGS: Jesus' death, Mark 15:21-40
Jesus' resurrection, Matthew 28:1-10; Mark 16:1-8; John 20:1-18

CATECHISM: WHAT IS ACCOMPLISHED BY THE DEATH AND RESURRECTION OF JESUS CHRIST?

By the death and resurrection of Jesus Christ, God conquers sin, death and the Devil, offering forgiveness for sin and assuring eternal life for those who follow Christ.

For God so loved the world that he gave his only Son, that whoever believes in him should not perish but have eternal life.

John 3:16, RSV

Out there in the distance I see a little hill called "Golgotha," where criminals are put to death. I keep picturing this hill in my mind as I try to describe what I might have seen if I had been an observer walking around Jerusalem the day when Jesus was crucified.

"I SAW HIM DIE"

As soon as Pilate has given permission to crucify Jesus, I see the soldiers grab him and put a crown of thorny branches on his head, and I hear them laugh and

shout, "Hail, King of the Jews." What a strange way to have fun! I wonder how it feels to a gentle person like Jesus to have them slap him and spit in his face and then ridicule him by kneeling down in front of him!

Then I see them take him over to that hill. I watch while they undress him and divide up his clothes among themselves. I feel sick all over as I see them stretch out his arms and nail his hands to a long board. Then I see his body sag and the nails tear at his hands as they lift him up and leave him hanging on a cross. I watch while they crucify two convicted thieves, one on each side of him.

A crowd has gathered around Jesus and I hear them shouting at him and telling him to come down from the cross if he really is the Son of God. They hate him so much that they keep on shouting at him even while he is dying!

I would not blame him if he would shout back at the people or curse them or if he would beg for mercy, but the first thing I hear him say is, "Father forgive them, for they know not what they do." He is actually praying for the people who are crucifying him! Then I hear one of the thieves who has been crucified with him say something to him, and I hear Je-

sus answer, "Today you will be with me in Paradise."

I see Jesus' mother standing by the cross and crying, and I see one of his disciples trying to comfort her. Then I hear him say to his mother, "Woman, behold your son," and to the disciple standing by her, "Behold your mother." I understand that Jesus is asking this disciple to care for his mother as her own son would do.

What kind of person can Jesus really be? Here, while he is suffering so terribly from the pain of being crucified, he seems to be concerned only for other people. He must be lonely up there on the cross, with so many people ridiculing him, and his disciples not daring to come to help him. I hear him cry out, "My God, my God, why have you forsaken me?" Even God seems to have deserted him. Then I hear him say that he is thirsty and I see someone dip a sponge in vinegar and touch it to his lips. After a while I hear him say, with a deep sigh, "It is finished." He seems to have finished doing something while he has been suffering on the cross, something which I do not understand. Then he says, "Father, into your hands I commit my spirit," and he dies.

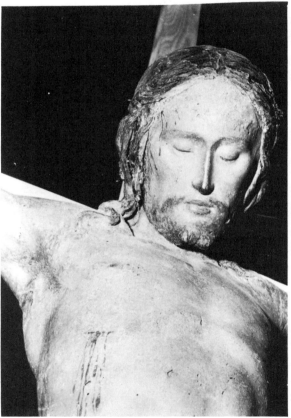

I had been impressed with Jesus as I had followed him from place to place with his disciples, teaching and healing people, but it seems to me that the way he died impressed me even more. The army captain in charge of the crucifixion must have had the same feelings when he said, "Surely this man was

194

the Son of God!"

No matter how impressive his death was, however, it brought to an end all the dreams of his friends and disciples about ruling with him in a new Kingdom. Now they had nothing more for which to hope. Joseph of Arimathea, a rich man, took Jesus' body from the cross and buried it in a cave he had dug for his own burial, and Pilate posted a guard to watch it.

The next day was the Sabbath, when his friends were not permitted to do anything except to mourn the death of their friend and teacher whom they had learned to love and in whom they had placed their hopes.

"I SAW HIM ALIVE AGAIN!"

Early Sunday morning, the day after the Sabbath, I watch some women as they go out to the cave where Jesus is buried. They are carrying sweet-smelling spices to put around his body. Suddenly things begin to happen so fast that I can't keep up with them!
• There is an earthquake.
• An angel appears and rolls away the stone that blocks the entrance to the cave.
• The guards faint at the sight of the angel. When they revive, they run away.
• I hear the angel tell the women not to be afraid, that Jesus is not here—he is risen from the dead. The angel instructs them to tell his disciples to meet him in Galilee.

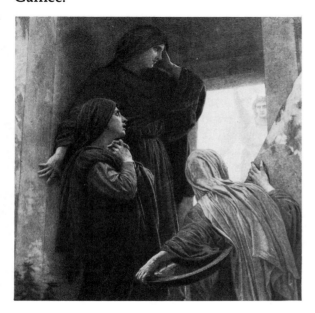

• The women are so frightened that they also run away.
• Peter and one of the other disciples come running up to the cave. They find it empty, except for the cloth which had been wrapped around the body of Jesus. Peter and the other disciple then leave.
• I see a woman go up to the cave. She seems to be talking with someone inside.

Now I see Jesus! There he is, alive! He is standing right behind the woman! She turns and sees him but does not recognize him until he calls her by name, "Mary!" Then she, too, recognizes him and realizes that Jesus is alive!

THE MEANING OF JESUS' DEATH AND RESURRECTION

This tragic death and this glorious resurrection, what do they mean? Two of Jesus' disciples were walking home from Jerusalem on the day of his resurrection, when Jesus joined them. They did not recognize him at first, but he explained to them from the Old Testament that the prophets had said that the Messiah would die and rise again from the dead. Therefore Jesus' death and resurrection was a fulfillment of these prophecies, and his death and resurrection proved that he really was the Messiah (see Luke 24:13-32).

The apostles in their preaching used many Old Testament prophecies to explain the meaning of Jesus' death and resurrection. One of these prophecies is in Isaiah, chapter 53. Part of this prophecy is:

> But he was pierced for our transgressions, he was crushed for our iniquities; the punishment that brought us peace was upon him, and by his wounds we are healed. All we, like sheep, have gone astray, each one of us has turned to his own way; and the LORD has laid on him the iniquity of us all (verses 5, 6, NIV).

On the basis of this and other prophecies, the apostles preached that Jesus died for our sins, so that we may be forgiven. God always wants to forgive sin, but he is also concerned about the suffering that has been caused by our sin. All of us have sinned, but God has provided a way to forgive us and also to correct the harm that we have caused.

That Jesus died for our sins means that God, through his Son, has accepted the responsibility for our sins. We may be forgiven and go absolutely free when we put our trust in Jesus and his death for us on the cross. This is the meaning of the death of Jesus.

The Apostles also used the Old Testament prophecies to explain the meaning of the resurrection of Jesus. Peter said, in his sermon, "God raised him from the dead . . . because it was impossible for death to keep its hold on him." The prophets had promised that the Messiah would rise from the dead. Therefore, because Jesus was the Messiah, it was not possible to keep him from rising from the dead (Acts 2:24-36).

By rising from the dead Jesus proved his power over death. When he comes again this power will be used to raise his followers to live eternally with him. "But the truth is that Christ has been raised from the dead, as the guarantee that those who sleep in death will also be raised . . . each one will be raised in his proper order: Christ, first of all, then, at the time of his coming, those who belong to him." (1 Corinthians 15:20, 23, TEV).

But Jesus' resurrection means even more. Jesus has risen from the dead so he can share his life with us while we are still living in this world. When we trust in him to forgive our sins, he begins to rule in our hearts, we enter God's Kingdom and receive a new life, which is the life of Jesus living in us. This does not make us perfect, but God will give us all the power that it took to raise Jesus from the dead to help us live this new life.

I have been crucified with Christ and I no longer live, but Christ lives in me. The life I live in the body I live by faith in the Son of God, who loved me and gave himself for me.

(Galatians 2:20, NIV)

Possible site of Jesus' tomb

The catechism for this chapter explains the meaning of the death and resurrection of Jesus. In order to help us understand it better, imagine that we are walking home from Jerusalem on the day of Jesus' resurrection, wondering about the meaning of all the things that had happened to him. If Jesus joined us on the road, he might say something like this:

"Don't you understand that I was *supposed* to suffer and die and rise again? I was wounded for your sins. When they beat me, it was for you that I suffered. When I died, I died for you. This is what the prophets said I would do. I won the victory over sin when they crucified me. I won the victory over death when I arose again. The Devil tried to destroy me, but I defeated him. Now I offer forgiveness for sins, and I promise a new and rich life to all who believe in me and follow me. That is what my death and resurrection mean."

Thank you Jesus for what you did for me.

Check Yourself

1. List at least three things that happened in connection with the resurrection of Jesus.

2. What is the value of the Old Testament in helping to explain the meaning of Jesus' death and resurrection?

3. Explain in your own words the meaning of the death and resurrection of Jesus.

In Class

Your teacher will make a list of several hymns about the meaning of death and resurrection of Jesus and will assign one hymn or part of a hymn to each member of the class. From the part of the hymn assigned to you, choose a sentence or part of a sentence that tells what the resurrection means to you.

For instance, if the hymn were "Amazing Grace," you might choose the sentence, "I once was lost but now am found, was blind but now I see." Rewrite the sentence or part of the sentence you have chosen into a one-sentence prayer. Write the prayer below:

_____

_____

_____

_____

_____

Your teacher will then explain how this sentence will be used, together with the sentences chosen by other members of the class to form a prayer.

Jesus Prepares His Disciples for Their Work   11

BIBLE READING: Matthew 28:16-20; John 21:1-19; Acts 1:3-11
Other suggested Bible readings: Luke 24:44-53; John 20:19-23

ASSIGNMENT: Interview two persons about what Jesus' resurrection means to them.
One of these persons may be one of your parents.

SIMON PETER'S STORY

I cannot describe how terrible I felt when I
heard that Jesus had died. When we were
having that last supper together, I had told
him I would be true to him even if everyone
else left him, but he warned me that, before
a rooster crowed, I would deny three times
that I even knew him. After he had been
taken to the high priest's house, another disciple and I followed along into the yard.
Then, when people started accusing me of
being one of his disciples, I lost all my courage. I was afraid they might arrest me, too,
and maybe kill me. I got so frightened that I
denied I knew him. After I had done this the
third time, Jesus looked straight at me, and
then the rooster crowed.

I knew then that I was nothing but a big
coward. I had failed Jesus when he needed
me most! I still thought he would be able to
get away from those people in some way, but
when I heard that he had died on that awful
cross, I felt even worse about what I had
done. I was a traitor, a liar and a coward!
Maybe if I had been loyal to Jesus I could
have gathered the other disciples together
and rescued him from death. It was because
of me, because I didn't have any courage,
that he died! I felt as though I were the most
unworthy person in the world! No one else
could have been as bad as I had been.

Then, when I was feeling the worst, some
women came running to say that Jesus was
missing from the place where he had been
buried. They were so excited that I could
hardly understand what they were trying to
say. They said something about his being
alive, but I knew that was impossible.
Another disciple and I ran as fast as we
could to the place where he had been buried.
There, sure enough, we found the cloth that
had been wrapped around his body, but his
body was gone!

I knew that something strange had happened, but I was so confused I didn't know
what to think. I remembered his saying
something about rising from the dead, but
even if he were risen from the dead, that
wouldn't do me any good. He wouldn't want
me for a follower any more after I had been
guilty of deserting him when he needed me
most.

But Jesus really was alive! It was unbe-
lievable; it was impossible; but it had happened! He appeared to some of us that night
when we had locked ourselves into a room
because we were afraid of the people who
had killed him. He gave us his blessing and
his peace, and he said he was going to send
us out into the world as God had sent him
into the world.

He appeared to us several times after that
and explained that his death and resurrection
were exactly what the prophets had said
would happen. He warned us that we would
be persecuted, but he gave us courage by telling us that he would always be with us.

One evening some of us decided to go back
to fishing again. We fished all night but did

not catch anything. Early in the morning a man standing on the shore called to us and asked us, "Have you caught any fish?"

"No," we replied.

"Throw out your net on the right side of the boat," he said.

As soon as we did that we got a whole net full of fish. Then I heard one of the men say, "It is Jesus!"

When I heard that I jumped out of the boat into the water and came to shore as fast as I could. The other men came following in the boat. There we found that Jesus had some fish frying on a fire and some bread. He asked us to bring some of the fish we had caught. When the fish were ready, we had breakfast together.

After breakfast, we had a wonderful talk together. As we were talking, Jesus asked me, "Simon, do you love me more than these?" I told him that I loved him, but he kept asking me over and over again if I loved him. By the time he had asked me the third time, I was quite upset. I felt embarrassed to keep telling him how much I loved him when I knew that I had denied him the night before he was crucified.

Yet, each time he asked me, he also told me to take care of his sheep and his lambs. I understood from this that he wanted me to care for other people who believed in him. That made me very happy because I knew he had forgiven me and wanted me to do his work even though I had been such a coward. Once again I was glad to belong to him.

PREPARING THE DISCIPLES FOR THEIR MINISTRY

Fortunately Simon Peter's story had a happy ending. It would have been far different for him if Jesus had not risen from the dead or if Jesus had not forgiven him and received him back again. Now he was restored to his place on Jesus' team of disciples. Judas had betrayed Jesus and had committed suicide when he realized what he had done, and a man named Matthias was later chosen to replace him on Jesus' team (Acts 1:15-26). Through this team Jesus was going to change the world and eventually bring hope and new life to millions of people. But first he spent forty days preparing them to continue his work.

DURING THIS TIME:

1. Jesus convinced the disciples that he had really risen from the dead.

In order to be true apostles, they had to be witnesses to Jesus' resurrection. It was to be on their word that other people could know that Jesus was really the Son of God and the Savior of the world because he had risen from the dead. Therefore, their faith must never waver. Whatever doubts unbelievers might have about Jesus' resurrection, these witnesses must be absolutely sure about what they were saying. During these forty days, therefore, Jesus spent enough time with them to make them sure that they were not just dreaming or imagining that the real Jesus was with them.

2. Jesus taught the disciples how to carry on their ministry and commissioned them for their work.

While Jesus was convincing his disciples that he had really risen from the dead he was also teaching them about their work and getting ready to send them out into the world. What Jesus told them is summarized in Matthew 28:18-20, which is known as "The Great Commission." Jesus gave it to them during a meeting with them on a mountain in Galilee:

> And Jesus came and said to them, "All authority in heaven and on earth has been given to me. Go therefore and make disciples of all nations, baptizing them in the name of the Father and of the Son and of the Holy Spirit, teaching them to observe all that I have commanded you, and lo, I am with you always, to the close of the age."

These instructions are for us as well as for the eleven disciples to whom Jesus first gave them. After they had died, oth-ers took their places until our own time. Now we are the disciples whom Jesus is sending out, and he intended the instructions for us as well as for them:

"Depend on my authority."—We are commanded to go with confidence. We need not fear ridicule, opposition, hatred, or persecution. If it seems hard to witness about Jesus, we may remember that he has more authority than any of his opponents. He will make sure that every faithful testimony will serve its purpose.

"Go . . . and make disciples."—We make disciples by the way we speak and act, by the way we take part in our churches, Sunday schools, and youth programs, by the way we support missionaries or become missionaries ourselves. We also make disciples by telling our friends about Jesus and what he means to us and inviting them to believe in him. We have different gifts and abilities which we may use in our ministry of making disciples, and this ministry is most effective when we work together with other Christians.

"Go . . . make disciples of all nations."—The Good News about Jesus meets the needs of all races and nationalities, and people of all nations respond to it. In order that they may hear the good news, Jesus has commanded us to bring it to all parts of the world. Missionary work is also a responsibility we share with other Christians. If we are willing to be true disciples of Jesus, God will help us discover what part he wishes us to have in this work. He may be calling us to become missionaries ourselves or to help support and encourage other missionaries.

"Baptizing them"—Jesus commanded us to baptize those who respond to the Good News and become disciples. Baptism signifies that a person's sins have been washed away by God through faith in Jesus. It also signifies that a person belongs to Jesus, and is one of his disciples.

"Teaching them to observe all that I have commanded you."—Jesus has asked us to teach new disciples what he has commanded so they may become mature in their faith. This is the reason we have Confirmation classes as well as Sunday schools. Teaching is an important ministry of the Church, and we need to continue to learn about him and how to be his disciples as long as we live.

"Lo, I am with you always, to the close of the age."—This is a promise rather than a command. It says that, when we are taking part in the work of making disciples and teaching them, we may be sure that Jesus will be present with us. Through his Spirit he will encourage us and give us strength right up until the time when he returns at the close of this age.

The Great Commission is a kind of "package" of three things from Jesus.

Jesus begins with an encouraging statement about his great authority.

Then he commissions us to go, and he tells us what to do.

Finally, he encourages us again by promising to be with us.

3. *Jesus told the disciples to wait for the power of God's Spirit.*

Even after Jesus had convinced his disciples that he really was risen from the dead, and after he had given them all these instructions, there was still one thing missing. Before they would be ready for their ministry they still needed God's power, which could only come from God's Spirit. Jesus promised to send the Spirit after he returned to heaven (Acts 1:4-8). He told the disciples to wait in Jerusalem until they received the Spirit and the power he had promised.

JESUS ASCENDS INTO HEAVEN

When Jesus had finished preparing his disciples for their ministry, he went with them up on a mountain. He reached out his arms and blessed them, and then he ascended into heaven. Although he would no longer be with them physically, he would now be with all his disciples around the world and in all generations through his Spirit. He continues to rule in their hearts as they serve him and live the life he has given them. He has promised to come back again some day, and his kingdom will then fill the earth with righteousness and peace. Therefore, as we continue the work which began with his first disciples, we also await the time when he will return.

Check Yourself

1. What question did Jesus ask Simon Peter when he talked with him after a breakfast, and what did he tell Simon to do?

2. What three things did Jesus do for his disciples during the forty days he spent with them after his resurrection?

3. Explain, in your own words, what Jesus commanded his disciples to do in the "Great Commission."

In Class

After the class discussion about the meaning of Jesus' resurrection appearances, complete the following sentence: "To me the resurrection appearances mean . . .

_____

_____

_____

_____

_____

REVIEW OF UNIT THREE

At his Last Supper, Jesus established a "New Covenant," which emphasizes our relationship with God, with ourselves, and with others. By his death and resurrection, Jesus opened the way for us to come to God and to live his new life. Before he ascended into heaven, Jesus spent forty days with his disciples to prove to them that he had risen from the dead and to prepare them to do his work.

The Early Days of the Church

UNIT FOUR

CHAPTER 12
Jesus' Disciples Begin a New Life Together

The Holy Spirit united the disciples into one body, which is the Church, and gave them the power to witness about Jesus.

CHAPTER 13
The Church Reaches Out

The Apostle Paul led the early Church in reaching out. He made three great missionary journeys and started many churches.

CHAPTER 14
Letters to Help the New Church

Letters were written to help believers deal with the problems of their new life. Most of these letters were written by the Apostle Paul. They are now part of the New Testament, and they are God's Word for us also.

CHAPTER 15
Relationships in the Early Church

Other letters of the New Testament were written to help Christians get along with each other and live in an unfriendly world.

CHAPTER 16
The Church Faces Persecution

There are letters in the New Testament to encourage Christians to hold out and not give up when they are persecuted and to give them hope for the future. These letters are also for us.

Birth of Jesus	Jesus' ministry, death, resurrection, ascension	Coming of the Holy Spirit	Three missionary journeys of the Apostle Paul	Roman persecution of Christians begins with Nero	
4 BC	27 AD	30 AD	47 AD 56 AD	64 AD	100 AD

Jesus' Disciples Begin a New Life Together

12

BIBLE READING: Acts 1:1-14; Acts 2:1-47

CATECHISM: WHO IS THE HOLY SPIRIT?

The Holy Spirit is God everywhere present and powerful, working in us, in the Church, and in the world.

And I will ask the Father, and he will give you another Counselor to be with you forever— the Spirit of truth. The world cannot accept him, because it neither sees him nor knows him. But you know him, for he lives with you and will be in you.

John 14:16, 17, NIV

Why would anyone want to turn to God when there are so many other interesting things to do? Things like sports, entertainment, hobbies, and parties are right here for us to enjoy. With all these things to make us happy, what else do we need?

The answer to these questions is: the "Holy Spirit" makes us realize how much we need God and causes us to feel sorry for our sins. Then, when we hear the Good News about Jesus, the Holy Spirit encourages us to repent and believe in

Jesus and shows us how satisfying the new life of being his follower really is. Because the Holy Spirit is so important to us, we need to know who he is and what he does.

THE HOLY SPIRIT IS ONE OF THE THREE PERSONS OF THE HOLY TRINITY

In order to know who the Holy Spirit is, we need to know that the Bible speaks of God in three ways:

1. As Ruler of everything he created, he is known as "God, the Father."
2. As the One who lived on this earth as a human being called "Jesus," he is known as "God, the Son."
3. As the unseen Spirit who is present in the world and draws people to himself, he is known as "God, the Holy Spirit."

Because God has revealed himself to us in these three ways in the Bible, we call him "the Triune God." "Father," "Son," and "Holy Spirit" are spoken of as "Three Persons," "the Holy Trinity" or just "the Trinity." The Bible emphasizes, however,

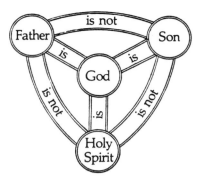

Father — is not — Son
Father — is — God — is — Son
Father — is not — Holy Spirit
Holy Spirit — is — God
Son — is not — Holy Spirit

that God cannot be divided into three compartments even though he expresses himself in these three ways. Father, Son, and Holy Spirit never act separately, but always as one Being. Whether we pray to God the Father or to Jesus or to the Holy Spirit, we are praying to the same one God, and the same one God hears us.

This means that the Holy Spirit is God, just as Jesus is God.

THE HOLY SPIRIT FORMS THE CHURCH

When Jesus went back into heaven, he promised his disciples that the Holy Spirit would come to give them special power to be his witnesses, and he told them to stay in Jerusalem until they had received this power (Acts 1:4-8). The disciples obeyed Jesus' command, and they met every day to pray while they waited for this promise to be fulfilled.

The tenth day after Jesus had ascended into heaven was the day of the festival of Pentecost, which the Jewish people celebrated fifty days after their Passover every year. Jews who lived in different countries and spoke different languages came to Jerusalem for this festival. On this day, as the disciples were praying together, there came a sound like a strong wind; and flames of fire, shaped like tongues, came down on their heads. The disciples then began to praise God in the different languages of the people who had come to Jerusalem. A great crowd gathered, and the people marvelled that they were hearing the disciples praising God in their own languages.

Through all these strange events the Holy Spirit was forming a new body, called "the Church." This body includes all believers in Jesus, both those who have already died and those who are still

They saw what seemed to be tongues of fire that separated and came to rest on each of them (Acts 2:3, NIV).

living. Since that day, the Holy Spirit has been giving life to the Church and working through it.

THE HOLY SPIRIT GIVES POWER TO WITNESS

On that day the Holy Spirit filled the disciples with power to witness, as Jesus had promised before he ascended into heaven. When the Holy Spirit filled Peter with power, he preached to the great crowd that had gathered. He explained that God was bringing forgiveness and salvation through the death and resurrection of Jesus. The Holy Spirit gave Peter such power that about three thousand people repented and believed in Jesus and were baptized.

THE HOLY SPIRIT GIVES MEANING TO BAPTISM

It was because the Holy Spirit had been at work that all those people could be baptized on the Day of Pentecost. The Holy Spirit had given Peter the power to preach the Good News about Jesus. The Holy Spirit had convinced the people that they needed to repent and turn from their old lives and believe in Jesus. Then their sins had been forgiven, and the Holy Spirit had created new life in them. If the Holy Spirit had not been at work, none of these things would have happened, and there would have been no baptisms.

If it were not for the Holy Spirit, baptism would be no more than an initiation into a club. Because of the Holy Spirit, baptism signifies that God has cleansed away our sins and that we have been welcomed into a loving family that God has created.

THE HOLY SPIRIT MAKES JESUS REAL TO HIS PEOPLE

After Jesus ascended into heaven, the disciples could no longer be with him as they had before. But Jesus had promised that the Holy Spirit would come to make him real to them (see John 15:26). Jesus was so real to those who believed in him that they witnessed about him to every-

one who would listen. They called him "the Christ," and they soon began to be called "Christ-ians" because they talked so much about the Christ and acted so much like him (see Acts 11:26).

THE HOLY SPIRIT UNITES THE CHURCH INTO A FAMILY

Because the Holy Spirit brings the love of God to his friends, he unites them into a family who care for each other as brothers and sisters. He also gives different gifts to different members of the Church, so they can work together as they serve God and witness about Jesus.
• Because of the Holy Spirit, the Church is not just an organization; it is a loving family serving God together.
• Because of the Holy Spirit, our faith is not just a religion; it is a new life centered in Jesus.
• Because of the Holy Spirit, we do not just have new life, we have new life *together.*

Check Yourself

1. What do we mean when we speak of God as the "Triune God"?

2. List three things the Holy Spirit does.

3. How does the Holy Spirit make a difference in the lives of those who believe in Jesus?

In Class

In this class session we have discussed Pentecost, which is really the "birthday" of the Church. Ask yourself how you fit into the experience of Pentecost. Are you a part of the crowd, wondering what is going on? (see Acts 2:12). Are you in the crowd making fun of what is happening? (see Acts 2:13). Are you like the disciples before Pentecost, all huddled up and not ready to take a stand? (see Acts 2:1) Are you filled with the Spirit and anxious to tell others the Good News? (see Acts 2:14) Are you taking part in the fellowship of the Church and growing more mature? (see Acts 2:41-42) After thinking about these questions, write a statement about where you are in relation to this new life:

_____

_____

_____

_____

_____

The Church Reaches Out

13

BIBLE READING: Mark 16:15; Acts 1:8; Acts 13:1-3; Acts 14:1-28
Other suggested Bible readings: Acts 16:11-34; Acts 19:13-41

CATECHISM REVIEW: WHAT IS THE KINGDOM OF GOD?
WHAT DID JESUS TEACH US CONCERNING LIFE IN THE KINGDOM OF GOD?
WHAT IS THE SACRAMENT OF THE LORD'S SUPPER?
WHAT IS ACCOMPLISHED BY THE DEATH AND RESURRECTION OF JESUS
  CHRIST?
WHO IS THE HOLY SPIRIT?

Becoming a Christian made such a difference to me that I wanted to tell everybody about it. It was wonderful to know that my sins were forgiven, that Jesus was my friend, and that I had something worthwhile to live for. Because I wanted other people to know about it, I joined in the things my church and Sunday school were doing to teach and preach about Jesus. I discovered that whenever people receive the Good News about Jesus they want to reach out and tell it to other people. It is the Holy Spirit who is causing them to want to share the Good News.

The Holy Spirit has always been causing Christians to reach out to others. This began with the very first Christians. As they worshiped together, ate together, and cared for the poor, they demonstrated the love that they preached about. Soon the Church increased to 5,000, and still it kept growing.

As the Church grew larger, the apostles could not care for all the needs of the people, and they chose seven men who were filled with the Holy Spirit to be their helpers. One of these helpers, a man named Stephen, was arrested because of the way he preached about Jesus. While he was making a speech in his defense, an angry crowd dragged him

out of the city and threw stones at him until he died. This was followed by a time of persecution that scattered the Christians all over the land of Judea and even into other countries. These Christians witnessed about Jesus wherever they went, and many more people became Christians.

All believers in Jesus considered themselves to be witnesses, and their testimonies caused the Church to grow and spread throughout Judea and Samaria and even into other countries. Philip, another one of the helpers chosen by the apostles, preached in Samaria. Some Samaritans believed in Jesus, received the Holy Spirit, and a Samaritan Church was formed. Philip then continued preaching in other places.

THE CHRISTIANS SHARE THE GOOD NEWS WITH THE GENTILES

At first the good news about Jesus was preached only to Jews. Everyone who was not a Jew was known as a "Gentile," and no one knew at that time that the Good News was also for Gentiles.

God told Peter to accept an invitation from a Gentile army officer to come to his house and tell his family about Jesus. When Peter preached to these people and they believed in Jesus, the Holy Spirit came to them just as he had come to the Jews at the Festival of Pentecost. Peter then baptized them. They were the first Gentiles to accept Christ and to become members of the Church. In this way God taught the Christians to reach out to Gentiles as well as to Jews. He showed his people that he wanted believers from all different nationalities and races to become members of one Church.

Since that time the Church has sent missionaries to all parts of the world. Missionaries may be teachers, doctors, administrators, agricultural specialists, evangelists, or they may have other skills. They bring the Good News of Jesus to people by helping them meet their needs and by telling them about him.

The Covenant Church has been actively engaged in missionary work ever since its beginning, and many people have become Christians through the work of its missionaries. In 1937, for instance, a mission was established in Zaire, Africa. Now the Covenant Church in Zaire has more members than the Covenant Church in North America.

now spent the rest of his life witnessing about him and working for him. (For the story of Saul's conversion, see Acts 9:1-22.) In his missionary work, Saul traveled widely in the Roman empire. After he began this work he used his Roman name, Paul, and he is known to us as "the Apostle Paul."

PAUL, THE FIRST GREAT MISSIONARY

The first great missionary of the Church was a man named Saul, who came from Tarsus (you can find Tarsus on the map on page 212). Saul was a strict Pharisee and he worked very hard to destroy the new Christian movement because he considered it to be a false religion. He got special permission to arrest Christians wherever he could find them and to have them thrown in jail or killed.

When Saul was on his way to the city of Damascus in search of Christians to arrest and bring back to Jerusalem, he had a vision of Jesus, who asked him why he was persecuting him. As a result of this vision, Saul became a believer in Jesus, and God called him to be an apostle. Instead of working against Jesus, he

PAUL'S FIRST MISSIONARY JOURNEY (47-48 AD) (Acts 13:1-14:28)

After becoming a Christian, Paul lived and worked as a tentmaker in the city of Antioch in Syria, and he was also a member of the church in that city. God led this church to send Paul and a man named Barnabas out as missionaries.

When they were on this journey many people heard them preach and became Christians, but others opposed them. Many people believed strongly that it was necessary to be circumcised and obey the Law of Moses in order to be acceptable to God. They objected violently to Paul's preaching that all people, Jews or Gentiles, could be saved by turning from their sins and believing in Jesus.

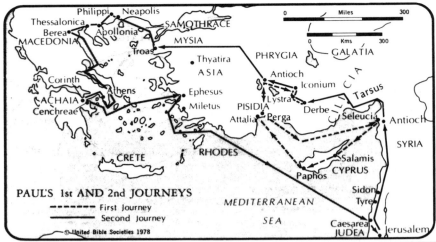

PAUL'S 1st AND 2nd JOURNEYS
- - - - - First Journey
————— Second Journey
© United Bible Societies 1978

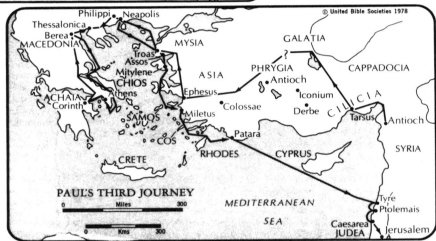

PAUL'S THIRD JOURNEY
© United Bible Societies 1978

Paul and Barnabas left groups of Christians in the cities where they preached, and these were organized into churches. After more than a year of traveling, they returned to Antioch and reported to the church what had happened on their journey.

THE JERUSALEM COUNCIL (49 AD) (Acts 15:1-31)

Some teachers were telling the Christians in Antioch that they could not be saved unless they would be circumcised and keep the law of Moses. Paul and Barnabas disagreed sharply with these teachers. Because of this disagreement the church in Antioch appointed Paul and Barnabas to talk with the apostles and other church leaders in Jerusalem. When they arrived in Jerusalem a conference or "council" was arranged to consider the disagreement.

Peter told the council how God had accepted Gentiles by giving them the Holy Spirit, and Paul and Barnabas reported on the wonderful things God had done among the Gentiles even though they had not been circumcised. Then James explained that the prophets had promised that God would accept both Gentiles and Jews as his people. At the end of the discussion it was decided not to require the Gentile Christians to be circumcised and to keep the Law of Moses. All people were to be accepted on the same basis, by faith in Christ alone.

PAUL'S SECOND MISSIONARY JOURNEY (49-52 AD) (Acts 15:36-18:22)

1. The Good News comes to Europe.
On Paul's second missionary journey he planned to visit the churches he had established on his first journey to see

212

how they were getting along. After he had visited these churches, however, God showed Paul a vision of a man calling him to Macedonia, a part of Greece. Up to this point Paul had been preaching in Asia, but Greece is in Europe. When Paul went to Macedonia, therefore, it meant that the good news about Jesus had now come to Europe and would some day be heard and believed throughout the whole Western world.

2. *How Paul worked as a missionary.*

Paul's visit to the city of Philippi is an example of the way he worked as a missionary. He first found where the Jews gathered to worship, and there he preached to them. Then he preached to the Gentiles. Later, both Jews and Gentiles who believed in Jesus were united in one church. Among those who met at the Jewish place of worship was a businesswoman named Lydia, who became a Christian. She invited Paul and Silas, his companion, to stay in her home. Her whole family also became Christians.

Paul made some slave owners angry by driving an evil spirit out of a slave girl who was making money for them by telling fortunes. They had Paul and Silas arrested and thrown in prison. In the prison Paul and Silas sang songs and prayed until midnight, and the other prisoners listened to them. At midnight an earthquake shook the prison so much that the doors came open. Fearing that the prisoners had all escaped, the jail-keeper was ready to kill himself when Paul assured him that all the prisoners

were still in prison. That night the jail-keeper and his whole family became Christians. In the morning Paul and Silas were released, and they went on their way. Paul continued to preach to the Jews and the Gentiles. In every city some people opposed him, but others believed, and he organized the believers into churches.

PAUL'S THIRD MISSIONARY JOURNEY (52-56 AD) (Acts 18:23-21:15)

After reporting again to his own church in Antioch, Paul went out for the third time to visit the churches he had started. On this journey Paul spent three years in the city of Ephesus, where many people became Christians. From Ephesus Paul traveled through Greece again, on his way back to Jerusalem.

PAUL'S ARREST AND LIFE IN ROME (Acts 21:16-28:31)

Soon after Paul arrived in Jerusalem he was attacked by a mob in the temple. He was rescued by the Roman commander, who also arrested him. Paul remained in prison in Caesarea until he appealed to the Emperor in Rome. In the last chapter of Acts we find Paul in Rome in the cus-

tody of a soldier, but permitted to live in a private house and receive visitors. He preached the Good News of Jesus to all who came to see and to hear him. The New Testament does not tell what happened to Paul after this, but it is believed that he was put to death some years later by the Roman Emperor Nero.

CHRISTIANS ARE STILL REACHING OUT

The Apostle Paul was the first of many missionaries, whom God has called to bring the message of Jesus to all parts of the world. Undoubtedly your church is helping to support one or more missionaries. Do you know who these missionaries are?

Not all Christians are called to be missionaries but all are called to be witnesses. Business people, teachers, homekeepers, salespersons, and others have lived in such a way that people have been attracted to Jesus, and then they have witnessed about him whenever they have had an opportunity. Through missionaries and through other witnesses the Church has continued to reach out with the Good News.

AND THIS IS STILL GOING ON!

Check Yourself

1. What was the name of the first great missionary? _____ What had his name been before he began his missionary career? _____ How many missionary journeys did he make?

2. What was the reason for the Jerusalem Council, and what decision did it make?

3. List some ways in which you can witness to your friends.

In Class

Read the following in class:

Although some Christians are called by God to a career as missionaries, all Christians are called to be witnesses. This means that God has something for each one to do in order to show others that God cares for them and to try to help them become believers in Jesus. Some young people have been witnesses by being kind to other young people, making friends with them, and inviting them to come to church. Others have visited people who are sick. Some young people have helped their friends to understand some hard part of their school work, and this has given them a chance to invite them to church or to tell them about Jesus.

There are many ways for young people to share the Good News about Jesus. Your teacher will lead you in a discussion about what it means to share the Good News. After this discussion, complete the following statement in the space below: If I were to take the words of the great commission in Matthew 28:19, 20 seriously, I would

_____

_____

_____

_____

_____

Letters to Help the New Church

14

BIBLE READING: 1 Corinthians 1:10-17; 1 Corinthians 5:1-13; 1 Corinthians 11:17-34
Other suggested Bible readings: 1 Corinthians 3:1-9; 1 Corinthians 14:1-5; 1 Corinthians 14:26-33; 1 Corinthians 15:12-28

CATECHISM: WHAT IS MEANT BY ATONEMENT?

Atonement means the work of God in Jesus Christ by which we, being guilty, are justified; being enslaved to sin, are redeemed; being alienated from God, are reconciled; and being unholy, are sanctified.

Now, by means of the physical death of his Son, God has made you his friends, in order to bring you holy, pure, and faultless, into his presence.

Colossians 1:22, TEV

Even though I was excited about being a new Christian, I still had many problems. One of my problems was that I liked to look at sexy pictures and I could not keep from thinking a lot about sex. I was able to figure out that God had created people with sexual desires, but I was sure God had not intended sex to be more important than anything else to me. Why was I having so much trouble with sex? Why was I so selfish? Why could I not forgive people whom I did not like? Why was I so jealous? Why did church and Sunday school seem so dull? Why didn't God change all these things when I became a Christian?

My Christian friends and my pastor helped me to understand that we don't become perfect when we become Christians. As we deal with our problems, we receive help from the Bible, Jesus helps us through the Holy Spirit, and we can also receive help from our Christian friends. I discovered that these were the ways that God was helping me. I learned that we shall always want certain things, that some of them are wrong and some are not. Anything is wrong if it becomes more important to us than obeying God.

I learned that I can make certain choices, and if I make the right choices I will grow stronger as a Christian. For instance, I can choose to take part in some of the things the church is doing to help other people. This helps me take my mind off myself and my own problems. I can choose to make friends with the pastor or other people who will be able to help me. I can talk from time to time with Christians in whom I have confidence.

One of the most important things I learned was that God knows I am still a human being, and he is always ready to forgive me and help me to do better. Two sentences from the Bible that helped me were 1 Corinthians 10:13, "You can trust God to keep the temptation from becoming so strong that you can't stand up against it" (LB), and 2 Timothy 2:13, "Even when we are too weak to have any faith left, he remains faithful to us and will help us" (LB). I often thought of these sentences, and they kept reminding me that God would help me overcome temptation and that he would not fail me even when I had failed. I found that prayer was also important, and as I kept struggling and praying, God kept teaching me new things.

Then I began to understand that all these struggles had a purpose. I was like a baby learning to walk. A baby learns by stumbling and falling, and I was learning in the same way. Through all these struggles I was becoming a stronger person, and I was learning to understand the struggles of other people.

LETTERS TO HELP CHRISTIANS

I was going through struggles very much like the struggles of the first Christians. They were excited about their new life, but they also had many problems. God called some of the leaders of the Church to write letters to help them with their problems. These letters, or "epistles," as they are sometimes called, later became a part of the New Testament. Beginning with Romans, all the rest of the books of the New Testament were once letters. Most of them were written by the Apostle Paul, but some of them were written by other leaders of the Church. The Holy Spirit inspired these authors to write God's Word to different churches. We have the same kind of problems as the early Christians did, and these letters are just as valuable to us as they were to them.

1 CORINTHIANS, AN EXAMPLE OF A LETTER TO A CHURCH

The epistles, or letters, of the New Testament and their authors and main purposes are listed on page 221, at the end of this chapter. Since we do not have time to study all of them, we shall look only at 1 Corinthians, which is a letter from Paul to help the church in Corinth deal with some of its problems.

The Problem of Divisions in the Church.

Different groups in the church in Corinth were arguing about which leader was the greatest. Was it Paul? Was it Apollos? Was it Peter? Was it Christ? Paul helped them to understand that Christ was the only true leader of the Church, and all other leaders were only his servants (see 1 Corinthians 1:10-17; 3:1-9).

The Problem of Immorality.

One of the members of the church in Corinth was having sexual relations with his stepmother, and the church in Corinth was accepting this kind of life as being proper for Christians. God is greatly concerned about relationships in families, and he desires that sexual relations be limited to husbands and wives. What was happening in Corinth would eventually destroy family life. This was so serious that it had to be stopped immediately (see 1 Corinthians 5:1-13).

The Apostle Paul meets with Aquila and Priscilla in Corinth (Acts 18) in a scene from the A.D. *television miniseries.*

Other Problems. Some people were causing disorder in the worship services (see 1 Corinthians 14:1-5 and 1 Corinthians 14:16-33). Some were not showing proper respect for the Lord's Supper (see 1 Corinthians 11:17-34). False teachers had told the Christians that those who had died would never be raised from the dead (see 1 Corinthians 15:12-23).

In this letter, Paul helped the Christians deal with problems like these, and, in the other letters, there is help for many other problems that Christians have even today.

A MESSAGE OF ENCOURAGEMENT

The New Testament letters not only dealt with problems; they also brought encouragement to the Christians. When, for instance, Paul corrected the false teaching about the resurrection, he also encouraged the Christians by reminding them of the wonderful promise that they would be raised from the dead to live forever with Jesus (see 1 Corinthians 15:20-28).

The catechism for this chapter is really a message of encouragement. But first we must define some of the big words. These words have simple meanings, and it is important for us to know them because they describe some important truths.

ATONEMENT means "at-one-ment" or "to unite people who have become separated and make them one again." Christ

"atoned" for our sins by giving his life so that we can be united with God as his friends.

JUSTIFIED means "to be declared righteous." To be justified through Jesus Christ means that, when we believe in Jesus and trust in what he did for us, God says to us, "I no longer consider you guilty; I forgive you and declare you to be righteous."

REDEEMED means "to be set free by paying a price." If you find that you have no money to pay for a meal in a restaurant, you may be asked to leave your watch for security. Then, when you bring the money and get your watch back, you have "redeemed" the watch. It cost Jesus his own life to "redeem" us or set us free from sin.

ALIENATED means "that we are separated from God and have become his enemies because of our sins."

RECONCILED means "to become friends again." God has made it possible for us to stop being his enemies and to become his friends.

UNHOLY means "to be unfit for friendship with God." Because we have sinned, we cannot be friends of God until our sins have been forgiven.

SANCTIFIED means "to be made fit to be in the presence of God." When we trust in Jesus for the forgiveness of our sins and ask him to rule in our hearts, we are accepted by God as his friends, even though we are still struggling with temptations.

If we put all these definitions together, perhaps we can translate the catechism into more simple language:

"At-one-ment," or being made one with

God, means the work of God in Jesus Christ by which God says to us, "I forgive you and declare you to be righteous." Though we were slaves to sin, God, through Christ, paid the price to set us free from slavery; though we were enemies of God, we may now become his friends again; though we were unfit for friendship with a pure God, he has now purified us and made us acceptable to him.

This is an encouraging message because it tells us that God has done everything necessary to make it possible for us to become his friends.

Check Yourself

1. Why were the letters or "epistles" of the New Testament first written? What is their value to us?

2. State two of the problems of the church in Corinth.

3. What do "justified" and "redeemed" mean to you?

In Class

Your teacher will give you a problem in Christian living and suggest how you can find help from one of the letters or "epistles" of the New Testament. Then you will be asked to work on the problem by finding out what the Bible says about it. Before you begin this work, read together the following statements. They are things that will help you to understand the Bible.

1. Pray before you begin. Since the Bible is God's message to us, we need the help of the Holy Spirit to understand it.

2. Keep praying as you read and study. Keep asking God to make you willing to accept his message even though you may not agree with it at first. Ask him to make you willing to change your mind.

3. Imagine the early Christians listening as this letter was being read to them. What would it mean to them? What are some differences between their world and yours? What should it mean to you, in your world?

4. Don't just read one or two verses. You cannot understand a letter by reading only one or two sentences. Read enough to help you understand why it was written and what kind of problem it was dealing with. Don't just think of it as a set of rules. Try to understand the underlying truth and how that truth applies to you.

5. If possible, use other books to help you understand the passage. These may include other translations or a concordance, which lists other places in the Bible where you can find the same subject.

6. Discuss the problem and the Bible passage with your friends. Can you find out what it means to your parents or to your pastor?

You may not be able to use all these suggestions, but try to follow as many as you can in order to help you discover how the Bible deals with the problem given you by your teacher.

THE LETTERS (EPISTLES) OF THE NEW TESTAMENT

LETTER	STATED AUTHOR	GENERAL THEME OR PURPOSE
Romans	Paul (1:1)	To explain the gospel and its power to reconcile both Jews and Gentiles to God and to one another. To prepare for a visit to Rome.
1 Corinthians	Paul (1:1)	To help the church in Corinth deal with problems in Christian living.
2 Corinthians	Paul (1:1)	To answer charges that Paul was not a true apostle. To appeal for money for needy Christians in Judea.
Galatians	Paul (1:1)	To correct the false teaching that salvation requires obedience to the whole Law of Moses.
Ephesians	Paul (1:1)	To describe the new life the Christians have because they believe in Christ.
Philippians	Paul (1:1)	To thank the church in Philippi for a gift, to encourage Christians to be humble servants of Christ.
Colossians	Paul (1:1)	To correct false teachings that claimed that Christ alone was not enough to give complete salvation.
1 Thessalonians	Paul, Sylvanus, Timothy (1:1)	To explain more fully about Christ's return and to encourage Christians to be faithful.
2 Thessalonians	Paul, Sylvanus, Timothy (1:1)	To correct the false teaching that Christ had already returned.
1 Timothy	Paul (1:1)	To instruct Timothy about his work as a church leader.
2 Timothy	Paul (1:1)	To urge Timothy to be faithful as a church leader. To instruct him about how to keep out of trouble.
Titus	Paul (1:1)	To instruct Titus about his work as a church leader.
Philemon	Paul (1:1)	To ask Philemon to forgive Onesimus, a runaway slave who had become a Christian, and to receive him back as a Christian brother.
Hebrews	not stated	To encourage and warn Christians not to turn away from Christ in times of temptation.
James	James (1:1)	To encourage Christians to express their faith by their actions.
1 Peter	Peter (1:1)	To give hope to persecuted Christians and to encourage them to remain faithful.
2 Peter	Peter (1:1)	To explain why Christ had not yet returned and to encourage Christians to be ready for his return.
1 John	not stated★	To warn against false teachings and to urge Christians to live in fellowship with God and with each other.
2 John	"the Elder"★	To urge Christians to love one another and to warn against false teachings.
3 John	"the Elder"★	A letter to Gaius, a church leader, commending him and warning him against a troublemaker.
Jude	Jude (1:1)	To encourage Christians to remain faithful and to warn against false teachings.
The Revelation	John (1:1-4)	A special drama of visions and symbols, written to seven churches, to encourage persecuted Christians with the assurance that God will win the battle against Satan and evil.

★*traditionally considered to be "John, the Elder."*

Relationships in the Early Church 15

BIBLE READING: 1 Corinthians 12:12-31; 1 Corinthians 13

CATECHISM: WHAT IS THE CHRISTIAN CHURCH?

The Christian Church is all who confess Jesus Christ as Savior and Lord and who are united in one body with Christ as head.

Speaking the truth in love, we will in all things grow up into him who is the Head, that is, Christ. From him the whole body, joined and held together by every supporting ligament, grows and builds itself up in love, as each part does its work.

Ephesians 4:15, 16, NIV

Once another fellow tried to take my girlfriend away from me. It made me feel good when she chose not to go with him, but he never liked me very much after that. I didn't like him very much either, even though we both were supposed to be good Christians. I learned that it is very easy for Christians to talk about loving each other, but it isn't easy to do, especially when things like this happen.

Getting along with others was one of my greatest problems. I got jealous of other people and sometimes I became very angry. I heard Christians quarreling with each other, and some of them got so angry that they would not even speak to each other. "What a terrible way for Christians to act!" I said to myself. Yet, I wasn't acting any better than they were.

It is terrible when Christians quarrel and become angry with each other, but nothing in all the world is more wonderful than when they love and care for one another. It is possible to suffer and to face great hardships with courage when we have Christian friends who love and care for us, who help us to do right and who accept and forgive us when we do wrong.

The letters to the early Christians,

which we now have in the New Testament, teach us to think of ourselves as parts of the same body. In 1 Corinthians 12:12-17, Paul says that the human body is not composed only of an eye or of an ear. There are many different organs, and they all need each other. The eye can't say to the hand, "I don't need you," and the head can't say to the foot, "I don't need you." The body to which all Christians belong is the Church. Christ is the head, and the Church is sometimes

The ruins at Corinth

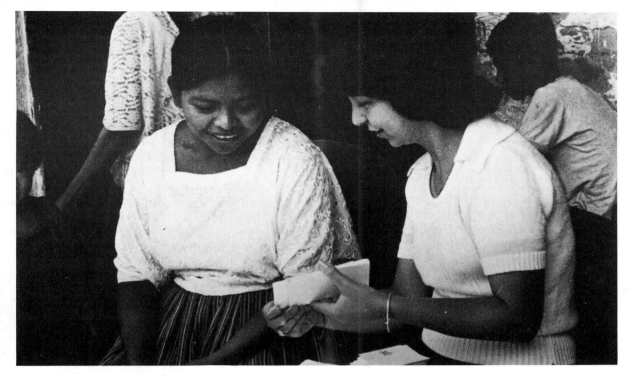

called "the body of Christ." When we all do our share, and when we depend on others to do their share, the Church is a healthy body.

On the other hand, if we put ourselves first, if we become jealous because we do not get as much praise as we think we should, if we become proud or dishonest, or if our feelings get hurt and we stop doing our part, the body of Christ becomes sick. Since it is easy for us to stop caring about others and to become interested only in ourselves, we need the Holy Spirit to help us be concerned about the whole body.

One reason the Holy Spirit came to the Church was to bring all the separate Christians together into this one body. How wonderful life can be when we let the Holy Spirit unite us and help all the different people in the body of Christ to do their part. Then we never need to feel deserted or alone, for the others are caring for us, and we are caring for them.

The problem is that there always seems to be at least one person who is messing up this happy relationship. If we let ourselves lose interest in the body because of those who are not doing their share, we become more like disconnected organs than like a whole body. Therefore,

we need to keep asking God to help us overlook the faults of others and to forgive them. This will help to keep the whole body healthy even though some of the members may not be doing their share.

THE NEED FOR LOVE

What we need most of all, in order to keep the Body of Christ healthy, is love. This love comes from God, but he has also put his love in our hearts so we can love others as he has loved us. Romans 5:5 tells us that "God has poured out his love into our hearts by the Holy Spirit, whom he has given us" (NIV). It is the Holy Spirit who makes it possible for us to love each other and to work together to keep the body of Christ healthy. Therefore, it is important for us to read and study the Bible so that we learn how the Holy Spirit wants to deal with the problems of loving each other. It is also important to ask the Holy Spirit to fill our hearts with his love. Learning to love other Christians is one of our greatest struggles as Christians, but when we let God help us, we are able to win this struggle. Then we really begin to enjoy living the Christian life together with other Christians.

The catechism for this chapter describes the Church as the body of Christ, in which we are all united. It tells how this body is held together with love. It is a description of the body of Christ when it is healthy (Ephesians 4:15, 16).

A SPECIAL KIND OF LOVE

Filling the blank in this sentence with each of the words or phrases that follow will give us an idea of the different meanings of love: "I love _____." (oranges, my dog, my bride, my husband to whom I have been married for fifty years, those people who need my help and can never repay me). Every time we change the ending of the sentence we give "love" a different meaning. When we say, for instance, "I love oranges," we mean something quite different from when we say, "I love those people who need my help and can never repay me."

God's love is a special kind of unselfish love. It is not a feeling; it is expressed in what we do. As far as we know, Jesus never said, "I love you," to anyone, yet we can never doubt his love because of the things he did. It would be impossible for us to love people in this way, but "God has poured out his love into our hearts." With the love that God gives us, we receive the greatest satisfaction from loving other people unselfishly.

God loves us even when we turn away from him and become his enemies. Nothing can stop him from loving us. Because he first loved us, we can love others. This love makes it possible for us to love people who do not love us or who are not very easy to love. It helps us to keep on loving them even when we do not feel like it or even if they do not seem to deserve our love.

One of the best descriptions of this kind of love is found in 1 Corinthians 13. Just imagine if everybody in the world would live this way:

"Love is very patient and kind, never jealous or envious, never boastful or proud, never haughty or selfish or rude. Love does not demand its own way. It is not irritable or touchy. It does not hold grudges and will hardly even notice when others do it wrong. It is never glad about injustice, but rejoices whenever truth wins out. If you love someone you will be loyal to him no matter what the cost. You will always believe in him, always expect the best of him, and always stand your ground in defending him."

1 Corinthians 13:4-7, LB

This kind of love is a gift from God to his people, and many others do not know anything about it. If we trust God and if we want to do his will, he will help us to love in this way.

224

Check Yourself

1. What is one of the things this chapter tells us the Holy Spirit does?

2. How does 1 Corinthians use the human body to illustrate the relationship of the individual Christians to the whole Church?

3. "Love" means many things. Describe the kind of love God gives to his people.

In Class

In class you will be exploring ways that Christians show love for one another. After you have finished this, write in the space below some specific ways you can show Christian love to those around you:

_____

_____

_____

The Church Suffers Persecution 16

BIBLE READING: Acts 6:7-15; Acts 7:57-60 1 Peter 3:13-18; 1 Peter 5:6-11
Other suggested Bible readings: 1 Peter 2:11-17; 1 Peter 4:1-6 1 Peter 4:12-16

CATECHISM: WHAT IS THE CHRISTIAN HOPE?

The Christian hope is a confident expectation of Christ's coming in triumph when he shall reign forever with his church.

Praise be to the God and Father of our Lord Jesus Christ! In his great mercy he has given us new birth into a living hope through the resurrection of Jesus Christ from the dead, and into an inheritance that can never perish, spoil or fade—kept in heaven for you . . .

1 Peter 1:3, 4, NIV

"We may be raided by the police tonight!" Raided by the police? Why would the police raid a home where a few people had gathered to praise God and to preach the Good News about Jesus? I was visiting in a country where it is against the law to preach about Jesus unless you have been approved by the government. These people were obeying Jesus, even though this meant to disobey their own laws.

It was the pastor who had warned me that we might be raided. "Since you are a visitor, you would no doubt be excused," he said, "but if we are raided the rest of us will have to go to jail."

At that meeting one man turned his life over to Jesus and became a Christian. "When his boss finds out that he has become a Christian," the pastor said, "he will be fired from his job."

Fortunately we were not raided, but this experience helped me to realize how much some people must suffer for being faithful to Jesus. It caused me to ask myself how faithful I would be if I might be raided by the police or lose my job for being a Christian. It helped me to remember that there are times, even in our own country, when it is hard to be a

Christian, and I prayed that God would keep me faithful even if it meant that I must suffer.

Jesus had warned his disciples that they would be persecuted. "If they have persecuted me," he said, "they will persecute you," and ever since the time of Jesus, many of his followers have suffered

226

from persecution. Christians know that the Bible teaches that they should obey the laws of their country, but they also know that the Bible teaches them to obey God, and when their government forbids what God has called them to do, they know that God's will comes first. God's new life in Christ is different from the old life of the world, and when these two kinds of life come into conflict with each other, persecution often results.

SOME REASONS FOR PERSECUTION

Following are some reasons why Christians have been persecuted:

1. Some people sincerely believed the Christian faith was against the will of God, and they believed God wanted them to destroy Christianity. This was the reason the Apostle Paul persecuted Christians before he was converted himself.

2. Some of the religious leaders opposed the Christians because they, them-

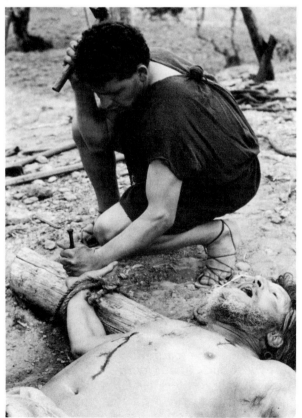

selves, had not been true to God and because they were afraid that they would lose their positions of authority if too many people turned to Jesus. They could not deny that God was blessing the Christians, but they tried to stop them from preaching to others (see Acts 4:16-18). This was the reason Stephen, the first Christian martyr, was killed (see Acts 6:8-15; 7:57-60).

3. Christians have often been persecuted because they have defended helpless people from injustice and oppression. This was the reason the people in Philippi who owned a slave girl started a riot against Paul. Paul had driven an evil spirit out of her so she could no longer make her owners rich by telling fortunes (see Acts 16:16-24).

4. Christians were persecuted by the Roman government because they refused to worship the emperor. Some of the Roman emperors, like Nero, became very jealous of their power and demanded to be worshiped as gods. The Romans did not care if people worshiped Jesus as long as they also worshiped the emperor, but the Christians insisted that since they recognized Jesus as Lord of all they would worship no one else.

5. Later, the governments of different European countries generally recognized a certain church or denomination to be the official religion of that country, and all religious practices which were not a part of that official religion were declared to be illegal.

6. Sometimes Christians have been persecuted simply because they are different from other people.

7. In recent times the governments of some countries have opposed all religion,

and believers of all faiths are forbidden to worship except by permission of the government.

OTHER KINDS OF PERSECUTION

We are grateful that our country recognizes our freedom to worship according to our own conscience. We believe that the only way people can be won to Christ is by telling them the Good News and showing them the love of Jesus. We believe that they must be permitted the freedom of making their own choice and not forced by law to say they are Christians. Nevertheless, even here Christians are sometimes persecuted. One example of persecution is when people are required by their employers to do things which are dishonest or illegal or contrary to their faith. Christian students may have difficulties in school because of a teacher who is prejudiced against faith in God. Another form of persecution is making fun of people who are Christians.

Even in a country that promises freedom of religion, we cannot be sure of freedom from persecution. The old life of the world will always be different from the new life in Christ, and we may expect to find opposition wherever we go as Christians.

IMPROPER CLAIMS OF PERSECUTION

If Christians do things that are dishonest or unkind, or if they do not respect the laws of their country, they cannot consider themselves persecuted for trouble they bring on themselves by their own misconduct (see 1 Peter 4:15, 16). A good question to consider or to discuss with your friends might be: If parents are forced to bring their sick children to a doctor even though they believe God does not approve of doctors, are they being persecuted?

HELP FOR PERSECUTED CHRISTIANS (1 Peter)

The New Testament contains encouragement and hope for Christians who are being persecuted. The First Epistle of Peter, for instance, was written for this purpose. This epistle was written especially to Jews who were living in foreign countries (see 1 Peter 1:1, 2), and who had become Christians. Many of them were being persecuted both because they were Jews and because they were Christians. This epistle is God's Word of help and encouragement to all Christians who are suffering persecution. Some of the ways in which 1 Peter encourages persecuted Christians are:

1. Be true to your faith and live so that you will gain the respect of your persecutors. They may even be won to Christ by the way you act when you are persecuted (1 Peter 2:11-17).

2. Follow the example of Jesus, who did not fight back at his persecutors but continued to love them (1 Peter 2:21-25).

3. Live in such a way that you do not bring suffering on yourselves for your own wrongs (1 Peter 3:13-18).

4. Consider it a privilege to suffer for Jesus, because he suffered for you (1 Peter 4:12-16).

5. Suffering will not last forever. Jesus will come again to relieve you of your suffering and reward you for your faithfulness (1 Peter 5:4).

THE HOPE OF JESUS' RETURN

Jesus had promised his disciples that he would come back again, and there are many references in the New Testament to his return. This promise is called "the Christian Hope." Jesus said that no one would know in advance when he would return, and he told his disciples to be ready, always, to welcome him back. He told a parable of ten young women who were invited to a wedding. Wedding customs in those days required the guests to have oil lamps with them. The wedding began late, and five of these young women did not bring enough oil. While they were out buying some, the wedding festivities began, and they were not permitted to enter. The lesson of this parable, Jesus said, was "Keep watch, because you do not know the day or the hour" (Matthew 25:13, NIV). Parables such as this are intended to warn us to be prepared always for Jesus' coming, but they are not intended to frighten us. The Good News about Jesus is that he has made it possible for us to be prepared so that we may look forward happily to his coming again.

For the wicked, who do not have eternal life, Jesus' return means the coming of judgment for their sins. For those who have eternal life, Jesus' return means the establishing of his kingdom of peace and righteousness over the whole earth. Most of all it means the end of sorrow and suffering for the friends of Jesus, the resurrection of his friends who have died, and the joy of being together with Jesus forever (see 1 Thessalonians 4:13-18).

Check Yourself

1. List three reasons why Christians have been persecuted.

2. What are two of the things that are written to comfort Christians in 1 Peter?

3. What is "the Christian Hope" and why is it particularly valuable to Christians who are being persecuted?

In Class

After the class discussion, read the following statements and rate yourself according to how you might respond. Ten is great. One is terrible.

1. I hang in there when the going gets tough.

   1_____ 10

2. I would die for my faith in Christ.

   1_____ 10

3. I would be tortured and still believe.

   1_____ 10

4. I am willing to be laughed at because I am a Christian.

   1_____ 10

5. My friends at school know that I am a Christian.

   1_____ 10

6. My friends know that I won't go along with the crowd because of what I believe.

   1_____ 10

"Eighty-six years have I served Christ, and he has never wronged me; how can I now blaspheme him, my King and my Savior?"

—spoken by Polycarp, Bishop of Smyrna, in 155 AD, when he was urged to save his life by denying Christ. Because he refused, he was burned to death.

REVIEW OF UNIT FOUR

The Holy Spirit united the followers of Jesus into one body, the Church, and gave them power to witness. The Church reached out to the world with the Gospel, especially through the Apostle Paul, who was the first great missionary. Paul and other church leaders wrote letters to help the Christians deal with their problems and to encourage them when they were being persecuted. The Holy Spirit inspired these writers so their letters are God's message to the whole Church, and they are now part of the New Testament.

The Church through the Centuries

UNIT FIVE

CHAPTER 17
God Gives His Friends a Book

We learn how we got our Bible and that it is a gift from God.

CHAPTER 18
What Must Christians Believe?

Christian leaders wrote statements known as "creeds" to define what Christians believe and to keep heresies out of the Church.

CHAPTER 19
The Church Struggles to Be the Light of the World

The church became the leader in a world that was falling apart. We follow the Church as it struggles to be a light to the world.

CHAPTER 20
The Church is Called Back to Its Purpose

Martin Luther and other leaders of the Protestant Reformation called the Church back to its purpose. We outline the principles of the Reformation. The Church divided into many denominations as it tried to discover its purpose.

CHAPTER 21
The Church in North America

Freedom of religion has allowed the Church to develop in a variety of ways and to reach out to many different kinds of people in the United States and Canada. It has also given people greater responsibility in making their own choices.

Life of Jesus	Council of Nicaea	Council of Carthage	Fall of Rome	GREGORY THE GREAT / Beginning of Moslem faith	Battle of Tours	Holy Roman Empire begins	The Church divides	Crusades begin	ST. DOMINIC / ST. FRANCIS OF ASSISI	The Inquisition	JOHN WYCLIFF / JOHN HUS	Reformation begins / LUTHER / ZWINGLI / CALVIN	JOHN WESLEY / JONATHAN EDWARDS / GEORGE WHITFIELD / CHARLES G. FINNEY	
30 AD	325 AD	397 AD	410 AD	622 AD	732 AD	800 AD	1054 AD	1096 AD				1517 AD	1800 AD	1900 AD

God Gives His Friends a Book **17**

BIBLE READING: Luke 24:26-32; John 5:39, 40; John 14:26; 2 Timothy 3:14-16

CATECHISM REVIEW: WHAT DO WE BELIEVE ABOUT THE BIBLE?

We believe in the Holy Scriptures, the Old and the New Testaments, as the Word of God and the only perfect rule for faith, doctrine, and conduct.

For all Scripture is inspired by God and is useful for teaching the truth, rebuking error, correcting faults, and giving instruction for right living.

2 Timothy 3:16, TEV

(This catechism is discussed in Part 1, Chapter 4.)

Let's suppose that you were one of the people who believed in Jesus when you heard him speak and saw him perform miracles. Let's suppose, also, that you were one of those who received the Holy Spirit on the Day of Pentecost when the Church was formed and that you had belonged to the Church from its very beginning.

You would have joined with other believers to worship and praise God, to take part in the Lord's Supper and to listen to one of the apostles speak. The apostles would talk about Jesus and explain the meaning of what he had com-

manded, and they would use the Old Testament to show how he had fulfilled what the prophets had said (Luke 24:27). The apostles spoke with great authority, and it was easy to believe them because they had actually seen and heard Jesus. You heard the story of Jesus from them until you knew it word for word, and then you told it to your children until they knew it word for word. They would be encouraged to believe when they saw how sure you were about your faith and how Jesus affected your life, and the Holy Spirit would help make Jesus real to them.

This was the way the Christian faith began to spread—by people who had been with Jesus telling and retelling the story until they knew it word for word, and by others who heard it from them telling and retelling it until they also knew it word for word.

WRITING THE MESSAGE OF JESUS

As more and more Gentiles became Christians and the Christian faith spread into the Roman world, it became necessary to have the message of Jesus in written form.

Both the Holy Spirit and human authors took part in writing the story of Jesus. God chose certain persons to write what they had seen and heard from Jesus. As they wrote the Holy Spirit taught them and reminded them, as Jesus had promised (John 14:26), so that the message was the message God intended it to be. Their writings were "inspired" by God, and the part the Holy Spirit had in the writing is called "inspiration."

We are already familiar with the four Gospels, Matthew, Mark, Luke, and John. We have seen how each one emphasized something different about Jesus. Yet, the Holy Spirit watched over their writing so that it was the Word of God, just as the Old Testament was.

We have also become familiar with some of the letters to the early churches, which the Holy Spirit inspired.

As churches received letters from the Apostle Paul, they immediately recog-

nized them as the Word of God. The four Gospels, the Acts of the Apostles, and other letters were also recognized as God's Word. During the second century, Christians were using the entire Old Testament, and most of the New Testament which we have today, as their Bible. It is important for us to remember that Christians themselves had recognized these writings as God's Word, before any official decision had been made.

Other authors were also writing books and letters. Some of them had had no contact with Jesus, and a decision needed to be made about which of these writings, if any, should be recognized as God's Word and included in the Bible.

Then, about 140 AD, a man named Marcion, from the church in Rome, began teaching that none of the Old Testament and very little of the New Testament should be accepted as God's Word. All he wanted to include in the Bible were the Gospel of Luke and some of the letters of Paul. He was expelled from the Church, but his teachings continued to add to the confusion.

In the caves at Qumran jars were discovered containing Jewish writings and scriptures dating from the first century AD.

THE NEW TESTAMENT CANON

This confusion was finally ended by the Council of Carthage in 397 AD, which adopted a "rule" or "measuring stick" to test whether or not any book should be included in the New Testament. The word "canon," which is the Latin word for "measuring stick," is used to identify the books that have passed the test. These books are said to belong in the New Testament "canon." The test that each book must pass was:

1. The book must have been written by an apostle or by a person who knew someone who had actually seen Jesus after he had risen from the dead.
2. The book must recognize the Old Testament as also being God's Word.
3. After a book had passed these two requirements, it was considered on the basis of several other requirements, such as:

• Did a large number of Christians already consider it to belong in the Bible?
• Was it in agreement with other books that had already been accepted?
• Did it speak of Jesus as the Son of God?

On the basis of this test the council took these three actions:

1. It declared what had already been generally recognized, that the four Gospels, the letters of Paul, Acts, and one or two smaller books belonged in the Bible. By doing this it rejected the teachings of Marcion, who refused to accept all of these books.
2. It accepted Hebrews, James, Revelation, and the other shorter books which make up the Bible. These had already been recognized in many churches but had been questioned by others.
3. It rejected other books that did not meet the test.

The Council did not have to consider the books of the Old Testament. The Old Testament canon had been settled by a similar process that ended at a conference of Jewish scholars in the city of Jamnia in 90 AD.

THE HOLY SPIRIT AND THE BIBLE

The service the Council of Carthage performed for us was to declare officially that the books the churches were already using as God's Word belonged in the "canon" of the New Testament. It also cleared up some confusion about a few of the books that had been questioned, and it saved us from having to wonder about other writings whose authors had not had direct contact with Jesus. Its action

confirmed that the Bible really was a gift from God.

The Holy Spirit inspired the authors of both the Old and the New Testaments to write God's message as he intended. The Holy Spirit led the early Christians to recognize the books of the New Testament to be God's Word. The Holy Spirit led the Council of Carthage to confirm the books of the canon. The Holy Spirit has protected God's message all the way down to our time. When we read the Bible prayerfully, the Holy Spirit helps us to understand its message and to put it into practice in our lives. This is the meaning of songs like "The Spirit Breathes Upon the Word," which we sometimes sing in church before the sermon. It is also a good song to read or sing before we read the Bible at home (see *The Covenant Hymnal,* No. 284). Because the Bible is so important to us, we are reviewing the Catechism from Part One, chapter 4, "What do we believe about the Bible?"

Check Yourself

1. What did Marcion teach about the Bible?

2. Name two of the tests a book had to pass before it was accepted into the "canon" of the New Testament.

3. What does the word "inspiration" mean when it is used in connection with the writing of the Bible?

In Class

Write your personal answers to the following questions:

1. How am I using the Bible? _I use the bible to learn about God and Jesus, and what they did._

2. In what way am I hearing God speak in the Bible? _To follow his way. (God)_

3. How much am I obeying God's voice as he speaks to me in the Bible? _I try to obey him as much as I can_

After thinking about your answers to these questions, write a prayer in the space below, asking God to help you in your use of the Bible: _____

What Must Christians Believe? 18

BIBLE READING: Philippians 2:5-11; Colossians 1:15-20

CATECHISM: WHAT IS THE SOURCE OF THE CHURCH'S LIFE?

The life of the Church has its source in God; Father, Son, and Holy Spirit. It is created and renewed by the Spirit and Word, the holy sacraments, and prayer.

Now to him who by the power at work within us is able to do far more abundantly than all that we ask or think, to him be glory in the church and in Christ Jesus to all generations, forever and ever. Amen.

Ephesians 3:20, 21, RSV

As the Christian faith spread out into the Roman world, it came in contact with many different ideas, and it became necessary for Christians to define their faith much more clearly than they had before. It was hard for some people to believe that God could be in human form, and they were tempted to accept a teaching that Jesus was not fully human. Other people were tempted by a teaching that Jesus was not fully God.

The New Testament warns against both of these temptations. 1 John 4:2, 3 is a warning against a teaching that Jesus was not a true human being: "Every spirit which confesses that Jesus Christ has come in the flesh is of God, and every spirit which does not confess Jesus is not of God. This is the spirit of the antichrist."

Colossians 2:8, 9 is a warning against a teaching that Jesus was not God: "See to it that no one makes a prey of you by philosophy and empty deceit, according to human tradition, according to the elemental spirits of the universe, and not according to Christ. For in him the whole fulness of deity dwells bodily."

A teaching known as "gnosticism" was popular in that day. It emphasized the value of a special kind of knowledge. 1 Corinthians 8:1 is a warning against this teaching. It says, " 'Knowledge' puffs up, but love builds up."

False teachings such as these are known as "heresies." The leaders of the Church wrote statements, known as "creeds," which did two things:
1) Creeds defined the faith of the Church
2) Creeds defended the Church against heresy.

NEW TESTAMENT CREEDS

The first Christian creed has only three words, "Jesus is Lord!" (see Romans 10:9; 1 Corinthians 12:3). The Roman emperor demanded that he be recognized as Lord, but the Christians refused to worship anyone else but Jesus. They confessed their faith by saying, "Jesus is Lord."

Two other statements from the New Testament that are really creeds are quoted below. As you read them, notice how they define the Church's basic convictions about Jesus Christ and how they defend the Church against heresies that are contrary to these convictions.

Have this mind among yourselves, which is yours in Christ Jesus, who, though he was in the form of God, did not count equality with God a thing to be grasped, but emptied himself, taking the form of a servant, being born in the likeness of men. And being found in human form he humbled himself and became obedient unto death, even death on a cross. Therefore God has highly exalted him and bestowed on him the name that is above every name, that at the name of Jesus every knee should bow in heaven and on earth and under the earth, and every tongue confess that Christ is Lord, to the glory of God the Father.

Philippians 2:5-11

He is the image of the invisible God, the first-born of all creation; for in him all things were created, in heaven and on earth, visible and invisible, whether thrones or dominions or principalities or authorities—all things were created through him and for him. He is before all things, and in him all things hold together. He is the head of the body, the church; he is the beginning, the first-born from the dead, that in everything he might be preeminent. For in him all the fullness of God was pleased to dwell, and through him to reconcile to himself all things, whether on earth or in heaven, making peace by the blood of his cross.

Colossians 1:15-20

The first passage emphasizes the humility and suffering of Jesus but ends with his being highly honored. The second passage begins with Jesus being honored but ends with his suffering on the cross. These two passages illustrate that sometimes it is important to emphasize the humility and suffering of Jesus, and at other times it is important to emphasize his greatness.

THE APOSTLES' CREED

A shorter statement of what we call "The Apostles' Creed" may have been used by the Church as early as the end of the second century AD. This statement was revised several times until, by the end of the eighth century AD, it had reached a form very much as we have it today. People were asked to confess their faith by reciting it before they were baptized. It is called "The Apostles' Creed" because it was considered to be a summary of the teaching of the apostles. The Apostles' Creed, like other creeds, was intended to help people know what they must believe to be Christians and to keep heresies or false teaching out of the Church.

THE NICENE CREED

After the Roman emperor Constantine became a Christian in 312 AD, the Roman government stopped persecuting Christians. This made it possible for the Church to work more openly, and a great church conference was held in Nicaea in 325 AD. This conference formed what is known as "The Nicene Creed," which was formally accepted at another church conference held in the ancient city of Constantinople in 381 AD. Revisions of this creed were adopted at later conferences.

The Apostles' Creed and the Nicene Creed are quoted side by side below to help you compare them.

THE APOSTLES' CREED

I believe in God the Father Almighty, maker of heaven and earth:

I believe in Jesus Christ his only Son, our Lord; who was conceived by the Holy Spirit, born of the Virgin Mary, suffered under Pontius Pilate, was crucified, dead and buried; he descended into hades; the third day he arose from the dead; he ascended into heaven, and sitteth on the right hand of God, the Father Almighty; from thence he shall come to judge the quick and the dead.

I believe in the Holy Spirit, the holy Christian Church★, the communion of saints, the forgiveness of sins, the resurrection of the body, and the life everlasting. Amen.

★"holy Christian Church" is a revision of the Apostles' Creed, which uses the words "holy catholic Church." The word "catholic," as used here, does not refer to the Roman Catholic Church. It means that there is only one Church, which includes all Christians of all times. Since "catholic" is the original word, you may wish to use it instead of the word "Christian."

THE NICENE CREED

I believe in one God, the Father Almighty, maker of heaven and earth, and of all things visible and invisible:

And in one Lord, Jesus Christ, the only-begotten Son of God, begotten of his Father before all worlds, God of God, Light of Light, very God of very God, begotten, not made, being of one substance with the Father, by whom all things were made; Who for us men and for our salvation came down from heaven, and was incarnate by the Holy Spirit of the Virgin Mary, and was made man, and crucified also for us under Pontius Pilate; he suffered and was buried, and the third day he rose again according to the Scriptures, and ascended into heaven, and sitteth on the right hand of the Father; And he shall come again with glory to judge both the quick and the dead; Whose kingdom shall have no end.

And I believe in the Holy Spirit, the Lord and giver of life, who proceedeth from the Father and the Son, who with the Father and the Son together is worshiped and glorified; who spoke by the prophets. And I believe in one catholic and apostolic church; I acknowledge one baptism for the remission of sins, and I look for the resurrection of the dead, and the life of the world to come. Amen.

COMPARING THE APOSTLES' CREED AND THE NICENE CREED

As we look at these two creeds we see that they both have three paragraphs or "Articles." The first is about God, the second is about Jesus Christ, and the third is about the Holy Spirit and the Church.

The first article

The first article of both creeds opposes a belief that the Almighty God did not create the heavens and the earth directly but that this was done by another god who was not as great. The Nicene Creed goes into greater detail than the Apostles' Creed and says that there is only one true God and that he created both the things that can be seen and the things that cannot be seen.

The second article

As you read the second article of the Apostles' Creed you see that it speaks both of Jesus being the Son of God and of his being human, but it places a great deal of emphasis on his birth, suffering, and death. This was to emphasize that Christians believe Jesus to be human, and to oppose a heresy that Jesus was not a true human being. The second article of the Nicene Creed places greater emphasis on Jesus being God. This would oppose a heresy which had become popular at the time this creed was written, that Jesus was not God in the fullest sense.

The third article

The third article of the Nicene Creed emphasizes, much more than the Apostles' Creed does, that the Holy Spirit is equal to the Father and the Son. This was to oppose a heresy that gave a lower place to the Holy Spirit than to the Father and the Son.

As we compare these two creeds we see how they define the faith of the Church and also oppose the heresies that were being taught when each of them was written. Notice that creeds do not speak directly about false teachings; they define what Christians DO believe, but this also means that they do NOT accept the teachings that deny what is said by the creeds.

Many other creeds have been written since the early days of the Church. Some examples are: the Athanasian Creed, the Augsburg Confession, and the Westminster Confession.

THE VALUE OF CREEDS

The creeds of the Church are important for us, as Christians, to help us define who we are and what we are expected to believe. When we confess our faith by reciting the Apostles' Creed, for instance, we confess that we believe the same things the Christians have believed in all the centuries since the Church began.

THE WEAKNESS OF CREEDS

It is not enough to confess that we believe certain correct teachings. We must also have a personal faith in Jesus as our Savior and Lord. The Catechism for this chapter says that the true Church has its source in God and that it is "renewed by the Spirit and Word, the sacraments, and prayer." This is possible because the Church is made up of people who have new life in Christ. A weakness of creeds is that they cannot give us this life.

Another weakness of creeds is that they may divide the Church into separate parts. Since Christians cannot always agree on which teachings are true and which are false, some creeds exclude some true Christians.

The Evangelical Covenant Church has not adopted any creed except a simple statement that it believes "in the Holy

Scriptures, the Old and New Testament, as the Word of God and the only perfect rule for faith, doctrine and conduct." It welcomes into membership all those who will accept the authority of the Bible, who confess to having a personal faith in Jesus Christ as Lord and Savior, and who are living his new life. Since it does not have a creed, its members may interpret many of the teachings of the Bible according to their convictions. The Covenant Church does, however, recognize the value of the ancient creeds, which define our Faith in the way that Christians have believed since the beginning of the Church. Those who worship in Covenant churches often confess their faith by reciting the Apostles' Creed.

Check Yourself

1. What two purposes do creeds serve?

2. Name two early creeds of the Church and tell which came first.

3. What is the main weakness of creeds?

In Class

After you have discussed several heresies in class, write a creed to help keep these heresies out of the Church. Be sure to use positive statements in your creed. That is, have it say what you DO believe, not what you do not believe. Write your creed, beginning with the words, "I believe

---

The Church Struggles to Be the Light of the World   19

BIBLE READING: Matthew 5:14-16; Matthew 6

CATECHISM REVIEW:
WHAT IS MEANT BY ATONEMENT?
WHAT IS THE CHRISTIAN CHURCH?
WHAT IS THE CHRISTIAN HOPE?
WHAT IS THE SOURCE OF THE CHURCH'S LIFE?

Imagine that you are in a time capsule and are going to speed through one thousand years in a few minutes. Fasten your seat belts; this will be like a fast roller coaster ride! The capsule will fly from 400 AD to about 1400 AD. Both good and bad things will be happening to the Church during this time, so keep alert and don't miss anything!

A WORLD OF DISORDER AND CONFUSION

Right now as we get started we look ahead and see a dark tunnel. The city of Rome is being invaded by barbarians! The Roman government continues to rule from Constantinople, far to the east, but the western part of the Roman Empire is falling apart.

The breakup of the Roman Empire leaves the people of Europe in confusion. They are poor and uneducated, and they need someone to help keep order and give them guidance. This disorder and confusion is the dark tunnel we saw as we started our journey through time.

Christians are encouraged by a book, *The City of God*, written by a bishop in North Africa named Augustine. This man is one of the greatest of the Christian leaders, and his book helps Christians to see how God is at work in the world through his Church.

410
Rome invaded by barbarians

354-430
Augustine,
The City of God

245

THE CHURCH STEPS IN

Now we see the Church in Rome stepping into the emergency and helping to restore order. The head of the Church in Rome is now the head of the whole Church, and he is called the "Pope."

As we continue our journey we see the Church becoming the spiritual and political leader of Europe. After about 200 years a pope named Gregory brings greater organization to the Church. He also defines its faith more clearly and sends missionaries as far as England. Under his leadership, the Church is now helping to establish order and government throughout Europe. Because of the great accomplishments of Pope Gregory, he becomes known as "Gregory the Great."

What can be better than to have the Christian Church in control? Everything around us seems to be getting brighter. Perhaps this is the end of the dark tunnel!

540-604
Gregory the Great

THE CHURCH BECOMES MUCH LIKE THE WORLD

As the Church tries to be a political leader as well as a spiritual leader, however, it becomes much like the world. We watch as the following things happen to it:

1. The Church becomes involved in warfare.

622
Moslem religion begins

Soon after we pass the year 600 we see the rise of a new religion, known as "Islam" or "the Moslem faith," established by Mohammed. We see this new religion spread through Palestine, Arabia, Persia and North Africa. From North Africa it spreads through Spain and into Italy and southern France. The Moslems are finally turned back at the Battle of Tours in France. In its struggle with both political and military enemies like the Moslems, the Church becomes involved in the wars of earthly nations.

732
Battle of Tours

2. Life in the Church becomes like life in the world.

In many countries everyone is included in the Church and all the citizens are considered to be Christians even though they may have no personal relationship with Christ. The result is that the morals of the Church have become much like the morals of the world. Some officials in the Church are honest, and others are corrupt, just as some officials of government are honest and others are corrupt. There is superstition in the Church just as there is in the world. Christians are worshiping pictures and statues and relics of famous Christians whom the Church has declared to be saints. There is little difference between life in the Church and life in the world.

3. The Church engages in worldly political struggles.

800
Charlemagne crowned emperor of the Holy Roman Empire

The Church has the same kind of political struggles that the world has. In the year 800 a pope crowns a king named Charlemagne as emperor of what is called "the Holy Roman Empire." It is hoped that the emperor will care for the earthly needs of the people so that the pope and the Church can concentrate on their spiritual needs. This action, however, results in struggles for power between popes and emperors.

The eastern and western parts of the Church are also struggling with each other, and in 1054 we see the Church divide into two parts. The Eastern Church now has its headquarters in Constantinople, and the Western Church has its headquarters in Rome.

1054
The Church divides into eastern and western parts

The Church is trying to be the light of the world, and it is making some changes in society. Moral standards in the world are higher. Ignorance is being dispelled, and many people have become believers. Yet, the world has also made changes in the Church. There seems to be as much ignorance, superstition, and immorality in the Church as there is in the world. The Church has become so much like the world that its own light has grown dim.

MONASTICISM—TRYING TO WITHDRAW FROM THE WORLD

During our whole journey we see people who are trying to deal with worldliness by withdrawing from the world. They engage in meditation, prayer, study, and work, and they serve God in different ways. They belong to "monastic orders," and they live in places called "monasteries." The men are called "monks" and the women "nuns." They believe they are pleasing God and earning special favors from him by living apart from the world as much as possible. This whole movement is called "monasticism." Even though the members of monastic orders may be limiting their influence on the world by withdrawing from it, they are receiving training in the monasteries that causes them to be chosen as leaders of the Church. As leaders, they are able to be of influence both in the Church and in the world.

SIGNS OF INCREASING LIGHT

As we pass the year 1100 we see the beginnings of universities at Bologna, Italy; Paris, France; Oxford, England; and at other places. Here the Christian faith and other subjects are being taught, and people are beginning to understand better what it means to live the Christian life. The Church is surviving the darkness, and its light appears to be shining brighter.

THE CRUSADES

About this time we keep hearing a slogan being shouted by many people: "It is the will of God!" Eloquent preachers are calling people to form an army to rescue the Holy Land from the Moslems. Those who respond are promised forgiveness of sins and other rewards from God. Prisoners are set free and others are excused from their responsibilities to join in a Crusade to the Holy Land. This large army succeeds in capturing Jerusalem from the Moslems and in holding it for a short time.

During the next two hundred years seven more crusades follow. Many people are killed. Two tragic crusades are made up of fifty thousand children. Most of them either die or are sold into slavery. As we view the crusades we again see the Church trying to use the methods of the world to accomplish God's will.

1096
The Crusades begin

1182-1226
St. Francis of Assisi

1170-1221
St. Dominic

ST. FRANCIS AND ST. DOMINIC

Among the lights we have seen shining in the darkness are many friends of God who have helped people follow Jesus more faithfully. One of these friends of God is a man named Francis, who was born in Assisi, Italy. He believes in living a godly life through serving others. He gathers a group of men who agree to give up everything they own to practice holy living, to preach, and to care for the poor. The pope recognizes the sincerity of Francis and permits him to organize a monastic order, later known as the "Order of St. Francis" or the "Franciscans."

Another of God's friends during this time is Dominic. He organizes a band of preachers through whom he hopes to correct false teaching in the Church. They give up their possessions and adopt a life of poverty. Dominic begins a monastic order. This band of men is the beginning of the "Dominican Order," which emphasizes preaching and teaching. The Dominicans have a strong influence in the universities.

1227
The Inquisition begins

THE INQUISITION

As we move toward the year 1300, we see spies searching for people who believe and teach against the doctrines of the Church. Suspects are arrested, and a trial or "inquisition" is conducted. If they are found guilty and do not reject these beliefs, they are tortured and put to death. Because the Dominicans are concerned about false teaching, they are put in charge of the Inquisition.

RUMBLINGS OF REVOLT

During all these centuries the Church has acted as a "parent" to people who were poor, illiterate, and often uncivilized. It has cared for them, tried to protect them, made many of their decisions for them, told them what they must believe, and punished them if they did not obey.

Now, as we approach the year 1400, we find that conditions have changed. Thousands of people are attending the universities. Superstition is giving way to learning. People are doing more thinking for themselves. The "children" have now grown up and are capable of taking more responsibility for their own faith. They are making some demands of their "parent" the Church, such as:

• People should have the right to try to understand the Bible and decide what it means.
• People should not be required to pay money or meet special requirements of the Church in order to receive forgiveness.
• Political leaders of countries should be free to act without asking permission from the Church.
• People should have the right to communicate directly with God without the interference of the Church.

248

Demands like these sound very much like the complaints of young people to their parents: *We want the right to make our own decisions, to reach our own conclusions, to take the responsibility for our own actions and to be free from parental authority.* The Church found it hard to let go and let its "children" have more freedom, just as parents often do.

As our time capsule moves on, the Church continues to struggle with this problem.

We see John Wycliff, translating the Bible into English. He is fired from his teaching position at Oxford University.

1320-1384
John Wycliff

We also see John Hus, teaching at the University of Prague. Because he is unwilling to give up his struggle for freedom and for reform in the Church, he is condemned to be burned to death. Although he dies for his beliefs, his followers, the "Hussites," continue to fight for religious and political freedom.

1369-1415
John Hus

OUR JOURNEY COMES TO AN END

On our long journey we have seen the Church struggling to be the light of the world and also struggling for power. When it placed too much emphasis on its power it lost its message and failed to be the light God intended it to be. Now, if the Church is to continue to be the light of the world, it must recover its message. As we bring our time capsule to a stop we remind ourselves that our lives are to be like lights shining in our world. (see Matthew 5:14-16)

Check Yourself

1. Describe: The Moslems, the Crusades, the Inquisition.

2. How did the Dominicans and the Franciscans originate?

3. Describe what happened to the Church when it became a political power.

In Class

Consider one of the following questions:
1. "What do I need in order to be a light to the world around me?"
If you believe that you used to be a light to the world around you but that you have lost your light, consider the second question:
2. "What do I need in order to regain the light?"
After you have considered one of these questions, write a prayer in the space below, about being a true light to the world around you:

_____

_____

_____

_____

_____

_____

_____

_____

_____

_____

The Church Is Called Back to Its Purpose 20

BIBLE READINGS: Romans 1:16, 17

CATECHISM: WHAT IS THE PURPOSE OF THE CHURCH?

The purpose of the Church is to glorify God, celebrate new life in Christ, build up one another in faith and love, proclaim and teach the gospel everywhere, and care for the needs of the world.

You are a chosen race, a royal priesthood, a holy nation, God's own people, that you may declare the wonderful deeds of him who called you out of darkness into his marvelous light.

1 Peter 2:9, RSV

When a living tree suffers through dry years or is battered by a heavy storm or passes through a fire, it does everything it can to survive and continue to grow. We often see scars on trees from disasters they have faced. We see how they have tried to heal their wounds and to strengthen themselves to face other changes and other disasters in the future.

The living Church, like a living tree, also struggles to heal its wounds and to adjust to new conditions. It can do this because it has new life in Christ, as our catechism for this chapter tells us.

In the last chapter we saw how the Church filled a need in the world by stepping in and becoming a leader in government. We saw how it became involved in so many worldly things that its light grew dim. The Church survived those hard years because its life kept being renewed, but it had been wounded in its struggles, just as a tree may be wounded in struggling through a storm.

One of the wounds of the Church was the corruption that came from its great political power. Another wound was its claim to be the only source of forgiveness of sin. It was asking people to give money and perform acts of "penance" to pay for forgiveness. The immorality and lack of responsibility of some of its leaders was another wound. Many people were now beginning to understand the Christian faith better, and they were becoming concerned about helping to heal the wounds the Church had received during its long struggle.

Most of the people who wanted to see changes in the Church were its loyal members and friends. They did not want to separate from the Church. They wanted to help it "reform" so that it would be a more effective light to the world and be better able to fulfill its purpose.

MARTIN LUTHER AND THE LUTHERAN CHURCH

The many struggles to bring reformation to the Church climaxed in a German priest named Martin Luther, who was born in 1483. After much prayer and study of the Bible, Luther came to realize that the Church could not forgive sins by requiring people to pay money or do certain good works as "penance." He reached the conclusion that, according to the Bible, people receive forgiveness by repenting of their sins and by having a simple faith in Christ.

During a trip Luther took to Rome he became greatly disturbed by the careless and irresponsible way some of the

251

Church leaders lived. After he returned from Rome, he became even more disturbed when a man named Tetzel came through Germany selling letters of pardon from the pope in order to raise money to build St. Peter's Cathedral in Rome. By paying money, a person could get a letter (known as an "indulgence") from

the pope, saying that his or her sins were forgiven. Luther believed that this was taking advantage of the superstitions of the people in order to raise money.

In 1517 Luther wrote a paper containing ninety-five statements of changes he believed were needed in the Church, and he nailed it to the door of his church in Wittenberg. When Luther did this he had no intention of starting a new church. He believed there should be only one Church, and he wanted to encourage the Church to correct the evils that had crept into it. He still remained loyal to the pope.

The Church authorities objected immediately, and since Luther could not be silenced, he was called before a gathering of German political and church leaders in the city of Worms. Here he was asked to take back the things he had said. His famous reply may be summarized as follows:

> "Until I am convinced by Scripture and reason, I cannot retract anything. Here I take my stand, I cannot do otherwise, so help me God!"

At that time Germany was divided into districts, with rulers known as "electors" over some of them. The elector of the district of Saxony was on Luther's side. He arranged to have Luther kidnapped and taken to a prison in Wartburg for nearly a year to protect him from his enemies. This time was not wasted because Luther spent it in translating the Bible into German.

Martin Luther

Luther was declared a heretic, which made it impossible for him to work in the existing church. He then began to organize the Lutheran Church, which became the official church of most of Germany, of Scandinavia, and of some of the other countries of Northern Europe. The Evangelical Covenant Church and the Evangelical Free Church came out of the Lutheran Church of Sweden, but they were also influenced by other reform movements. We shall look further at the Evangelical Covenant Church in chapters 23 and 24.

THE ROMAN CATHOLIC CHURCH AND THE PROTESTANT CHURCH

The Church of Luther's time was called the Roman Catholic Church. It was called "Roman" because its headquarters was in Rome. The word "catholic" means "universal." It was called "Catholic" because it recognized that there was one worldwide Church. Those who were protesting the evils in the Church were called "Protest-ants" or "Protestants." Since they were trying to reform the Church, they were also called "Reformers." The movement they started was called "the Protestant Reformation." The church groups or "denominations" that came out of the Protestant Reformation are called "the Protestant Church."

ZWINGLI, CALVIN, AND THE REFORMED CHURCH

Another part of the Protestant Reformation began in Switzerland, where the leading reformers were Ulrich Zwingli and John Calvin.

Ulrich Zwingli

Zwingli was born in Switzerland in 1484, and he led the reformation in Zurich. Under his leadership parts of Switzerland became Protestant. Zwingli emphasized the Bible and biblical preaching. Zwingli's followers later became a part of the Reformed Church, which began with John Calvin.

John Calvin

Calvin was born in France in 1509. He studied to become a priest, and he also studied law. When he was 23 years old he became associated with the Reformation. He helped to organize the city government of Geneva, Switzerland according to Protestant principles. Calvin emphasized God's sovereignty and God's right to rule, and he also emphasized human helplessness. While Luther spoke much more about "Christ," Calvin spoke more about "God." Except for a few differences such as these, Calvin's emphasis was much the same as Luther's.

The teachings of Calvin and of the Reformed Church deeply influenced the Puritans, the Congregationalists, the Presbyterians, and most Baptists.

THE ANABAPTIST MOVEMENT AND THE MENNONITE CHURCH

The Anabaptist movement began in Switzerland and Germany and in other parts of Europe. One of the strongest of the Anabaptist groups was started by some followers of Zwingli in Zurich, Switzerland, in 1525. The word "Anabaptist" means "to baptize again." The Anabaptists did not believe in baptizing their infants, and they baptized adult believers again if they had been baptized as infants. They believed in complete separation of Church and State. Many of them were persecuted because they refused to take part in war, but they have also been respected as peace-loving people. A denomination that came from the Anabaptist movement is the Mennonite Church.

John Calvin

THE PRINCIPLES OF THE PROTESTANT REFORMATION

Although there were some differences in the beliefs of the different reformers and the churches they organized, they agreed on many principles. Some of these principles are:

1. *The Bible is the final authority for the Christian.*

The Bible is to be read by the common people. They have as much right to read, study and apply it as the leaders of the Church. The Bible is to be their final authority for what they should believe and teach and for the way they should live.

2. *Salvation is by grace through faith alone, apart from any required good works.*

The Reformers said that the Church has no right to require either good works or payment of money to make up for sins. Sinners become acceptable to God, not by doing good things, but by true repentance and simple faith in Jesus Christ. "By grace" means that forgiveness and new life are free gifts from God. The Reformers believed that those who are truly repentant and sorry for their sins will want to correct the wrongs they have done, but no one can pay for forgiveness, and the Church has no right to demand such payment.

3. *Christ is head of the Church.*

The reformers taught that people are responsible to Christ, and not to the pope, as their final authority. They believed that each country should have the right to make its own decisions. They did not go as far as to say that each person should have the right to decide what his or her religion should be. This freedom came much later, and many people were still persecuted because they did not agree with the religious views of their leaders.

4. *Everyone has the right to come to God directly through Christ.*

Priests, pastors, and Church leaders may counsel and pray for their members, but they cannot claim to stand between them and God. Luther said that all Christians are "little Christs" to each other. By this he meant that all Christians may help other Christians to deal with their sins, but Christ is the only person through whom they receive forgiveness. They come directly to God through him.

THE REFORMATION AND THE PURPOSE OF THE CHURCH

The Reformation was a call to the Church to return to the purpose for which God created it. This purpose is illustrated in the life of a man named John Wesley, who was the founder of the Methodist Episcopal Church, now known as the United Methodist Church.

Wesley was born in England in 1703. He became a minister of the Church of England and went to America as a missionary to the Indians. His missionary work was a failure because he could not be sure he had received God's gift of salvation, and, therefore, he had no Good News to bring to the Indians.

Before Wesley returned to England, however, he met some Moravian missionaries. They belonged to a group that had been in Bohemia with John Hus nearly 300 years earlier. Wesley was so impressed with the joyfulness of these missionaries that he later went to a Moravian Church in London. During the service someone read from Luther's introduction to the Book of Romans, and the Holy Spirit gave Wesley the joy of knowing that his sins had been forgiven through simple faith in Christ for salvation.

The purpose of the Church, as described in the Catechism for this chapter, was fulfilled in Wesley by the following things that happened to him after he received this assurance:

• He and the Christians who gathered with him celebrated new life in Christ by the joy of knowing their sins were forgiven.

• He formed groups to build up one another in faith and love.

• He proclaimed and taught the gospel all over England.

• Through his preaching the whole nation of England became more concerned about caring for the needs of people.

• In all these things, he and those who worked with him glorified God, as the catechism suggests.

In John Wesley we also see how the different denominations bring together their different emphases and their different experiences to fulfill the purpose of the whole Church:

1. Wesley learned about Jesus and the Christian life from his background in the Church of England.

2. Wesley learned about the joy of the Christian life from the Moravian missionaries.

3. Wesley learned from Martin Luther that this joy comes from simple faith in Christ for salvation.

Check Yourself

1. List four principles of the Protestant Reformation.

2. What conclusion did Martin Luther reach about the teachings of the Bible that led to his becoming a reformer?

3. Explain how the different denominations can work together to fulfill the purpose of the whole Church.

In Class

After you have discussed Romans 1:16-17 in class, fill in your name in the blank space in the following quotation of Romans 1:16: "For I am not ashamed of the gospel; it is the power of God for salvation to _____, who has faith."

Remembering your class discussion, write, in the space below, what this verse, with your name in it, means to you:

_____

_____

_____

_____

BIBLE READING: Joshua 24:15

REVIEW: THE TEN COMMANDMENTS

The President of the United States and the Prime Minister of Canada have declared that the official religion of these countries shall be the Church of Modern Christianity. The practice of all other religious faiths is forbidden. All other denominations will be dissolved and their property will be taken over by the government. Special classes are being offered to explain the teachings of the Church of Modern Christianity, and all persons will be required to become members of this church. Regular attendance at the services will be required. Failure to obey this proclamation may result in heavy fines, long imprisonment, or even death.

NEWS ITEM: "Several members of Baptist, Presbyterian, Pentecostal, Covenant, and Catholic churches were arrested yesterday for failure to comply with the recent proclamation establishing the Church of Modern Christianity as the only official religion. They were charged with worshiping illegally. If convicted, they face stiff prison sentences. Their pastors, who were charged with preaching an illegal religion, face possible death sentences. When interviewed, all those arrested emphasized that they were loyal to their country but that their first responsibility was to their religious convictions. They said that they were willing to die, if necessary, for the freedom to worship according to their own convictions."

Freedom of religion has been guaranteed in both Canada and the United States to make sure that no action like this will ever be taken in either country. In the years following the Reformation in Europe this freedom did not exist. Each country had its official church, everyone was required to worship in a way that was approved by that church and the government, and no one was permitted to teach any other doctrine. Then, when a king with different religious views came to the throne, the people were required either to change their religion or be persecuted.

To escape persecution a group of Congregationalist Puritans (known to us as the Pilgrims) sailed to America in a ship called the *Mayflower*. They landed on the shore of Massachusetts, at Plymouth Rock, on November 11, 1620. Here they formed the Congregational church and found the freedom to worship according to their convictions. Other Puritans followed them, and soon there was a large colony in Massachusetts.

However, the Puritans were not willing to grant the same freedom to others that they asked for themselves. They permitted no worship that was not in agreement with the Congregational Church. A man named Roger Williams and some of his friends left Massachusetts to escape persecution. He founded a new colony in Rhode Island, which he called Providence. He also established the first Baptist church in America. In this colony people were permitted to worship according to their own convictions, but this

was not true in all the other colonies.

A group of Roman Catholics sailed to America to escape persecution in England. They settled in what is now Maryland on March 26, 1634. From the beginning they guaranteed freedom of worship for both Protestants and Catholics. When the Protestants came into control they passed laws that denied Catholics the freedom to worship according to their conscience.

It was only after many struggles that the value of complete religious freedom was recognized. In the United States, in 1791, it was guaranteed by adopting the First Amendment to the Constitution, which said (in part):

"Congress shall make no law in respect to an establishment of religion or prohibiting the free exercise thereof . . ."

In Canada the situation was somewhat different. By the time the Canadian provinces had been united into the Dominion of Canada in 1867, many religious groups were already active, and religious freedom was generally being practiced. The Canadian Bill of Rights is one of a series

of acts adopted by the Canadian government to guarantee that freedom of religion, as well as other freedoms, would be continued. It was passed in 1960 and says (in part):

"It is hereby recognized and declared that in Canada there have existed and shall continue to exist . . . the following human rights and fundamental freedoms, namely . . . freedom of religion . . . "

It was a new idea for governments to permit people with different religious views to have equal rights to practice their religion. Because of this new freedom, the Church in North America developed in a new and different way.

THE EFFECTS OF RELIGIOUS FREEDOM

Following are some of the things that happened to the Church in North America because of religious freedom:

1. *Many New and Different Churches.*

Even before there was complete freedom of religion, the restrictions were not as great as they had been in Europe. This allowed immigrants from Europe to establish churches in the new country where they could worship in the same languages and according to the customs they had followed in the country from which they had come. In this way these new churches became places where people could meet and associate with other people who had come from the same country. In other cases, people who were unhappy with their church simply decided to start another church.

One of the effects of religious freedom, therefore, was the establishing of many new and different churches to meet the needs and wishes of many different people. On the chart at the end of this chapter, "One Body—Many Members," you can trace some of these different churches or denominations and see where they originated. The chart is too small to include more than the major denominations, but one way to learn about the origins and teachings of other denominations is to look in an encyclopedia.

2. A Great Loss of Membership.

Many people came to North America for other reasons than to find freedom to worship. In many cases they came for adventure or to seek a more comfortable life. Although they had been members of the official churches of their own countries, many of them did not know Christ personally and had no interest in the Christian faith. Therefore, they never took the trouble to join a church when they came to this new world. As a result only about ten percent of the people belonged to any church. There was much drunkenness, immorality, dishonesty, crime, and corruption. Since people did not have to belong to any church, most of them chose not to do so, and the result was a great loss of church membership.

3. The Great Revivals.

Whenever people turn away from God, he is faithful to call them back to himself, and this is what happened in North America. Since before the Revolutionary War, there have been times when great numbers of people became Christians. These times were called "revivals" or "awakenings."

"The Great Awakening," which began about 1726, was the first of these revivals. About 40,000 people on the East Coast became Christians. Two of the great preachers of this revival were Jonathan Edwards and George Whitfield. During the Revolutionary War in the United States, the Great Awakening continued in eastern Canada, where Henry Alline was the leading preacher.

"The Second Great Awakening" began in churches in New England and reached its climax about 1800 at Yale University, where many students became Christians. About the same time, in Kentucky, people began to gather in great "Camp Meetings." These outdoor meetings lasted several days and attracted large crowds of people who came from as far away as one hundred miles. Among them were many who were not Christians, who heard the Good News about Jesus and became believers.

"The Finney Revival" was the result of the preaching of Charles G. Finney, who conducted meetings throughout the northeastern part of the United States. Thousands of people responded to his invitation to repent of their sins and become Christians.

"The Prayer Meeting Revival" began in 1857 when a pastor in New York City invited people to come to Wednesday noontime prayer meetings in his church. Six came on the first Wednesday, twenty on the second Wednesday, forty on the

third Wednesday, and within six months ten thousand people were meeting every day in many churches in New York and other major cities. Within two years one million people had become Christians.

These revivals helped the people in different churches to learn to appreciate one another and to think of each other as members of one great body. Baptists, Methodists, Congregationalists, Reformed and Presbyterians worked and prayed and worshiped together in the revivals. During the years from 1800 to 1960 more people joined the Christian Church than ever before in its history.

4. A Struggle With the Problem of Making Responsible Choices.

In Joshua 24:15, which is the Bible reading for this chapter, we read how Joshua told the people that they must make a choice about serving the Lord. In very much the same way, the revival preachers in North America reminded the people of their responsibility to choose for themselves, and this was one of the main reasons why so many people became Christians during this time.

In the United States the Civil War and the slavery problem divided Christians and required them to make choices. Sometimes these choices were made on the basis of true Christian convictions. At other times choices were made on the basis of what seemed to be the most popular view. People on both sides of the Civil War chose to interpret the Bible in such a way that it would prove their side to be right. Large denominations like the Baptist Church, the Methodist Episcopal Church, and the Presbyterian Church divided over the question of slavery.

The Civil War also brought Christians face to face with their responsibilities to black people, who had been uprooted from their own culture and forced into slavery in a strange land. We Christians still have this responsibility. We must continue to help both black and white people, as well as people of other races and cultures to relate to one another as equals.

5. A Greater Concern for Missionary Work.

As more and more people became Christians, they became more concerned about all the people in other parts of the world who did not have anyone to tell them the Good News about Jesus. Churches of many denominations, as well as special missionary societies, invited young people to give their lives to missionary work. Cities like Chicago and Toronto became missionary centers from which missionaries were sent to all parts of the world. The time since 1800 has been the greatest time for missionary work in the history of the Church.

Early scene from Covenant missions in Africa.

This concern for missions continues today in most denominations, including the Evangelical Covenant Church. "Go . . . and make disciples of all nations," Jesus' words from Matthew 28:19, are still calling Christians, young and old, to commit themselves to missionary service. Is it possible that God is calling you to this way of serving him?

6. A Spirit of Friendly Cooperation Among Christians.

Since the beginning of the twentieth century a spirit of friendship and cooperation among Christians has expressed itself in several ways:

• Some denominations have united. For example, in 1934 three Methodist denominations united to form the Methodist Church, which joined with the Evangelical United Brethren Church in 1968 to form the United Methodist Church. Another example is the United Church of Canada, which was formed by the union of Congregational, Methodist and Presbyterian Churches in 1925.

• Some denominations or groups of Christians are working together through associations such as the World Council of Churches, the National Council of Churches, and the National Association of Evangelicals.

• Even more significant than the forming of new organizations is a spirit of friendship that has grown up among people of many different denominations. Without being bound together by any special organization, members of both Catholic and Protestant churches fellowship and work together wherever they recognize that the Holy Spirit is present.

This emphasis on friendly cooperation among Christians is known as "the ecumenical movement." It gives Christians an opportunity to demonstrate the oneness of the Church without giving up the freedom to worship according to their own conscience.

SPECIAL MEANINGS OF THE FREEDOM OF RELIGION

Freedom of religion has two special meanings for us. It means that we cannot be forced to accept a certain official or "established" religion, but it also means that we have a greater responsibility for making the right choices ourselves. Where there is freedom of religion, no one else will make these choices for us.

Check Yourself

1. According to this chapter what do Jonathan Edwards, George Whitfield, Henry Alline, and Charles G. Finney have in common?

2. List four effects of freedom of religion on the churches in North America.

3. What signs of freedom of religion do you find in your community?

In Class

You have considered the influence of the church in your country and the advantages of religious freedom. In the space that follows list the privileges and responsibilities that are yours because you live in a country where there is freedom of religion.

Privileges:_____

_____

_____

Responsibilities:_____

_____

_____

REVIEW OF UNIT FIVE

We followed the Church from its early days down to modern times. We learned how we got our Bible and the meaning of the "canon." We also learned about the "creeds" that were written to define the faith of the Church and to keep out heresy. The Church took over many worldly responsibilities and struggled to continue to be the light of the world. With the Protestant Reformation, the Church divided into many denominations in its struggle to return to its original purpose. In North America the Church has served people from many different cultures. With freedom of religion, individuals have a greater responsibility to make their own choices. During the great awakenings more people chose to become Christians than at any other time in the history of the Church.

The Church Reaches out to Us

UNIT SIX

CHAPTER 22
Living as Good Friends of Our Country

We consider ways for Christians to be good citizens of their country.

CHAPTER 23
The Story of
The Evangelical Covenant Church

We discuss the influences that produced The Evangelical Covenant Church. We examine the history of our denomination and some of the ways in which it serves.

CHAPTER 24
The Evangelical Covenant Church: A Family of Believers

We consider the principles of the Evangelical Covenant Church and the way these principles make it possible for our denomination to be a family of believers.

CHAPTER 25
Worshiping God in Our Own Church

With Isaiah as a guide, we examine the nature of Christian worship.

CHAPTER 26
Serving God in Our Own Church

We see how God gives us different abilities to serve him in different ways. These are all needed in the Church.

Life of Jesus	Council of Nicaea	Council of Carthage	Fall of Rome	GREGORY THE GREAT / Beginning of Moslem faith	Battle of Tours	Holy Roman Empire begins	The Church divides	Crusades begin	ST. DOMINIC / ST. FRANCIS OF ASSISI	The Inquisition	JOHN WYCLIFF / JOHN HUS	Reformation begins / LUTHER / ZWINGLI / CALVIN	JOHN WESLEY / JONATHAN EDWARDS / GEORGE WHITFIELD / CHARLES G. FINNEY / Covenant Churches organized: Sweden—1878 / United States—1885 / Canada—1904
30 AD	325 AD	397 AD	410 AD	622 AD	732 AD	800 AD	1054 AD	1096 AD				1517 AD	1800 AD 1900 AD

Living as Good Friends of Our Country

22

BIBLE READING: Romans 13:1-10

CATECHISM REVIEW:
  WHO IS GOD?
  WHAT DO WE BELIEVE ABOUT THE BIBLE?
  WHAT IS GOD'S RELATIONSHIP TO THE WORLD?
  WHAT DOES IT MEAN TO BE A HUMAN BEING?
  WHAT IS SIN?
  WHAT ARE THE RESULTS OF SIN?

REVIEW THE BOOKS OF THE BIBLE

ASSIGNMENT: Ask your parents (and other relatives if possible) about their "faith roots." What churches have they attended. What were their special beliefs and customs? What caused them to choose to become Christians? Report to the next class what you have learned.

"Our country is a Christian nation."
"Our country is NOT a Christian nation."
"IT IS"
"IT IS NOT"
"IT IS!"
"IT IS NOT!"
"IT IS!"
"IT IS NOT!"
' . . . It is! . . . " " . . . It is not!"
There would be no way to end an argument like this because both sides are right and both sides are wrong. There is a sense in which our country is a Christian nation, and there is a sense in which it is not.

"OUR COUNTRY IS A CHRISTIAN NATION"

Although we have freedom of religion, our country is founded on Christian principles. Even freedom of religion is a Christian principle because Christians believe that God created people with the ability to make their own choices. We be-

266

lieve in the principles of justice, freedom, and equality, which are taught in the Bible. Our military forces have Christian chaplains, and public officials take their oath of office with their hands on a Bible. Many of the founders of our country were Christians, and our laws and customs are based on the teachings of the Bible. In these ways our country is a Christian nation.

"OUR COUNTRY IS NOT A CHRISTIAN NATION"

The laws of our country promise complete freedom of religion. People of other religions have the same right to worship in their own way and to spread their faith just as Christians do. People are not required to practice any religion. They cannot be forced to believe as Christians do or to adopt Christian practices. In this sense our country is not a Christian nation.

BEING CHRISTIAN FRIENDS OF OUR NATION

Romans 13:1-10 teaches us that, as Christians, we should be friends of our government. It tells us that governments are gifts from God. Through government, God gives us laws which make it possible for us to live orderly and safe lives. Therefore, we should recognize that our government is God's gift to us, even though government leaders may not always be Christians.

According to this passage, we should obey the laws, except when they require us to be disobedient to God, and we should pay our debts and be honest about paying our taxes. This passage also tells us that we should love our nation and care enough for our neighbors to keep from doing things we know to be wrong.

THINGS WE CANNOT EXPECT OF OUR NATION

We have no right to expect our nation to pass laws that force people to do things that are expected only of Christians. For instance, we have no right to try to pass laws that would require people to go to church or take part in other Christian activities. We have no right to expect the government to pay money to help support missionaries who go out to preach the gospel. We cannot expect our government to pass laws that favor Christianity above any other religion.

THINGS WE CAN EXPECT OF OUR NATION

As friends of our nation, we expect it to promote those things that are valued by all people, whether they are Christians or not. For instance, we expect our nation to provide justice for all people and to protect the rights of all because we believe that justice and human rights are valued by everyone. Our Christian faith teaches us to care for the poor and the suffering, but we believe our govern-

Martin Luther King, Jr. (middle)

ment should also have the same concern because this concern is important to the entire nation. Since both the Christian faith and our nation emphasize the value of human life, we have the right and duty to try to influence our government to protect the life of all human beings, from the very young (who may not yet have been born) to the very old (who may have no one to care for them), regardless of their race or nationality or whether they be rich or poor.

To care for the children of our country is important to everyone, and since Jesus taught us to be concerned about children, we have the responsibility to make sure that adequate provision is made for their education. Even though we cannot expect the public schools to encourage students to become Christians, we do have the right to insist that the schools do not prejudice the students against our faith or against any other religion.

To serve as friends of our nation, we should try to discover which candidates for office are honest and capable persons and have the welfare of the people in mind. We should use our influence to have such people elected.

SOME WAYS IN WHICH CHRISTIANS HAVE TRIED TO BE FRIENDS OF THEIR NATION

There have always been Christians who have proven themselves to be friends of their country. Through the influence of John Wesley, for instance, the people of England became much more concerned about the poor. Finney, the revival preacher, condemned slavery as well as selfish business interests that put money before righteousness. The college of which he was president was the first to admit women to its classes. Many other Christians fought against slavery, and

Billy Graham

others fought for the right of women to vote.

Following are three persons who are examples of ways that Christians have tried to influence their country for good:

Martin Luther King, Jr.
Dr. Martin Luther King, Jr. was a minister who fought for equal rights for black people and for other minorities.
• His emphasis was to get the people of America to enforce the rights guaranteed by the Constitution. He held great rallies and conducted "marches" in which large numbers of people demonstrated that they were strongly in favor of justice and fairness for black people.
• He insisted that those who were demonstrating never use violence and never fight back when they were attacked.
• He was a great orator, and his addresses helped to stir the people to action.
• Unfortunately he was shot and killed in 1968. Both by his life and by his death he increased the concern for justice throughout the nation.
Dr. King served as a friend of his country by trying to convince the nation to protect the rights of all its people.

Billy Graham
Dr. William "Billy" Graham is an internationally-known evangelist and revival preacher.
• He does not believe in making laws to force people to live as Christians. He believes people should be responsible to make their own choices on such matters.
• He applies the message of Jesus to problems like racial prejudice, injustice, crime, alcohol, and drug abuse, home life, and relations with other countries. He teaches that knowing Jesus and following him helps us deal with problems like these.
• He teaches that, if a great many people will become Christians, they will become concerned about the problems of the world, and their influence will affect the life of their whole nation.
Dr. Graham has served as a friend of his country by trying to get as many people as possible to believe in Jesus and to use their influence for righteousness and justice.

Ernest Manning
Mr. Ernest Manning was premier of Alberta, Canada from 1943 to 1968. During the time he was in office he taught a Sunday school class every Sunday morning and conducted a Christian radio broadcast every Sunday afternoon.
• Even though only a minority of the people agreed with his strong religious convictions and many disagreed with his political views, they kept voting his party into office term after term. One important reason was the way he practiced his Christian faith.
• He did not try to force his religious convictions on the people. Even those who disagreed with him respected his fairness.
• During his time in office his government was not involved in any scandals.
• He made sure that the large profits from the new oil industry were used to benefit the public.
Premier Manning served as a friend of his country by his fairness, honesty, and concern for the people.

In the accounts of these three people you will discover several issues about which Christians have been concerned. You can no doubt think of other issues in which you can be a friend of your country by being an influence for God.

Ernest Manning

Check Yourself

1. In what sense is your country a Christian nation? In what sense is it not a Christian nation?

2. Name one thing we can expect from our country as a free nation. Name one thing we do not have a right to expect from it as a free nation.

3. What were the three different ways in which the three persons used as examples in this chapter served as friends of their country?

In Class

After discussing the issues which face our nation and the part that Christians have taken in dealing with them, write a statement, in the space below, on "How I believe I should take part, as a Christian, in helping my country deal with the issues it is facing."

_____

_____

_____

_____

BIBLE READING: Ephesians 4:3-6

ASSIGNMENT: Memorize the third article of the Apostles' Creed and Luther's explanation of it, as stated in the answers to the two following questions:

1. What is the third article of the Apostles' Creed?

I believe in the Holy Spirit, the holy Christian Church★, the communion of saints, the forgiveness of sins, the resurrection of the body, and the life everlasting. Amen.

2. What does this mean?

I believe that I cannot by my own understanding or efforts believe in Jesus Christ, my Lord, or come to him. But the Holy Spirit has called me through the gospel, enlightened me with his gifts, and sanctified and kept me in true faith.

In the same way he calls, gathers, enlightens, and sanctifies the whole Christian Church on earth, and keeps it united with Jesus Christ in the one true faith and with the whole Church body on earth and in heaven.

In this Christian Church day after day he fully forgives my sins and the sins of all believers.

On the last day he will raise me and all the dead and give me and all believers in Christ eternal life.

This is most certainly true.

★*If you prefer, you may substitute the words "holy catholic Church" for "holy Christian Church." See footnote on page 241.*

Three streams came together in the mountains near a place where I once lived. The first of these was a big, quiet stream into which the others flowed. It was not a good stream for swimming or wading because it had sharp rocks and big holes in the bottom.

The second stream was great for wading because it had a soft, sandy bottom and it had a place for swimming and for rowing boats. This was a place where we could have fun all day.

The third was a tiny stream that trickled down the side of the mountain until it fell over a tall cliff into the place where the other two streams joined. The sun made rainbows in the mist that formed where it splashed into the other two streams.

Three great teachings flowed together like these three streams to form The Evangelical Covenant Church. The first of these was the teaching that salvation is by grace through faith in Christ alone. This teaching came from the Lutheran Church in Sweden. It is one of the great teachings of the Bible that was recovered by the Protestant Reformation and emphasized by the Lutheran Church. This was like the big quiet stream into which the others flowed.

In Sweden, however, everyone was baptized as a Lutheran and everyone was a member of the Church. To be a citizen meant to be known as a Christian. All the people had been taught that salvation is by grace through faith in Christ, but many of them did not have any personal relationship with Christ. Something more was needed to make this great teaching real.

This need was met by the second great teaching, which was that Christians must also have a personal relationship with Christ by faith. This was like the second stream—the one that invited people to dive in and swim. People, who had been taught that salvation is by grace through faith trusted him as Savior and Lord. Now they were no longer like people standing on the banks; they were like people who were swimming in the stream.

This emphasis on a personal relationship with Christ came from a movement known as "Pietism." The Pietists believed that only those who have a personal relationship with Christ should be considered to be Christians and be members of the Church. The teachings of one form of Pietism were spread throughout Germany by Lutheran ministers like Philip Jacob Spener and August Hermann Francke. They stressed that Christians should be serious about their relationship with

Christ and that they should depend on the Holy Spirit to help them follow Jesus faithfully. Sometimes, however, they became so serious about their faith that they missed the joy of being Christians.

Joyful Christian living was emphasized by a form of Pietism that was being spread through Germany by the Moravians. They had been befriended by a Count named Zinzendorf, who was also a Pietist. His friendship had a large part in reviving the Moravian movement after it had been almost wiped out by persecution. Zinzendorf helped the Moravians understand that the Christian life is also a joyful celebration of the forgiveness of sins.

When these two forms of Pietism were brought to Sweden, many people learned to know Jesus personally. For them this was the beginning of a new and exciting life. They gathered in little groups to worship and study the Bible. They wrote new songs to describe their relationship with Jesus, and they told others about their new life as Christians.

Among them were some people known as "Mission Friends," who met in groups called "Mission Societies." One of these groups asked a Lutheran minister named Paul Peter Waldenstrom to serve them communion at a separate meeting to which only the people who had a personal relationship with Christ would come. They met in their own chapel, because the church officials would not allow them to use the Lutheran church. Because Pastor Waldenstrom was disciplined by the church officials for serving communion at this separate meeting, he resigned from his position and became a leader among the Mission Friends. The Mission societies then began to form "Mission churches." In 1878 these churches joined together to become the Covenant Church of Sweden.

THREE STREAMS THAT JOINED TOGETHER IN THE EVANGELICAL COVENANT CHURCH

1. The stream from the Protestant Reformation and the Lutheran Church:
   The biblical teaching of salvation by grace through faith in Christ alone.

2. The stream from Pietists like Spener and Francke:
   The experience of a personal relationship with Christ.

3. The stream from Zinzendorf and the Moravians:
   The joy that turns the Christian life into a celebration.

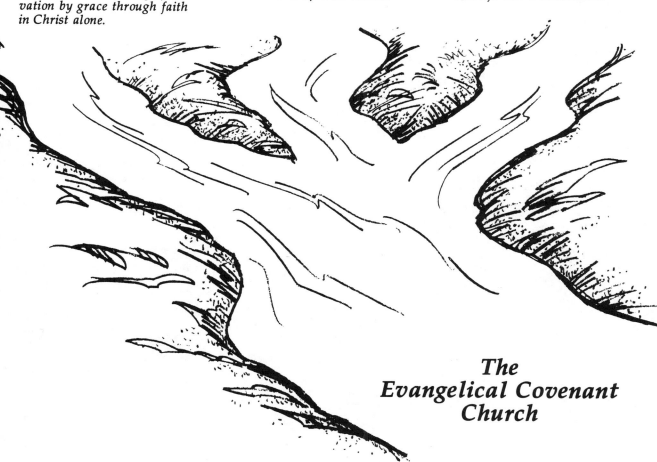

The Evangelical Covenant Church

THE EVANGELICAL COVENANT CHURCH IN NORTH AMERICA

During this time many Swedish people were migrating to North America in search of more land to farm or better jobs and better living conditions. After landing on the East Coast, many of them migrated westward to places like Minnesota, Iowa, Illinois, Manitoba, Saskatchewan, and California. Many of them joined Lutheran churches, and those who had belonged to Mission Societies in Sweden formed similar societies in their new communities.

A man named Carl Bjork (pronounced Byork) moved to Swede Bend, Iowa, and became active in the Lutheran church there. He invited people to his home for prayer and Bible study. A new pastor who came to the Lutheran church became critical of the group that was meeting with Bjork. He believed they placed too much emphasis on their personal relationship with Christ and not enough emphasis on proper Lutheran teachings. His criticism led to disagreements, and this group left

the Lutheran church and formed the first "Mission church" in North America in 1868. Soon other Mission churches were formed.

At a meeting in Chicago on February 20, 1885, representatives of these churches formed what became known as the Swedish Mission Covenant Church of America, now known as The Evangelical Covenant Church. The word "evangelical" means that this church believes in a personal relationship with Christ, and the word "covenant" refers to the agreement among the churches to work and to serve in one body. The Evangelical Covenant Church of Canada was organized in Winnipeg, February 20, 1904.

SOME WAYS IN WHICH THE EVANGELICAL COVENANT CHURCH SERVES

Following are some of the ways the Holy Spirit has led the Covenant Church and its people to serve:
• Within a year after the Covenant Church was organized it made plans to

Swede Bend, Iowa, Covenant Church, with inset of C.A. Bjork

build a "Home of Mercy" to care for poor people who were sick or in need of special attention. This was later divided into a hospital and a retirement center. The Covenant Church has since built another hospital and several other retirement centers.

• Covenant people have established homes for orphan children or for children whose parents cannot care for them. They have also provided places where sailors can receive care and hear about Jesus.

• They established a Christian school in Minneapolis, which was later moved to Chicago and was named North Park College and Theological Seminary. They established a Christian high school in Minneapolis, known as Minnehaha Academy, and the Covenant people of Canada established Covenant Bible College in Prince Albert, Saskatchewan.

• The Covenant Church has built many new churches and helped these churches to begin their ministries.

The First Mission House in Chicago.

• Covenant people have tried in many other ways to bring the good news about Jesus to other people. Eric August Skogsbergh, for instance, is an example of traveling evangelists who preached to Swedish immigrants and persuaded many people to become Christians.

Sunday school in Alaska

• From the very beginning the Covenant Church has been interested in Christian missions. It assumed responsibility for missionary work which had just been started in Alaska by the Covenant Church of Sweden. It established several churches in Alaska and built a Christian high school for Alaskan young people. Later it set up a Christian radio station in Nome. Under the leadership of a missionary named Peter Matson it started a mission in China, which continued until the Chinese Communist revolution.

The Covenant Church now conducts missionary work in the following countries: Zaire (since 1937), Mexico (since 1946), Ecuador (since 1947), Japan (since 1949), Taiwan (since 1952), Colombia (since 1968) and Thailand (since 1971).

275

THE EVANGELICAL COVENANT CHURCH TODAY

Covenant churches in North America and in other countries now include members from many races and nationalities. They are united in one body by their faith in Christ, as the Bible reading for this chapter tells us. A sentence from Luther's explanation of the third article of the Apostles' Creed helps us understand that it is the Holy Spirit who unites the whole Church: "He calls, gathers and sanctifies the whole Christian church on earth, and keeps it united with Jesus Christ in the one true faith."

Check Yourself

1. Define the three beliefs that joined as "streams" to form The Evangelical Covenant Church.

2. Define "Pietism" and "Mission Friends." Define "evangelical" and "covenant" as these words are used in "The Evangelical Covenant Church."

3. List four of the countries, besides the United States and Canada, where the Covenant Church now conducts missionary work.

In Class

After discussing the three beliefs that joined like streams in The Evangelical Covenant Church, write, in the spaces below, what each one means to you:

1. To believe in salvation by grace through faith in Christ means to me that

_____

_____

_____

_____

_____ .

2. To have a personal relationship with Christ means to me that _____

_____

_____

_____

_____

_____ .

3. To celebrate the joy of forgiveness of sins means to me that _____

_____

_____

_____

_____

_____ .

BIBLE READING: Romans 12:1-8; Romans 1:16, 17

CATECHISM: WHAT IS THE SACRAMENT OF BAPTISM?

Baptism is the sacred use of water, commanded by Jesus Christ, to signify God's cleansing of our sins and our welcome into the family of God.

Go therefore and make disciples of all nations, baptizing them in the name of the Father and of the Son and of the Holy Spirit, teaching them to observe all that I have commanded you; and lo, I am with you always, to the close of the age.

Matthew 28:19, 20, RSV

One of the best ways to define The Evangelical Covenant Church is to say that it is a family of people who believe in Jesus. Its members are bound together in a family by their common faith in Jesus Christ, by their personal relationship with him, and by their love for each other. Their many differences make it possible for them to fill different places in the one body to which they belong (See Bible reading, Romans 12:1-8), and this body is a family, not just an organization.

THE PRINCIPLES OF THE EVANGELICAL COVENANT "FAMILY"

This family spirit has been strengthened and encouraged by certain principles that the Covenant Church has followed since its beginning. Some of the more important of these principles are:
1. *The authority of the Bible.*

The founders of The Evangelical Covenant Church began by recognizing the Bible as the final authority for Christians. They adopted the statement about the Bible that is part of our catechism. "We believe in the Holy Scriptures, the Old and New Testaments, as the Word of

God and the only perfect rule for faith, doctrine, and conduct." The Covenant Church believes that Christians should read the Bible prayerfully, asking God to let its message become the center of their lives.

2. *The necessity of being born again.*

The Covenant Church believes that it is not enough just to know what the Bible teaches and to try to follow its teachings. Every Christian must also have a personal relationship with Christ. Those who have this relationship also have his new life, which they receive by faith. To have his new life is what it means to be "born again." This is a joyful life that turns Christian living into a happy celebration.

3. *The Church as a fellowship of believers.*

The Covenant Church believes that all those who have received Christ as Lord and Savior should be able to have fellowship together in the same church. People of all races and nationalities, people who have little or much wealth, people of different backgrounds and cultures who recognize the authority of the Bible and have a personal relationship with Christ are welcome in Covenant churches. Some of the great joys of the Christian life come to those who learn to appreciate the values that are brought by Christians from different cultures.

4. *The freedom of Christians.*

The Covenant Church emphasizes that Christ makes people free. Since God's love in the hearts of Christians causes them to wish to obey him and to do good to other people, they are free to do as they wish as God fills their hearts with his love.

Christians learn from the Bible how to express God's love and to live as free people. Since they do not always understand the Bible perfectly, they often interpret it in different ways. Members of Covenant churches have the freedom to hold these different interpretations of the Bible that have sometimes divided Christians. In the Covenant Church they have the opportunity to learn to love and respect each other even though they sometimes disagree.

When Christians give in to temptations, they are no longer filled with God's love. Then they lose their freedom and become slaves of their own desires. Whenever this happens, God calls them to repent and seek his forgiveness so they may become free again.

5. *The work of the Holy Spirit.*

The Covenant Church believes that it is the Holy Spirit who makes it possible for people to be Christians. He gives Christians strength to overcome temptations and helps them care for other people and bring the Good News about Jesus to those who do not know him. The Holy Spirit unites the Church into one body and gives it the life of Jesus. It is the Holy Spirit who causes the Church to become a family and helps Christians feel that they belong to this family.

BAPTISM AND CHURCH MEMBERSHIP

In these last two chapters we have followed the story of The Evangelical Covenant Church, its beginnings, the ways it is serving, and its basic principles. These chapters have brought us right down to ourselves. We are talking about *our church!* The people of whom we are speaking are our church family. They belong to us, and we belong to them. One day the members of this and other confirmation classes will be leaders of Covenant churches and of the Covenant denomination.

The final weeks of our confirmation study will be a good time for you to think seriously about your faith in Christ and about applying for membership in your church. Becoming a church member means taking your place as part of your own church family. It is saying to your Christian brothers and sisters, "Yes, I'm a Christian, too, and I belong here. I need you. I want to worship regularly with you, and you can depend on me to do my part in serving Jesus together with you."

Since baptism is a sign of belonging to the Church, your church will no doubt request that those who become members will have been baptized, either as little children or as adults. Whether or not you have already been baptized, therefore, you will want to know something about the meaning of baptism. The Catechism for this chapter tells us that:

1. Baptism is the sacred use of water, commanded by Jesus.

Baptism, like the Lord's Supper, is a sacrament of the Church. A sacrament is an action, commanded by Jesus, that uses an ordinary substance in a sacred way. In baptism we use water in a sacred way. Nothing magical happens to the water. It has a special meaning and becomes sacred only because we are using it for the purpose Jesus commanded.

2. Baptism signifies God's cleansing of our sins.

We do not receive cleansing or forgiveness of our sins by being baptized. Baptism signifies that God has already forgiven our sins through faith in what Christ has done in his death and resurrection. Every service of baptism is a celebration of the forgiveness of sins.

3. Baptism signifies our welcome into the family of God.

Every service of baptism is also a welcome party into God's family. Baptism is a sacred event, but this does not keep it from being a happy event. It is a time for rejoicing.

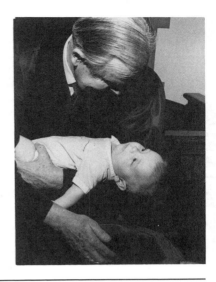

INFANT AND ADULT BAPTISM

Some of you may have been baptized as little children. Your parents presented you for baptism because they knew that you belonged to God before you were able to make your own choices. They were celebrating the fact that God's grace was reaching out to you even before you could either accept or reject it. Because little children already belong to God, your parents were baptizing you to be welcomed into God's family. Others of you may not have been baptized as little children. Your parents also believed that you belonged to God before you were able to make your own choices, but they believed your baptism should take place after you have made your own decision to receive God's gift of salvation.

Each of these views has been held by thousands of Christians, and we shall never be able to prove to all that either view is correct. Members of the Covenant Church have the freedom to use the form of baptism that is in accord with their beliefs. We are all united by our being baptized "in the name of the Father and of the Son and of the Holy Spirit," and we must never permit our differences to divide us.

Your church has cared for you in Christian love ever since its first contact with you. It is doing everything possible to help you respond in faith to God and to live in his will. Now, if you have not already done so, you are being called by God to turn from sin and begin Christ's new life by believing in him. Whether you were baptized when you were a little child or will be baptized after you have responded to God's call, you give meaning to your baptism by saying "Yes," to God.

Whenever you wish, your pastor will be happy to talk with you about your faith in Christ and explain how you may apply for membership in your church. If you have not been baptized, he will be glad to talk with you about your baptism.

Check Yourself

1. List five basic principles of The Evangelical Covenant Church.

2. Members of Covenant churches have the freedom to interpret the Bible differently. Suppose a member says, "According to my interpretation, the Bible gives me freedom to lie and steal and commit murder." Explain why this interpretation should or should not be permitted in a Covenant church.

3. State one difference in the beliefs of Christians who present their children for baptism and those who do not.

In Class

1. One of the early Covenant leaders described The Evangelical Covenant Church as a "family of faith." The word "family" implies that we are all brothers and sisters in the Covenant because of our faith. How are you (or are you not) a part of this family of faith?

_____

_____

_____

Covenant churches, missions, and institutions would not exist without people like you. Have you ever thought that God may be calling you to serve The Evangelical Covenant Church as a missionary, a pastor, a Christian education director, a youth pastor, a camp director, or in any other way? Pray about it. It is an exciting vocation. If you have considered serving God in this way, be sure to tell your pastor about it.

Worshiping God in Our Own Church

25

BIBLE READING: Isaiah 6:1-8

CATECHISM REVIEW:
WHAT IS MEANT BY A COVENANT BETWEEN GOD AND HIS PEOPLE?
WHAT IS GOD'S PROVIDENCE?
WHAT IS SALVATION?
WHO ARE THE PROPHETS?
WHO IS THE MESSIAH?
WHAT IS THE KINGDOM OF GOD?
WHAT DID JESUS TEACH US CONCERNING LIFE IN THE KINGDOM OF GOD?

Once, at a Bible camp, a camper said to me, "I always pay attention and listen at camp meetings because I know that the camp is for me, but I don't ever pay attention in my own church because I don't think of church as being for me."

I had this same attitude when I was young. I never thought of church as be-ing for me; I just assumed it was for adults. Therefore, I didn't pay attention to what was going on. It was only after I began to realize that it was for me that it became interesting.

Someone has described a church wor-ship service as a kind of drama in which all of us are a part. The drama includes

God, the pastor, and the congregation. The drama has an audience, an actor, and a prompter to help the actor know what to do next. Think of God as the audience, the congregation as the actor, and the pastor as the prompter. This helps us to understand that worship has something for us to do. We don't just sit and listen. God is listening to us as we worship. Then, during some of the time, we sit quietly and listen to God.

CHRISTIAN WORSHIP IS A CELEBRATION OF WHAT GOD HAS DONE

We Christians do not worship God to try to get him to do something for us. Christian worship is a celebration of the great things God has already done. In worship we think of the things God has done for his people from the very beginning, but we think especially of what he has done through Jesus.

We also think of what God has done for our own church and for us personally. Sometimes it helps us to worship if we look around the sanctuary and think of the people who have learned to know Christ here, who have worshiped here, and for whom God has done many great things. These people are part of our family. God has brought us together and helped us to love each other, and now we belong to one another. We do not think only of ourselves when we worship; we remember that we belong to a family for whom God cares very much. Everything good that has happened to our church since its beginning represents what God has done. All this helps us to think of worship as a celebration.

Thinking about all that God has done for us helps us to understand that worship is not trying to get God to do something for us. Rather, *worship is celebrating what God has already done for us, especially in giving us his son, Jesus.*

ISAIAH'S VISION ILLUSTRATES THE NATURE OF OUR WORSHIP

The prophet Isaiah saw a vision in the temple in Jerusalem. This vision is described in Isaiah 6:1-8, which is our Bible reading for this chapter. This was a very important time of worship for Isaiah, and from it we learn some things about what it means to worship God.

1. Worship is reverence.

There was God on a great throne, with strange six-winged creatures flying around the room. When they spoke to each other the whole room shook and was filled with smoke. What an awesome sight! It must have been frightening to Isaiah, and it made him respectful and reverent.

It is awesome to think that the Almighty and Eternal God wants us to be his friends, and this feeling of awe causes us to be respectful and reverent when we worship.

2. Worship is praise.

The winged creatures were worshiping God by singing his praises. Since worship, for Christians, is celebrating what God has done, we take our hymnbooks and sing with enthusiasm. While we worship we keep reminding ourselves of all that God has done for us.

3. Worship is confessing our sins.

"My doom is sealed, for I am a foul-mouthed sinner, a member of a sinful, foul-mouthed race; and I have looked upon the King, the Lord of heaven's armies" (Isaiah 6:5, LB). This is what Isaiah said when he saw God. Whenever people come into the presence of the Holy God, they realize how unworthy and how sinful they are. Although we know that Christ has died for our sins, we still feel badly about the things we have done wrong, especially when we are in the presence of God. We know how much pain and suffering sin has caused and how much God hates sin. Therefore we take our sins seriously and confess them to God, as Isaiah did.

4. Worship is receiving the assurance of forgiveness.

When Isaiah confessed his sin, one of the creatures took a coal from the fire and touched his lips. In his vision, this was a sign that his sin had been cleansed away. "Now you are pronounced, 'Not guilty' because this coal has touched your lips. Your sins are all forgiven." (Isaiah 6:7, LB)

In Christian worship we receive the assurance that we are forgiven. "If we confess our sins, he is faithful and just, and will forgive our sins and cleanse us from all unrighteousness" (1 John 1:9). One of the great moments of worship comes when we realize that it is really true that God has forgiven our sins. We are clean and pure enough to be in the presence of God! Then, when we realize that we have not earned this forgiveness by anything we have done—that it is a gift from God because of what Christ has done—we become even more thankful.

5. Worship is saying "yes" to God.

Then God spoke from his throne in Isaiah's vision: "Whom shall I send, as a messenger to my people? Who will go?" Isaiah was so happy to know that God had forgiven and accepted him that he said to God, "Lord, I'll go! Send *me.*"

The relief of being cleansed from sin and being accepted by God would soon fade away if worship did not also include a response. Now that we have been assured that God has cleansed away our sins, we feel all clean and new inside, and we are ready to respond to his call to serve him. "Lord, I'll go! Send *me,*" is our answer. Saying "yes" to God's call is our response in worship. We leave the church with excitement because we know we have the privilege of serving the God whom we love.

HOW ISAIAH'S VISION APPLIES TO OUR WORSHIP

Isaiah's worship included the following:
1) Reverence
2) Praise
3) Confession of sin
4) The assurance of forgiveness
5) Saying "yes" to God's call to serve him.

When we worship we usually follow Isaiah's vision in the things we do:

1. In our prayers.

In different prayers during a worship service, we express our reverence for God, and we confess our sins and thank God for forgiveness. We also pray for other people and ask God to help us minister to them.

2. In the singing.

The hymns we sing usually include at least some of Isaiah's vision for worship. For instance:

A hymn of reverence is "Joyful, Joyful We Adore Thee" (No. 36, *The Covenant Hymnal*).

A hymn of praise is "Praise the Lord, Each Tribe and Nation" (No. 56, *The Covenant Hymnal*).

A hymn of confession is "Just As I Am, Without One Plea" (No. 304, *The Covenant Hymnal*).

A hymn of assurance of forgiveness is, "Through the Love of God, Our Savior" (No. 397, *The Covenant Hymnal*).

A hymn of response (Saying, "Yes," to God) is "Lead On, O King Eternal" (No. 532, *The Covenant Hymnal*).

3. In the Sermon.

During the sermon we hear God speaking to us through the Bible. This is the time for listening quietly and attentively so we do not miss the message God has for us. During the sermon the pastor becomes God's messenger. He or she has studied the text carefully so as to explain its meaning to the congregation, and has prayed that God will help him or her speak clearly and emphatically.

4. *In the Lord's Supper.*

We come to the Sacrament of the Lord's Supper with reverence because we know that we are celebrating the most sacred of all of God's acts. We praise God, through the prayer and the songs, for what Jesus did for us when he died on the cross. We confess that we are sinners who have not earned the right to sit at the Lord's table. But we receive the assurance of forgiveness and take the elements of the communion with thanksgiving because we know that we have been forgiven. Before we leave, we respond to all that God has done for us, and we go out from the worship to serve and obey him joyfully.

PERSONAL WORSHIP

Having personal devotions is another way of worshiping God. One good way to do this is to find a quiet place to be alone. Here we may meditate and think about how God has been at work in our lives. We may read our Bibles prayerfully, trying to learn what God wants to say to us. Then we may pray about the things that trouble us, confess our sins to God, and accept his forgiveness, thank him for what he has done, and pray for other people. In our personal worship we don't have to use religious or "church" language, and God will not be angry with us if we speak frankly to him and tell him the things we would not dare tell anyone else.

Check Yourself

1. What does Christian worship celebrate?

2. In what five ways does Isaiah's vision help us understand our worship?

3. Think of a worship service you recently attended and list the things you remember from Isaiah's vision in the prayers, the hymns, or the sermon.

In Class

Close your eyes and imagine that you are in your church sanctuary or go to the sanctuary and sit quietly. Imagine that the walls have been listening and observing you as you worship each week. Write in the space below, what you think the walls would say about your faith and actions if they could speak.

_____

_____

_____

_____

_____

_____

_____

Serving God in Our Own Church

26

BIBLE READING: Romans 12:4-20; 1 Timothy 3:1-16

ASSIGNMENT: Interview a church leader or staff member whose name you will receive from your teacher. Introduce yourself to that person and ask questions like, "What is your job in the church?" "What do you do in your job?" "How did you get this job?"

CATECHISM REVIEW:
  WHAT IS THE SACRAMENT OF THE LORD'S SUPPER?
  WHAT IS ACCOMPLISHED BY THE DEATH AND RESURRECTION OF JESUS CHRIST?
  WHO IS THE HOLY SPIRIT?
  WHAT IS MEANT BY ATONEMENT?
  WHAT IS THE CHRISTIAN CHURCH?
  WHAT IS THE CHRISTIAN HOPE?

A greasy old car in a church building? There it was, in a back room of the old church. Someone had enlarged the door to get the car in, and now it stood there with the engine taken apart. What was this car doing in the church? And what about nine bicycles locked in a room behind the sanctuary of another church? Should bicycles be in a church building? Here, in another church building, were dozens of children's dresses and pants, all nicely pressed and hanging from hangers. Is this a clothing shop or a church? What about this box half filled with old eyeglasses in the narthex of another church? Or the pile of old sheets lying in a basket beside four sewing machines in a back room? You would expect to find hymn books in church, but a car, bicycles and old eyeglasses? What do they have to do with worship?

Yes, all these things do belong to the work of the Church. The old car was being repaired by a car club sponsored by the church. Their leader was an auto mechanic who served in this way. The mem-

bers were young people who came off the street, where almost everything they did would get them into trouble. The bikes in the back room belonged to the members of a youth group who were on a hike with their leader. The room behind the sanctuary was the only place that could be securely locked. The clothes on hangers were given by members and friends of the church. People who could not afford clothes for their children came and picked out what they needed. The old eyeglasses were to be sent to the mission in Africa, where they would be fitted to people who needed them. The old sheets were to be torn into strips, sewn together, and sent to the mission hospital where they would be sterilized and used as bandages.

WAYS IN WHICH CHRISTIANS SERVE GOD IN THEIR OWN CHURCH

I have seen all of these examples of ways in which Christian people share the love of Christ with other people. Dif-

ferent people have different abilities, and God can use them all. The Church is the body of Christ. It is like the human body in that it has many different parts. Every member of the Church should have some share in serving Christ. When the members use their different abilities, the whole church becomes a healthy body. The chart at the end of this chapter on page 293, shows some of the ways in which Christians serve God and other people through their churches. As you look at this chart, you may discover ways that you could serve in your church.

SPECIAL GIFTS THAT GOD GIVES

Romans 12:4-8 tells us that God gives each person the ability to do the work he wants done in the Church. The special ability that God has given you is called your "gift." You may have one gift or you may have several.

HOW TO DISCOVER WHAT YOUR SPECIAL GIFTS ARE

Here are seven questions to help you discover what your special gifts may be:
1. *What are you interested in?*
Very often the thing you enjoy doing the most is the thing God wants you to

do, and he will help you develop the gift to serve in this way.
2. *What are your natural abilities?*
The gift that God has given you may not be the thing you enjoy most. Sometimes it is the thing you do best.
3. *What skills are you developing?*
For instance, you may be taking piano lessons, and you have learned to play well enough to be the pianist for a Sunday school class or for your youth group. This may be what God wants you to do, and he will help you as you play.
4. *What things on the chart at the end of this chapter fit your interests or skills or natural abilities?*
God may use this chart to lead you to something you had not thought of.
5. *What does your church need?*
Sometimes there is a special need in your church, and no one else is available to help out. You may not feel that you are prepared for it, and you may not particularly enjoy it, but you might agree to try. The very fact that it is needed may be God's call to you. If it is, he will give you the gift to do it and also help you enjoy it.
6. *What do people usually ask you to do?*
Sometimes the leaders of the church may ask you to work in the nursery or to form a singing group or to serve in some other way. This may mean that they have recognized gifts in you that you may not

What is wrong with this picture?

know you have. This may help you discover what God wants you to do.

7. What are the things that come to your mind when you are praying?

The Holy Spirit may be speaking to you while you are praying by bringing to your mind something for which God will give you a special gift.

You should not depend entirely on any one of these questions, but by comparing the answers to all of them you will begin to discover what part God wants you to take in your church. This does not necessarily mean that God wants you to do this all of your life. From time to time he may lead you to different things he wants you to do, and when you obey him he will give you the gift you need.

VOLUNTEER AND PAID POSITIONS IN THE CHURCH

Most of the work of any church is done by volunteers who receive no pay. They give some of their time to serve because they love Jesus and because God has given them a love for other people. They find great satisfaction in doing what God has called them to do. You may offer to do something that needs to be done, or you may be asked to help in some way. Do not be offended if you are asked to do something that does not seem to be important to you. Remember that Jesus never hesitated to take the lowliest place. You will usually come closest to Jesus when you are doing something that seems very ordinary.

In most cases pastors are paid for their work. I served as a pastor most of my life, and the churches I served paid me a salary. This made it possible for me to give all my time to the work of being a leader of the congregation. The pastor is not paid to do all the work of the church, however. Even two or three pastors would not have all the gifts that are needed in the church. The pastor is paid so that he or she can use his or her time and training to lead the members of the church in doing the work together. The pastor is like a coach, and the members of the church are like the players. They

use their different gifts and have the joy of serving Christ. Then the whole church works together like a healthy body.

Some churches have more than one pastor. Others have a youth minister and a minister of music, who are also paid. Church secretaries, custodians, organists and pianists are often paid so they can give more time to their work.

WHAT THE BIBLE TEACHES ABOUT SERVING GOD IN OUR OWN CHURCH

Romans 12:4-8, which is part of our Bible reading for this chapter, lists some gifts that God gives for working in a church. They are:

1. The gift of preaching God's Word, which is called **prophecy.**
2. The gift of caring for people's needs, which is called **service.**
3. The gift of explaining what the Bible means, which is called **teaching.**
4. The gift of encouraging people to be faithful, which is called **exhorting.**
5. The gift of giving money liberally, which is called **contributing.**

6. The gift of being a leader in the church, which is called **giving aid.**
7. The gift of relieving suffering, which is called **mercy.**

These are only some of the ways to serve God in our own church. The other part of Romans 12, from verse 9 to verse 20, explains how we can serve God in practical ways like being loving, patient, and forgiving, being enthusiastic and hopeful, being hospitable, being kind to those who mistreat us, being humble, and living in harmony and peace with each other.

Check Yourself

1. What is the meaning of "gifts" as the word is used in this chapter?

2. How can Christians discover what their special "gifts" are?

3. Suggest some ways in which you can serve God in your church.

In Class

1. On _____ (today's date) the members of my confirmation class told me that I have the following skills, gifts, or abilities.

_____

_____

_____

2. Turn to the list of ways in which people serve God in their church and list some of the ways suggested that interest you either for now or in the future.

_____

_____

_____

3. How could you use your skills, gifts, or abilities to serve God?

_____

_____

_____

SOME WAYS IN WHICH PEOPLE SERVE GOD IN THEIR CHURCHES

(Check some ways in which
you may be able to help)

IN WORSHIP
_____Providing music
_____Ushering
_____Bringing flowers for services
_____Giving offerings
_____Preparing, serving, and clean-
ing up after the Lord's Supper
_____Special festivals (such as
Christmas and Easter)
_____Conducting prayer meetings
_____Conducting worship services
_____Preaching

IN TEACHING
_____Sunday school
_____Vacation Bible school
_____Weekday Bible classes
_____Special interest classes
_____Confirmation classes
_____Classes for new members

IN YOUTH WORK
_____Fun and game times
_____Youth meetings
_____Young people's mission and
work projects
_____Camps

IN EVANGELISM AND MISSIONS
(Telling others about Jesus)
_____Showing love to our neighbors
_____Being witnesses in the way we
live
_____Being hospitable—inviting peo-
ple to our homes
_____Visiting people to tell them
about Jesus
_____Writing letters to missionaries
_____Praying for missionaries and
other Christian workers
_____Helping support missionaries
_____Inviting people to respond to
God's call to become
missionaries
_____Preaching and teaching the
good news about Jesus

IN CARING
_____Being friends
_____Helping older people
_____Collecting used toys for
Christmas
_____Caring for children of working
mothers
_____Helping people who are poor
_____Giving to world relief
_____Visiting and caring for sick
people
_____Praying for people with special
needs
_____Counseling with people with
special problems

IN STEWARDSHIP
(Being responsible for what God has
given us)
_____Giving a certain part of our
income
_____Keeping the church buildings
clean and comfortable
_____Maintaining and repairing the
buildings
_____Counting and depositing
offerings
_____Paying bills
_____Keeping financial records
_____Teaching people about giving
to God

IN BEING GOOD CITIZENS OF OUR COMMUNITY
_____Caring for needy people in the
community
_____Conducting language classes
_____Cooperating with other
churches
_____Helping solve community
problems

IN SPECIAL SERVICES
_____Welcoming new members
_____Anniversary celebrations
_____Special recognition services
_____Confirmation services
_____Baptisms
_____Dedications
_____Weddings
_____Funerals

REVIEW OF UNIT SIX

The Church has survived through the centuries, right down to our time, just as Jesus had promised. In Unit Six we considered what it means for us to live in countries where there is freedom of religion, what we may expect from our country, and how we, as Christians, can serve as its friends. We learned about our own denomination, The Evangelical Covenant Church. We saw how it began with the joining of three important Christian beliefs. We followed its beginnings in North America and learned how it is now serving. We saw how the basic principles of our denomination help it to be a family of believers. We learned about the meaning of worship and discussed ways to serve God in our own church.

Called to Believe and to Belong

Looking Back at the Friends of God   27

CATECHISM REVIEW:
  WHAT IS THE SOURCE OF THE CHURCH'S LIFE?
  WHAT IS THE PURPOSE OF THE CHURCH?
  WHAT IS THE SACRAMENT OF BAPTISM?

Review the three articles of the Apostles' Creed and Luther's explanation of them.

Let's get into our time capsule again. We are going to make an imaginary journey through time to visit some of the friends of God whom we met during this Confirmation course. We remember that the Bible, which is God's story, is also our story and the story of God's friends. We would like to know if these friends of God are really like us or if they are entirely different from us.

We fly all the way back to the beginning of everything, and we hear the voice of God saying "Let there be Light" and light appears. At the command of God the earth and the sky separate, the water gathers in oceans, and we see dry land which is beginning to turn green with new plant life. As the mists disappear, the sun begins to shine, and all kinds of animal life appear. Then right below us, we see Adam and Eve! They have just been driven from the beautiful garden God had given them because they had disobeyed him.

"Why did you disobey God?" we ask them.

"We didn't think of it as being so bad," they reply. "The tempter made it seem so good to us." As we pass by Cain and Abel, we see that sin is becoming an epidemic that infects everyone.

Suddenly a heavy storm breaks upon us. It rains so hard that water covers everything. We see Noah and his family, with some animals, in the ark God had

commanded him to build. After the water sinks away and the ark comes to rest on dry land, Noah says to us, "We have learned that God is always faithful to his people."

When our time gauge reads about 2000 BC we stop to visit with Abraham and his wife, Sarah. "What does it really mean to live by faith?" we ask Abraham.

"God made a covenant, or agreement, with me and my descendants," he replies. "He promised to be faithful to us, and he asked us to believe his promise. I left my home country at his command and went to a place he showed me. Of course, I had my doubts at times, but the important thing was that I obeyed God."

We pass by Abraham's son, Isaac, and his grandson, Jacob, and we visit a while with one of Jacob's sons, Joseph. Joseph's brothers had sold him to become a slave, but, as things turned out, he rescued his whole family from starvation.

"They meant to do me harm," says Joseph, "but God meant it for good." We see Joseph's family move down to Egypt, and we watch as their descendants become slaves. After several hundred years we stop for a visit with Moses, the man who led the children of Israel (as

they are now called) from slavery to freedom. "Why did it take you so long to get started?" we ask him.

"I tried to do it my way," he replies, "and that ended in disaster. When I did it God's way he gave me the strength I needed to lead the people to freedom."

We pass by Joshua as he leads the people into the land God had promised them. We see the people ruled by judges like Ehud, Gideon, Deborah, and Samson, and we remember that God's friends were sometimes far from perfect.

Here we notice the "vicious circle" for the first time. The people turn away from God when things go well. Then God allows their enemies to make slaves of them. This causes them to repent and cry out to God, who rescues them from their enemies. Then the whole cycle is repeated. The people never seem to learn to obey God. It is a relief to visit a few moments with Ruth and her family, and to find people who want nothing more than to live in quietness and peace.

We pass by Saul, the first king of Israel, who turns out to be a failure because he has made the wrong choices. At about 1000 BC we stop to visit David, the shepherd boy who has become Israel's greatest king. "I have a close relationship with God," he tells us. "I am sorry for the sins I committed, but I am grateful to God for forgiving me when I repented."

"You have written some psalms. How are they used?" we ask David. "They are our hymns of worship," David replies. "We praise God and express our feelings and our faith through the psalms."

Along the way we meet some writers of the Wisdom literature. "It really is stupid to do wrong," they explain. "If you are wise, you will do what is right and keep yourself out of trouble."

We watch the kingdom of Israel divide into two parts after King Solomon, and we become acquainted with prophets like Amos, Hosea, Isaiah, Micah, and Jeremiah. Jeremiah tells us that the prophets warned the people of what would happen if they did not repent, but that they also encouraged them with the hope of the coming of the Messiah. "It is a hard and thankless work," he says. "Much of the time we have to stand alone."

We have already seen the people of the Northern Kingdom taken captive by the Assyrians. Now we see the people of Jerusalem and Judah taken captive to Babylon. There they learn that God does not forsake them when they are captives in a faraway land. Their God is the God of all the earth, they learn, and he is as close to them when they are in Babylon as when they were in Jerusalem. After about 70 years they go back to their own land again.

The time gauge drops to zero, and we realize that we have just passed through the greatest moment in God's great plan. The Messiah has come as the little baby Jesus! We follow him as he is baptized by John the Baptist and as God's Spirit

comes on him to give him power to begin his work. We see him out in the desert, where he is tempted by the Devil to use his power to make himself great and popular rather than to use it to serve other people. We are glad that he passes the test by resisting the Devil's temptations.

We meet some of the special friends of Jesus, like Peter and the other disciples. They go from place to place with him as he announces the coming of God's Kingdom, and they learn from him as he performs miracles and explains about life in this Kingdom. We also see that Jesus has many other friends and disciples.

Peter later explains, "After Jesus had ascended into heaven, the Holy Spirit came to the Church. The Holy Spirit helped me to understand that the death and resurrection of Jesus were exactly what the prophets had said would happen. It is because of what he did that we can be saved by faith and become friends of God. Three thousand people became believers when I preached on the day the Holy Spirit came."

We follow Paul on his missionary journeys, and we see him writing inspired letters to help the new churches with their problems and to encourage them to be faithful. "I have one ambition," he tells us. "It is to really know Jesus and to have the power that raised him from the dead, and also to know more about what it means to suffer with him."

We would like to stop and visit with many other friends of God, who wrote creeds to define the faith of the Church and keep out heresy and who determined the canon of the Bible. We would also like to visit with some of the people who struggled to keep their lights shining in their world. However, we move on until our time gauge reads about 1521 AD. Here we stop to visit with Martin Luther, the great leader of the German part of the Protestant Reformation. "I have become convinced," says Luther, "that salvation comes by grace alone, through faith, and not by doing good things required by church officials. Even though I must suffer for my convictions, here I take my stand, I cannot do otherwise, so help me God."

After visiting with John Calvin and Zwingli, two of the other reformers, we head on toward the twentieth century. On the way we stop to visit with John Wesley, the founder of the Methodist Church. He tells us that he had been very religious but still did not have peace in his heart until one evening while he was in a meeting. "I felt my heart strangely warmed," he said. "I felt I did trust Christ alone for salvation, and an assurance was given me that he had taken away my sins."

We also stop to visit briefly with Pietist leaders Philip Spener, August Francke, and Count Zinzendorf in Germany, and with revival preachers Jonathan Edwards, George Whitfield, and Charles Finney, in America.

Our last visits are with three of the early leaders of The Evangelical Covenant Church: Peter Waldenstrom in Sweden, and Carl Bjork and E. August Skogsbergh in America. "We believe in the importance of the Bible and in having a good understanding of our faith," they tell us, "but we also believe it is necessary to have a personal experience of knowing Jesus by faith as Savior and Lord." As we take off Skogsbergh shouts, "Don't forget to celebrate the forgiveness of your sins!"

We park our time capsule in Chicago, in front of the headquarters of The Evangelical Covenant Church, and our long journey comes to an end. It brought us back to many different kinds of people who were friends of God. We were reminded that they were like us in many ways and different from us in other ways. They were not perfect, and sometimes they made the wrong choices, yet God kept calling them back to himself, as he does to us when we go astray. God called all his people to believe in him and belong to him. He gave to the world his own son, Jesus, who announced the coming of God's kingdom, taught people how to enter and live in it, and established the Church. We were reminded that Jesus died and arose again in order to give eternal life to those who have a personal relationship with him and who trust in him. Through it all God has continued to be faithful to his friends, right up to our own time.

Check Yourself

Number the following list of names in chronological order.

_____Peter
_____Ruth
_____John Wesley
_____Eve
_____Isaac
_____Paul Peter Waldenstrom
_____Amos
_____Deborah

_____John Calvin
_____Philip Spener
_____Abraham
_____Jesus
_____David
_____Paul
_____Martin Luther
_____Moses

In Class

1. List several ways in which you consider yourself to be like the friends of God mentioned in this chapter.

_____

_____

_____

_____

2. List several ways in which you consider yourself to be different from the friends of God mentioned in this chapter.

_____

_____

_____

_____

How to Receive God's Gift of Salvation   28

BIBLE READING: Ephesians 2:8, 9; Acts 3:19; 1 John 1:9; Romans 1:16; Romans 10:9

CATECHISM: HOW DO WE BECOME CHRISTIANS?

We become Christians by faith in what God has done for us in Christ's death and resurrection. This is God's gift which we receive through personal repentance of sin and acceptance of Jesus Christ as Savior and Lord.

For it is by grace you have been saved, through faith—and this not from yourselves, it is the gift of God—not by works, so that no one can boast.

Ephesians 2:8, 9, NIV

ASSIGNMENT: Review any other parts of the catechism that your teacher may assign.

GOD OFFERS SALVATION AS A FREE GIFT

Once I saw a runaway horse come galloping up the road. Some men tried to stop him, but he turned off the road and ran into a big pile of old wire. His legs got tangled in the wire, and he fell to the ground. This frightened him more than ever, and he tried desperately to get his legs free, but the more he struggled, the more tangled he became. Everything he tried to do for himself only made things worse for him. Several people tried to untangle the wires, but as soon as they came near, the horse struggled even more to free himself and became even more entangled.

Then my father came. He loved and understood horses, and after he had talked quietly to the horse for a long time, he approached calmly and began to pat him gently. When the horse began to relax, my father took a big pair of pliers and began cutting the wire away. As long as the horse trusted my father, all went well, but whenever he tried to help by struggling to get free, he only made

things worse. Finally the horse gave up and let my father cut away the wires until he was free.

This horse was saved from the tangled wire when he gave up and let my father save him. He was free again! It was as though he had received a gift of new life!

That was what it meant to me to re-

ceive God's gift of salvation. I was free! I had new life, and it was a gift from God!

> Ephesians 2:8, 9: *For it is by grace you have been saved, through faith—and this not from yourselves, it is the gift of God—not by works, so that no one can boast. (NIV).*

Ephesians 2:8, 9 tells us that we cannot save ourselves; we must depend on God to do it. From this passage we learn that we are saved by "grace." "Grace" means that God gives us salvation freely, as a gift, without our doing anything that we could boast about. Just as that frightened horse had to stop trying to save himself before he could be saved from the tangled wire, so we must stop trying to save ourselves and trust God to save us. *We must accept salvation as a gift from God.*

GOD HAS DONE EVERYTHING THAT IS NECESSARY FOR OUR SALVATION

God has sent his Son, Jesus, who died for our sins and arose again. This, according to 1 Corinthians 15:3, 4, is the Good News about Jesus. Jesus is called "the Lamb of God" who was sacrificed to take away the sin of the world (see John 1:29).

> 1 Corinthians 15:3, 4: *For I delivered to you as of first importance what I also received, that Christ died for our sins in accordance with the scriptures, that he was buried, that he was raised on the third day in accordance with the scriptures.*

The catechism for Chapter 10, "What is accomplished by the death and resurrection of Jesus Christ?" tells us that "In the death and resurrection of Jesus Christ, God conquers sin, death, and the Devil, offering forgiveness of sins and assuring eternal life for those who follow him." This is "Good News" about what God has done to save us from our sins. *God has done everything that is necessary for our salvation.*

GOD INVITES US TO ACCEPT HIS GIFT BY FAITH

From Romans 1:16 we learn that God has the power to save everyone who has faith. This faith is also a gift from God. The Holy Spirit works in us and encourages us to turn to God. He also makes it possible for us to believe.

> Romans 1:16: *For I am not ashamed of the gospel: it is the power of God for salvation to everyone who has faith, to the Jew first and also to the Greek.*

God then asks us to be willing to believe the Good News of what Jesus has done. Faith in Christ means three things: *1. Faith means to depend on what God has done.*

To help us understand what is meant by faith, let us imagine that we are trapped on the roof of a building that is on fire. There is another building just a little too far away to jump over to it. Then, suppose there is a board lying on the roof, and this board is long enough to put across to the other building and wide enough to walk safely across. Now we have a choice. We can either depend on our own ability to jump, which will end in disaster for us, or we can depend on the board to hold us up as we walk

across it.

This board represents what Jesus did for us by his death and resurrection. When we depend on what he did for us, we will be saved from our sins, and God will accept us, not only as his friends, but also as his children, no matter how great our sins are.

2. Faith means repentance.

God hates sin because it has separated the people he loves from himself; it has brought violence and suffering to the world and it has robbed people of his friendship and the hope of eternal life.

Therefore, if we have faith in God and desire to be his friends, we must also be freed from our sins.

> Acts 3:19: *Repent therefore, and turn again, that your sins may be blotted out.*
> 1 John 1:9: *If we confess our sins, he is faithful and just, and will forgive our sins and cleanse us from all unrighteousness.*

We cannot overcome our sins by ourselves. The more we try to get away from them the more tangled up we become. Therefore, we must confess them to God

and ask for his forgiveness. This is what is meant by repentance. The promise in Acts 3:19 and 1 John 1:9 is that God will forgive us when we repent and turn to him.

3. Faith means confessing Jesus as our Lord.
Having faith in Jesus also means that we trust him enough to turn our lives over to him and to obey him. Even though we will fail him at times, he will help us to overcome our temptations and to live useful and satisfying lives.

> Romans 10:9: *If you confess with your lips that Jesus is Lord and believe in your heart that God raised him from the dead, you will be saved.*

We have seen that faith in Jesus Christ means:

1) Choosing to accept Christ as our Savior and depending on him rather than on ourselves.

2) Repenting of our sins

3) Accepting Christ as Lord of our lives.

The Holy Spirit helps us to make this

303

choice and even helps us to believe and to obey Jesus as our Lord. Receiving God's gift of salvation is what it means to become a Christian. It is saying to God, "Yes, I do want to be your friend!"

The answer to the catechism for this chapter, "How do we become Christians?", summarizes very well what this chapter is all about. You may turn this answer into a prayer and pray it yourself as you make your decision to accept God's gift of salvation, or you may pray it with someone else who is making this decision:

God, I put my faith in what you have done for me through Christ's death and resurrection. I confess to you that I am a sinner and I repent of my sin and ask your forgiveness. I accept Jesus Christ as my Savior and I want to obey him as my Lord. I know that I cannot earn the right to be a Christian. I ac-cept this as a free gift from you by faith in Jesus Christ. Thank you that you have forgiven my sins and accepted me as your friend and your child. Help me to be a faithful servant of Jesus Christ. Amen.

If you have just made this decision, welcome to God's family. God has called you to believe in him, and you have responded to his call. Now you are beginning a new life, which you have received as a gift from him. You belong to God, and he will give you the strength to live this life by faith. A good promise to believe is: "Everyone who calls upon the name of the Lord will be saved" (Romans 10:13). You also belong to the family of God. Your pastor will be glad to talk with you and to explain what this means. He will help you begin your new life as a Christian.

Check Yourself

1. What does "grace" mean, as it is used in the New Testament?

2. What three things does faith in Christ mean?

3. Explain briefly, in your own words, how to receive God's gift of salvation.

In Class

Each mark on the line below represents a year of your age. Write in any important events in your life, such as starting school, moving, special awards. If you are a Christian and can remember when you made this decision, write this in also:

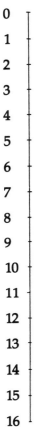

0
1
2
3
4
5
6
7
8
9
10
11
12
13
14
15
16

Are you a "friend of God?" Why or why not? If you are a "friend of God" you may have a friend who needs to hear that God wants to be his or her friend, too. List that person's name here and begin praying for an opportunity to talk to that person about God and his special kind of friendship.

_____

_____

_____

_____

_____

Living the Life of a Christian

29

BIBLE READING: John 10:1-5; 1 John 4:7-12; James 2:14-19

CATECHISM: HOW DO WE GROW AS CHRISTIANS?

We grow as Christians as we regularly receive God's grace in Word, worship, and sacrament, in study and prayer, and in fellowship and service with the Church.

But grow in the grace and knowledge of our Lord and Savior Jesus Christ. To him be the glory both now and to the day of eternity. Amen.

2 Peter 3:18, RSV

ASSIGNMENT: Review any other memory work that your teacher may suggest.

I was out walking with my dog one evening, when a man came rushing up to me, shouting, "You've got my dog! Give me back my dog!"

Since my dog is shy and timid, I picked her up as quickly as I could and said, "I'm sorry, sir, this is my dog."

With that he grabbed her by the hind legs and began to pull. I held on to one end of her, and he pulled on the other end until I became afraid that he would hurt her. Finally I had an idea, I said, "I'll put my dog down if you will let go of her, and you can call her. If she comes to you, you can have her."

He agreed, and I put the dog down. He began to call her by a name that neither she nor I had ever heard before. I just stepped back and called her by her right name, and she turned and followed me, leaving the man standing on the sidewalk. He said, in an apologetic voice, "I guess I was mistaken. She looked just like my dog."

What if she had chosen to go with him instead of me? I would have lost my dog. That, however, did not worry me. She knew her name, and she knew my voice, and I knew that she would not follow a stranger.

Jesus told a story that was very much like this experience I had with my dog. Jesus said that the shepherd "calls his own sheep by name and leads them out. When he has brought out all his own, he goes before them, and the sheep follow him, for they know his voice. A stranger they will not follow . . . for they do not know the voice of strangers" (see John 10:3-5).

We may be sure that if the sheep are following a certain shepherd, they belong to that shepherd. Jesus was speaking about Christians. Living the life of a Christian means to follow Jesus just as the sheep followed their own shepherd.

LIVING THE LIFE OF A CHRISTIAN BY FOLLOWING JESUS

My dog followed me because she has a feeling of "belonging" when she is with me. Sheep have the same feeling of "belonging" when they are with their own shepherd as he leads them out to their pasture. In the same way, the Holy Spirit gives us Christians a comfortable feeling of "belonging" that makes us want to be with Jesus. We may be sure we are Christians because we want to follow Jesus as he leads us through life.

THE MARKS OF A CHRISTIAN

There are certain marks by which we can be recognized as followers of Jesus. It will help us to remember some of them by noticing that they begin with the letters of the word "LEAD." The marks are:

L ove
E ndurance
A ction
D evotion

1. The Mark of Love.

Love for God and love for one another is the most important mark of being true Christians. "He who does not love does not know God; for God is love" (1 John 4:8). "We know that we have passed out of death into life, because we love the brethren" (1 John 3:14). The Holy Spirit makes it possible for us to love people whom we could not otherwise

love. The Holy Spirit also gives us a love for Jesus and a desire to follow him. Therefore, we are comfortable and we feel at home only when we are letting Jesus lead us.

2. The mark of endurance.

We know how important endurance is in sports. Athletes stay in training so they will grow stronger and be able to endure. As Christians we are trained to endure by letting Jesus be our coach. Some things that are included in Jesus' endurance training program are:
• Regular study of the Bible. We learn to endure by continuing to take part in a Sunday school class or some other regular Bible class.
• Regular practice in Christian living. As we put our faith into practice and learn

from our experience, we grow strong so that we can endure temptations.
• Building a team spirit by having fellowship with other Christians. Having Christian friends with whom we can talk and play and worship builds endurance.

3. The mark of action.

Our Christian faith is expressed in what we do. In James 2:17 we read, "Faith by itself, if it is not accompanied by action, is dead" (NIV). Following are some of the ways our faith will express itself in our actions:
• Being honest, unselfish, and responsible.
• Being kind and considerate of other people.

• Being witnesses by the way we live and by the way we speak.
• Giving some of our money to our church and to other Christian causes.
• Taking part in the life of our church.
• Caring for people who need our help.
• Doing any other things that Jesus has commanded us.

4. *The mark of devotion.*

To have devotion to God means that we want to worship him. We Christians worship God because we love him, because we want to celebrate his faithfulness, and because we appreciate his love and care. This means that we take part regularly in the worship services of our church, we pay attention to the preaching of God's message, and we join regularly with other Christians in the Sacrament of the Lord's Supper.

As Christians, we also want to have personal devotions alone with God. Times for reading the Bible and prayer become like "green pastures" and "still waters" to refresh us and to help us follow our Shepherd.

LIVING THE LIFE OF A CHRISTIAN BY FAITH IN JESUS

The whole Christian life, from beginning to end, is a life of faith. Just as we receive God's gift of salvation by faith in Jesus, we continue to live as Christians by faith in him. The secret of living as Christians is to have *faith in Jesus to lead us through life.*

• Because we have faith in Jesus, the Holy Spirit fills us with *love* for God and for other people.
• Because we have faith in Jesus, the Holy Spirit shows us how to gain *endurance* through study, exercise and fellowship with other Christians.
• Because our faith in Jesus is expressed in what we do, we take *action* in ways that show that we are Christians.
• Because our faith leads us to respect God, we show our *devotion* by worshiping him with other Christians and in

personal devotions.

As we approach the end of our time together in the Confirmation class, we look forward to continuing our lives as Christians. It will help us in days to come if we will remember the four words that begin with the letters of the word "LEAD." Jesus wants to lead us into a life of love, endurance, action, and devotion.

A PRAYER

After you have read through this prayer once, you may wish to pray in these words, or pray in your own words, asking God's help as you continue to live the life of a Christian—as his friend: *Jesus, my shepherd, help me to follow where you LEAD. Thank you for loving me so much. Fill my heart with your LOVE. Help me to do the things that will give me strength and ENDURANCE to face temptation. Show me how to express my faith in my ACTIONS. I love you and want to show my DEVOTION by worshiping you, my Lord and my Savior. Help me to live the life of faith and to have the marks of a Christian. Amen.*

Check Yourself

1. List the four marks of a Christian that are described in this chapter.

2. What are four ways in which our faith expresses itself in action?

3. What do we mean when we say that the Christian life is a life of faith?

In Class

List some of the marks of a Christian which you have discussed in this class:

_____

_____

_____

_____

_____

Tell, in the space below, which marks are a special problem to you and explain how you plan to work on them:

_____

_____

_____

_____

_____

_____

_____

_____

_____

_____

An End— and a Beginning

30

BIBLE READING: Joshua 4:1-7

CATECHISM: Review any parts of the catechism and other memory work that you still do not know very well.

"AN END—"

As I have been writing this book, I have imagined you sitting in class or taking part in some class activities and I have felt as though I have become your friend. I have shared a little of my life with you to let you know that I am a human being who needs friends very much and to encourage you to share some of your life with other members of the class.

There are few things more important than friendship, and it has always been exciting to me to know that God wants me to be his friend. The Bible, which we have been studying, is a true story about God and human beings and how they became separated from each other. During this time together, we have seen how much God has sacrificed to win our friendship back. We have also seen how he has succeeded in making friends of all who are willing to trust in Jesus. He has given to his friends a rich and satisfying life that will never end. I hope you have made the decision to trust in Jesus and to accept all the good things God has promised to those who belong to him.

One purpose of this Confirmation course has been to help you understand the Bible and the teachings of the Christian faith better. Now, as we come to the end of the course, you have a much better understanding of what it means to be a Christian. As we have discovered during this time together, it is not enough just to understand these things. I hope that you have also become a friend of

Jesus because you "believe" in him and that the Holy Spirit has helped you to know that you "belong" with him and with his friends.

We have also discovered that an important part of being a Christian is celebrating the forgiveness of our sins. I wish for you a Christian life that is like a happy celebration.

"—AND A BEGINNING"

But this is not just an end for us. In the Bible reading for this chapter we see Joshua and the people of God as they came to the end of their life in the desert. Now God was calling them to begin a new life in the land he had promised them. In the same way, God is calling us to a new and exciting chapter in our life of faith in Jesus and of belonging to him.

This is the time for us to remember that we are so valuable to God that he has given his own Son to win us back to himself. Since we are valuable to God, we are also valuable to other people. There are people who need love. There are problems that need to be solved. There are hurts that need attention. There are

people that need to hear about Jesus. If it seems to you that you cannot be of much help, remember what God's people learned from their escape from slavery in Egypt—that *God gives strength to do the impossible.* Jesus is living in our hearts through the Holy Spirit, and wherever we go, Jesus goes with us. We receive the greatest satisfaction from living our new life when we reach out to care for other people as God reached out to care for us.

Of course, God never intended us to do this alone. We need to be a part of the Church. We worship together regularly with other Christians, we continue to study regularly with them in Sunday school, we have times of fun together, and we work together. The life of serving God together with other Christians is the most satisfying life in the world.

This is also an end and a beginning for me. Writing these chapters has been a big part of my life for these last two years. As I have come to the end of this work, I look forward to something else that God wants me to do. After serving him for many years, I can think of nothing more exciting than to continue serving him for the rest of my life.

Since the time has come for us to say "goodbye," I wish you many years of happiness as a friend of God. Let's remember that:

• No matter how pleasant it may be to live for ourselves,
  Living for God offers far more pleasure.
• No matter how much we have sinned,
  God's willingness to forgive is greater than our sin.
• No matter how badly we have failed,
  God's ability to restore us is greater than our failure.
• No matter how much we try to do for God,
  he will do still more for us.
• No matter how many things we give up for God,
  The rewards of obedience are greater than our sacrifices.

Now to him who by the power at work within us is able to do far more abundantly than all that we ask or think, to him be glory in the Church and in Christ Jesus to all generations, for ever and ever. Amen.

Ephesians 3:20, 21

THE END—AND THE BEGINNING!

Memory Work

THE TEN COMMANDMENTS
Exodus 20

[1]And God spoke all these words, saying,

[2]"I am the LORD your God, who brought you out of the land of Egypt, out of the house of bondage.

[3]"You shall have no other gods before me.

[4]"You shall not make for yourself a graven image, or any likeness of anything that is in heaven above, or that is in the earth beneath, or that is in the water under the earth; [5]you shall not bow down to them or serve them; for I the LORD your God am a jealous God, visiting the iniquity of the fathers upon the children to the third and the fourth generation of those who hate me, [6]but showing steadfast love to thousands of those who love me and keep my commandments.

[7]"You shall not take the name of the LORD your God in vain; for the LORD will not hold him guiltless who takes his name in vain.

[8]"Remember the sabbath day, to keep it holy. [9]Six days you shall labor, and do all your work; [10]but the seventh day is a sabbath to the LORD your God; in it you shall not do any work, you, or your son, or your daughter, your manservant, or your maidservant, or your cattle, or the sojourner who is within your gates; [11]for in six days the LORD made heaven and earth, the sea, and all that is in them, and rested the seventh day; therefore the LORD blessed the sabbath day and hallowed it.

[12]"Honor your father and your mother, that your days may be long in the land which the LORD your God gives you.

[13]"You shall not kill.

[14]"You shall not commit adultery.

[15]"You shall not steal.

[16]"You shall not bear false witness against your neighbor.

[17]"You shall not covet your neighbor's house; you shall not covet your neighbor's wife, or his manservant, or his maidservant, or his ox, or his ass, or anything that is your neighbor's."

PSALM 23

[1]The LORD is my shepherd, I shall not want; [2]he makes me lie down in green pastures.
He leads me beside still waters;
[3]he restores my soul.
He leads me in paths of righteousness for his name's sake.

[4]Even though I walk through the valley of the shadow of death,
I fear no evil; for thou art with me;
thy rod and thy staff, they comfort me.

[5]Thou preparest a table before me in the presence of my enemies;
thou anointest my head with oil,
my cup overflows.
[6]Surely goodness and mercy shall follow me all the days of my life;
and I shall dwell in the house of the LORD
for ever.

PSALM 139

[1]O LORD, thou hast searched me and known me!
[2]Thou knowest when I sit down and when I rise up;
thou discernest my thoughts from afar.
[3]Thou searchest out my path and my lying down, and art acquainted with all my ways.
[4]Even before a word is on my tongue, lo, O LORD, thou knowest it altogether.
[5]Thou dost beset me behind and before, and layest thy hand upon me.
[6]Such knowledge is too wonderful for me; it is high, I cannot attain it.

[7]Whither shall I go from thy Spirit?
Or whither shall I flee from thy presence?
[8]If I ascend to heaven, thou art there!
If I make my bed in Sheol,
thou art there!
[9]If I take the wings of the morning and dwell in the uttermost parts of the sea,
[10]even there thy hand shall lead me,
and thy right hand shall hold me.

¹¹If I say, "Let only darkness cover me,
and the light about me be night,"
¹²even the darkness is not dark to thee,
the night is bright as the day;
for darkness is as light with thee.

¹³For thou didst form my inward parts,
thou didst knit me together in my
mother's womb.
¹⁴I praise thee, for thou art fearful and
wonderful.
Wonderful are thy works!
Thou knowest me right well;
¹⁵my frame was not hidden from thee,
when I was being made in secret,
intricately wrought in the depths of
the earth.
¹⁶Thy eyes beheld my unformed sub-
stance; in thy book were written,
every one of them,
the days that were formed for me,
when as yet there was none of them.
¹⁷How precious to me are thy thoughts,
O God!
How vast is the sum of them!
¹⁸If I would count them, they are more
than the sand.
When I awake, I am still with thee.

O that thou wouldst slay the wicked,
O God,
and that men of blood would depart
from me,
²⁰men who maliciously defy thee,
who lift themselves up against thee
from evil!
²¹Do I not hate them that hate thee,
O LORD?
And do I not loathe them that rise
up against thee?
²²I hate them with perfect hatred;
I count them my enemies.
²³Search me, O God, and know my heart!
Try me and know my thoughts!
²⁴And see if there be any wicked way
in me,
and lead me in the way everlasting!

LORD'S PRAYER

Our Father who art in heaven, hallowed
be thy Name, thy kingdom come, thy will
be done, on earth as it is in heaven.
Give us this day our daily bread.
And forgive us our debts as we forgive
our debtors.
And lead us not into temptation, but
deliver us from evil.
For thine is the kingdom, and the power,
and the glory forever. Amen.

THE APOSTLES' CREED

I believe in God the Father Almighty,
maker of heaven and earth:
And in Jesus Christ his only Son, our
Lord; who was conceived by the Holy
Spirit, born of the Virgin Mary, suffered
under Pontius Pilate, was crucified, dead,
and buried; he descended into hades; the
third day he rose again from the dead; he
ascended into heaven, and sitteth on the
right hand of God, the Father Almighty;
from thence he shall come to judge the
quick and the dead.
I believe in the Holy Spirit, the holy
Christian church, the communion of
saints, the forgiveness of sins, the
resurrection of the body, and the life
everlasting. Amen.

Student Journal

God

Jesus

Holy Spirit

317

Bible

Church

Worship

Baptism

Lord's Supper

Salvation

Human Beings

Sin

322

Believe

Belong

Confirmation

Catechism

PART ONE

1. *Chapter 2*

WHO IS GOD?

God is personal, eternal Spirit, creator of the universe, Father of our Lord Jesus Christ, and our Father.

"Lord, you have been our dwelling place throughout all generations. Before the mountains were born or you brought forth the earth and the world, from everlasting to everlasting you are God."

Psalm 90:1, 2, NIV

2. *Chapter 4*

WHAT DO WE BELIEVE ABOUT THE BIBLE?

We believe in the Holy Scriptures, the Old and New Testaments, as the Word of God and the only perfect rule for faith, doctrine, and conduct.

"All Scripture is inspired by God and is useful for teaching the truth, rebuking error, correcting faults, and giving instruction for right living."

2 Timothy 3:16, TEV

3. *Chapter 5*

WHAT IS GOD'S RELATIONSHIP TO THE WORLD?

God created the world by his Word, sustains it by his power, and entrusts it to the care of human beings.

"The earth is the Lord's and the fulness thereof, the world and those who dwell therein."

Psalm 24:1, RSV

4. *Chapter 7*

WHAT DOES IT MEAN TO BE A HUMAN BEING?

To be a human being is to be created by God in his likeness, free and responsible in relation to God, the world, neighbor, and self.

"Then God said, 'And now we will make human beings; they will be like us and resemble us. They will have power over the fish, the birds, and all animals, domestic and wild, large and small.' "

Genesis 1:26, TEV

5. *Chapter 8*

WHAT IS SIN?

Sin is all in thought, word, and deed that is contrary to the will of God.

"Everyone has sinned and is far away from God's saving presence. But by the free gift of God's grace all are put right with him through Christ Jesus, who sets them free."

Romans 3:23, 24, TEV

6. *Chapter 9*

WHAT ARE THE RESULTS OF SIN?

The results of sin are broken relationships, a weakening of ability to obey God, and finally, eternal separation from him.

"For the wages of sin is death, but the gift of God is eternal life in Christ Jesus our Lord."

Romans 6:23, NIV

7. *Chapter 10*

WHAT IS MEANT BY A COVENANT BETWEEN GOD AND HIS PEOPLE?

A covenant between God and his people is an agreement in which God promises his care and faithfulness as his people respond in faithful obedience.

"Know therefore that the Lord your God is God; he is the faithful God, keeping his covenant of love to a thousand generations of those who love him and keep his commands."

Deuteronomy 7:9, NIV

8. *Chapter 11*

WHAT IS GOD'S PROVIDENCE?

God's providence is the care by which he upholds all that he has created and guides all according to his wisdom.

"Look at the birds of the air: they neither sow nor reap nor gather into barns, and yet your heavenly Father feeds them. Are you not of more value than they?"

Matthew 6:26, RSV

9. *Chapter 16*

WHAT IS SALVATION?

Salvation is the work of God through Christ which liberates people from sin and restores them to a right relationship with God.

"Salvation is to be found through him alone; in all the world there is no one else whom God has given who can save us."

Acts 4:12, TEV

10. *Chapter 24*

WHO ARE THE PROPHETS?

Prophets are chosen by God to show nations and individuals their sin, to call them to obedience, and to present the hope of the Messiah.

"The Sovereign Lord has filled me with his Spirit. He has chosen me and sent me to bring good news to the poor, to heal the broken-hearted, to announce release to captives and freedom to those in prison. He has sent me to proclaim that the time has come when the Lord will save his people and defeat their enemies."

Isaiah 61:1, 2a, TEV

11. *Chapter 28*

WHO IS JESUS CHRIST?

Jesus Christ is the Messiah, God's son, promised through the prophets. He came into the world to free people from sin and establish his kingdom on earth.

" 'Who do you say that I am?' Simon Peter answered, 'You are the Christ, the Son of the Living God.' "

Matthew 16:15b, 16, NIV

PART TWO

12. *Chapter 6*

WHAT IS THE KINGDOM OF GOD?

The kingdom of God is the reign of God expressed in the hearts and lives of his people both now and through eternity.

"The kingdom of God does not come visibly, nor will people say, 'Here it is,' or 'There it is,' because the kingdom of God is within you."

Luke 17:20b, 21, NIV

13. *Chapter 7*

WHAT DID JESUS TEACH US CONCERNING LIFE IN THE KINGDOM OF GOD?

Jesus taught us that life in the kingdom of God means we are to live in a loving relationship with God, self, and others.

"And he said to him, 'You shall love the Lord your God with all your heart, and with all your soul, and with all your mind . . . . You shall love your neighbor as yourself.' "

Matthew 22:37, 39, RSV

14. *Chapter 9*

WHAT IS THE SACRAMENT OF THE LORD'S SUPPER?

The Lord's Supper is the sacred use of bread and the cup as commanded by Jesus Christ. In communion with one another we remember his suffering for us, proclaim his death until he comes, and partake of him in faith.

"For I received from the Lord what I also delivered to you, that the Lord Jesus on the night when he was betrayed took bread, and when he had given thanks, he broke it, and said, 'This is my body which is broken for you. Do this in remembrance of me.' In the same way also the cup, after supper, saying, 'This cup is the new covenant in my blood. Do this, as often as you drink it, in remembrance of me.' For as often as you eat this bread and and drink the cup, you proclaim the Lord's death until he comes."

1 Corinthians 11:23-26, RSV

15. *Chapter 10*

WHAT IS ACCOMPLISHED BY THE DEATH AND RESURRECTION OF JESUS CHRIST?

By the death and resurrection of Jesus Christ, God conquers sin, death, and the Devil, offering forgiveness for sin and assuring eternal life for those who follow Christ.

"For God so loved the world that he gave his only Son, that whoever believes in him should not perish but have eternal life."

John 3:16, RSV

16. *Chapter 12*

WHO IS THE HOLY SPIRIT?

The Holy Spirit is God everywhere present and powerful, working in us, in the church, and in the world.

"And I will ask the Father, annd he will give you another Counselor to be with you forever —the Spirit of truth. The world cannot accept him, because it neither sees him nor knows him. Buy you know him, for he lives with you and will be in you."

John 14:16, 17, NIV

17. *Chapter 14*

WHAT IS MEANT BY ATONEMENT?

Atonement means the work of God in Jesus Christ by which we, being guilty, are justified; being enslaved to sin, are redeemed; being alienated from God, are reconciled; and being unholy, are sanctified.

"Now, by means of the physical death of his Son, God has made you his friends, in order to bring you holy, pure, and faultless into his presence."

Colossians 1:22, TEV

18. *Chapter 15*

WHAT IS THE CHRISTIAN CHURCH?

The Christian Church is all who confess Jesus Christ as Savior and Lord and who are united in one body with Christ as head.

"Speaking the truth in love, we will in all things grow up into him who is the Head, that is, Christ. From him the whole body, joined and held together by every supporting ligament, grows and builds itself up in love, as each part does its work."

Ephesians 4:15, 16, NIV

19. *Chapter 16*

WHAT IS THE CHRISTIAN HOPE?

The Christian hope is a confident expectation of Christ's coming in triumph when he shall reign forever with his Church.

"Praise be to the God and Father of our Lord Jesus Christ! In his great mercy he has given us new birth into a living hope through the resurrection of Jesus Christ from the dead, and into an inheritance that can never perish, spoil, or fade—kept in heaven for you . . ."

1 Peter 1:3, 4, NIV

20. *Chapter 18*

WHAT IS THE SOURCE OF THE CHURCH'S LIFE?

The life of the Church has its source in God; Father, Son, and Holy Spirit. It is created and renewed by the Spirit and Word, the holy sacraments, and prayer.

"Now to him who by the power at work within us is able to do far more abundantly than all that we ask or think, to him be glory in the church and in Christ Jesus to all generations, for ever and ever. Amen."

Ephesians 3:20, 21, RSV

21. *Chapter 20*

WHAT IS THE PURPOSE OF THE CHURCH?

The purpose of the Church is to glorify God, celebrate new life in Christ, build up one another in faith and love, proclaim and teach the gospel everywhere, and care for the needs of the world.

"You are a chosen race, a royal priesthood, a holy nation, God's own people, that you may declare the wonderful deeds of him who called you out of darkness into his marvelous light."

1 Peter 2:9, RSV

22. *Chapter 24*

WHAT IS THE SACRAMENT OF BAPTISM?

Baptism is the sacred use of water, commanded by Jesus Christ, to signify God's cleansing of our sins and our welcome into the family of God.

"Go therefore and make disciples of all nations, baptizing them in the name of the Father and of the Son and of the Holy Spirit, teaching them to observe all that I have commanded you; and lo, I am with you always, to the close of the age."

Matthew 28:19, 20, RSV

23. *Chapter 28*

HOW DO WE BECOME CHRISTIANS?

We become Christians by faith in what God has done for us in Christ's death and resurrection. This is God's gift which we receive through personal repentance of sin and acceptance of Jesus Christ as Savior and Lord.

"For it is by grace you have been saved, through faith—and this not from yourselves, it is the gift of God—not by works, so that no one can boast."

Ephesians 2:8, 9, NIV

24. *Chapter 29*

HOW DO WE GROW AS CHRISTIANS?

We grow as Christians as we regularly receive God's grace in Word, worship, and sacrament, in study and prayer, and in fellowship and service with the Church.

"But grow in the grace and knowledge of our Lord and Savior Jesus Christ. To him be the glory both now and to the day of eternity. Amen."

2 Peter 3:18, RSV

Glossary

(Numbers in parenthesis indicate one or more chapters in this book in which the word is used)

action   Deeds done by a person. See also "conduct." (II:29)

adultery   Willing sexual intercourse between two persons, either or both of whom are married but not to each other. *Adultery in the heart:* A desire to have forbidden sexual intercourse (Matthew 5:28). *Spiritual adultery:* Idol worship, unfaithfulness to God (Jeremiah 3:9). (I:14)

age   A period of time during which God works in a certain way. The present age, also known as "this world," will come to an end at the return of Christ (see "this world"). (II:11)

alienated   Separated, broken relationships, because of sin. Human beings have been alienated from God ever since Adam and Eve first sinned. (II:14; See also I:8)

apostle   A person who has been "sent out," especially the twelve disciples chosen by Jesus to be with him, whom he sent out to be witnesses of his resurrection. (II:4)

Apostles' Creed   An ancient creed of the Church, understood to be a summary of the teachings of the Twelve Apostles. (I:6; II:3, 18, 23)

ark of the covenant, or *ark of the testimony:* The golden chest, containing the Ten Commandments written on stone, which stood in the most holy place in the tent of worship in the desert. The top, known as "the mercy seat," held two angelic figures and represented the presence of God among his people. (I:13)

ascension: Jesus' return to heaven, forty days after his resurrection, to rule with all authority both in heaven and on earth. (II:3, 11)

assurance: To have confidence, to be made sure. Those who repent and believe in Jesus have the assurance of forgiveness of sins and of eternal life because of the promise of God. (I:20; II:10; see also II:28)

atonement: "At-one-ment." An act of sacrifice that makes it possible to be united again. Christ died on the cross for our sins so that we may be united with God as his friends. (II:14)

authority: (See also "rule") The right and power to command obedience. The Bible is the Christians' "authority" or "rule." Jesus has been given all authority (Matthew 28:18-20). (I:4; II:11)

Babylon: Ancient city, located between the Tigris and Euphrates rivers in what is now Iraq, to which the people of Judah were taken captive in 587 BC. The word "Babylon" also symbolizes a wicked culture or civilization. (I:26)

baptism: The sacred use of water, commanded by Jesus Christ, to signify God's cleansing of our sins and our welcome into the family of God. (II:3, 11, 12, 24)

Bible: The book, composed of the Old and New Testaments, recognized by Christians as the Word of God and the only perfect rule for faith, doctrine and conduct. (I:3, 4; II:17)

birthright: Special privileges of the firstborn son in ancient times. (I:11)

blood of Christ: The death of Christ, in which he shed his blood for the sins of human beings. Also called "precious blood" because of its great value. (II:3)

body of Christ: See "Church."

Book of the Law: The ancient teachings God had given to his people through Moses, which explained how God wanted his people to live and worship and serve him. Lost and rediscovered while repairing the temple in Jerusalem under the direction of King Josiah (2 Chronicles 34:8-18). (I:23)

born again: Having new life in Christ. All those who believe in Jesus Christ as Savior and follow him as Lord have been born again whether or not they remember a time when they received this new life. (II:6) (For a description of this new life in Christ see II:10, 18, 29.)

Canaan: The Promised Land, located at the east end of the Mediterranean Sea; the land to which God led Abraham, and the land to which Moses led the Children of Israel. (I:16)

canon: A "rule" or "measuring stick." The rule which was used to test writings to determine if they belonged in the New Testament. The list of books approved for inclusion in the Bible. (II:17)

captivity: See "exile."

Carthage, Council of: The church council, held in Carthage, North Africa, in 397 AD, at which the canon of the New Testament was recognized. (II:17)

catholic: "Universal." Refers to the Church as a whole, including all Christians of all places and in all times; not to be confused with "Roman Catholic Church." (II:18)

Children of Israel: The descendants of Jacob, whose name was also Israel. God's ancient people, through whom Jesus came, also known as "Israel" or "Israelites." In Galatians 6:16 Christians are called "The Israel of God." (I:12)

Christ: Greek word for "Messiah." The rightful title of Jesus, the King, Savior and Son of God. See also "Jesus." (II:12)

Christian: A follower of Jesus Christ. The name first given to the disciples of Jesus in the city of Antioch (see Acts 11:26). (II:4)

Christian faith: The body of teachings believed by Christians, as defined by the apostles and found in the Bible. (II:18)

Christian hope: A confident expectation of Christ's coming in triumph when he shall reign forever with his church. The Christian hope includes the expectation of the resurrection of all believers in Jesus who have died. (II:16)

Church, or Christian Church: All who confess Jesus Christ as Savior and Lord and who are united in one body with Christ as head. Also known as "the Body of Christ.""Church" is also used to define a local body of Christians or a denomination. (II:12)

circumcision: Removal of the foreskin, to be performed on all males in Israel. A sign of belonging to the covenant God made with Abraham. *Circumcision of the heart:* To have a repentant and trusting spirit, seeking to do God's will (Romans 2:28, 29). (II:13)

commandments: The rules God has given, especially the Ten Commandments, by which his people may live as free people. The things Jesus told his disciples to do, the greatest of which is to love God and one another (see Luke 10:27; John 13:34). (I:10; II:7, 29)

commission: The responsibility Jesus has given to his followers to be his witnesses and to make other disciples. "The Great Commission" is found in Matthew 28:18-20. (II:11)

communion: See "fellowship;"see "Holy Communion."

community, Christian: The Christians in a local church or a certain area having fellowship, worshiping and serving God together as a body. (II:1, 4)

concordance: An index of the words in a certain version of the Bible with reference to passages where the words may be found. (I:3)

condemned: To be declared guilty and worthy of punishment. All human beings since Adam and Eve are condemned until they have been forgiven. (II:3, see also I:8, 9)

conduct: General way of living and behaving. (I:4; see also II:7, 14, 15, 29, which describe the conduct of the Christian)

confession: 1) An honest acknowledgement of having sinned, made either to God or to another person. (I:10; II:28)
2) A written statement of the beliefs of a certain church or other body of believers, or a personal statement of faith. (II:18, 28)

covenant: 1) (Between God and his people): An agreement in which God promises his care and faithfulness as his people respond in faithful obedience. See also "new covenant." (I:10, 25; II:9)
2) (as used in "The Evangelical Covenant Church"): An agreement among certain groups of Christians to unite in serving God and in carrying on his mission, forming what is now The Evangelical Covenant Church. (II:23)

covet: To have a strong desire for something that is forbidden. (I:14)

Creator: God, who calls all things into existence by his Word. (I:4)

creed: A written statement of beliefs, especially the beliefs of the Church. (II:18)

cross: The cross, made of wooden beams, on which criminals were hung to die, used mostly by the Romans. "The cross of Christ" symbolizes Christ's death on a cross for our sins. (II:9, 28)

crucify: To hang on a cross to die. *spiritual crucifixion:* To turn from sin and become identified with Christ (see Galatians 2:20). (II:8)

crusade: One of a series of military marches from Europe beginning in 1096 AD to rescue the Holy Land (Palestine) from the Moslems. (II:19)

Day of Atonement: A special holy day, beginning in ancient Israel, when the high priest made sacrifices for the sins of all the people and sprinkled blood from the sacrificial animal on the Ark of the Covenant. (I:13)

denomination: "name" or "title." An organized group of churches within the Church, carrying the same name, such as "Presbyterian," "Methodist," or "Covenant." (II:20)

descendant: An offspring of any number of generations. (I:10)

Devil: Satan, the Tempter, the Evil One. Sometimes also used for a demon. (II:3)

devotion: A deep affection for God expressed in worship. Often used to describe personal, individual worship. (II:25, 29)

disciple: "Learner." A follower of Jesus, who is learning from him. Often used especially for Jesus' Twelve Disciples. (II:4)

Divided Kingdom: The nation of Israel after 922 BC, when it divided into northern and southern parts. (I:20, 23)

doctrine: A teaching or a set of teachings of a certain faith or religion. (I:4)

ecumenical movement: "Worldwide." A movement for uniting the church, or parts of the Church, either in spirit or through an organization. (II:21)

Egyptians: Inhabitants of Egypt, a nation in northern Africa which made slaves of the Children of Israel. (I:12)

endurance: Strength to keep from giving up. (II:29)

epistle: "Letter." Especially one of the books of the New Testament which are letters. (II:14)

eternal life: A rich, satisfying and useful life that never ends, is a gift from God, to those who believe in Jesus Christ. Also called "everlasting life." (I:10; II:8, 10, 28)

eternal separation: Unending separation from God, the final punishment for unrepentant sinners. See also "hell." (I:9)

evangelical: Emphasizing "the evangel," which is the Good News about Jesus. Used to describe a church or other body of Christians that preaches and encourages people to respond to Jesus Christ as Savior and Lord. (II:23)

everlasting life: See "eternal life."

Eucharist: Another name for the Lord's Supper. (II:9)

exile: The captivity of the people of Judah in Babylon, which began in 587 BC and lasted 70 years. (I:26)

faith: Confidence in, trust in, belief in. Faith in Christ is a gift from God which makes it possible to respond to the gospel of Jesus. Also, a certain religion or body of beliefs, as "the Christian faith," (I:10; II:28)

faithful obedience: Obedience that results from faith. (I:10; II:29)

false testimony: Dishonesty, an untrue statement, a lie. Lying is forbidden in both the Old and New Testaments (Exodus 20:16; Ephesians 4:25). (I:14)

false witness: See "false testimony."

family of God: The Church, the body of Christ, or a local church seen as God's family. (II:24)

Feast of Booths: A festival of God's people, Israel, to remind them that they had lived in small huts when they came out of Egypt. Also known as "the Feast of Ingathering" (see Leviticus 23:26-32). (I:13)

Feast of harvest: A festival of God's people, Israel, in which they brought the first of their new crops as an offering to the Lord (Exodus 23:14-17). (I:13)

Feast of Ingathering: A festival of God's people, Israel, which they celebrated when the crops had been harvested (see Exodus 23:14-17). (I:13)

Feast of Unleavened Bread: A festival of God's people, Israel, to remind them of how God saved them from Egypt. During this time they also celebrated the Passover to celebrate their deliverance from Egypt (see Leviticus 23:5-8). (I:13)

fellowship: A relationship of love, understanding and shared responsibilities among a group of Christians. Also known as "koinonia." (II:4)

festival: A gathering of God's people to celebrate one or more of God's special favors. Christmas and Easter are major festivals of the Church. (I:13)

forgiveness: Canceling of all guilt and acceptance of a person as having committed no wrong. (I:9; II:14)

freedom: Release from all slavery, especially the release from the guilt and power of sin, to be free to live for God. We receive this freedom through faith in Jesus Christ. (I:14; II:28)

Genesis: "Beginning." First book of the Bible, describing the beginning of all things. (I:5)

gentile: A person who is not one of God's people, Israel. According to the New Testament, a Christian is no longer either a Jew or a gentile (see Galatians 3:27, 28). (II:13)

gifts: Different abilities the Holy Spirit gives to different Christians to do his work. Sometimes known as "talents." Salvation is also called a "gift" because God gives it freely. (II:26, 28)

Gnosticism: A popular heresy in the early days of the Church, based on the word "gnosis" or "knowledge," that salvation comes through a special kind of secret knowledge. (II:18)

God's image or likeness: The uniqueness of human beings as created by God, not like God physically, but having personalities able to respond to God and to his love and able to make choices. God's image in human beings was marred by sin. (I:6)

golden calf: A form of idol worship, practiced in ancient times, that tempted Israel during much of its early history. (I:13)

golden rule: The name given to the statement of Jesus which is recorded in Matthew 7:12. (II:7)

Golgotha: "skull." The Hebrew name for "Calvary," the hill outside Jerusalem on which criminals were crucified and on which Jesus was crucified. (II:10)

Good News: See "gospel."

gospel: "Good News." The message of Jesus, his coming, his Kingdom, and the salvation he brings. Also used to define the first four books of the New Testament. (II:2)

gossip: To spread damaging rumors. (I:22)

grace: What God does freely, as an undeserved gift. Salvation is by "grace" through faith because it is a gift from God. (II:20, 28)

Great Commission: See "commission."

guilty: A state of being worthy of punishment for wrongdoing. All human beings are guilty before God unless forgiven through faith in Christ. (I:9; II:14)

Hebrews: The Israelites. A name by which they became known while they were slaves in Egypt. (I:12)

hell: Name given to the place of eternal punishment for unrepentant sinners. Also used as the place from which the power of evil and death comes. "Hades," the place of the dead. See also "judgment," "punishment." (I:9)

heresy: False teaching. (II:18)

holy: Pure, undefiled, as God himself is. Cleansed and made worthy to fellowship with God and to serve him. God is holy. God, the Spirit, is called "the Holy Spirit."

338

People are made holy by faith in Jesus Christ. (I:13; II:14)

"Holy Communion:"   Another name for the Lord's Supper. (II:9)

holy place: The first room of the tent of worship in the desert, separated by a curtain from the most holy place. (I:13)

Holy Scriptures: "Holy writings." Another name for the Bible. (I:3)

Holy Spirit: See "Spirit."

Holy Trinity: The Christian definition of God as being one, but expressing himself in three Persons: Father (creator and sustainer of all), Son (God as Jesus, our Savior and Lord), and Holy Spirit (unseen but always at work and always present with his people). These three Persons are equal, one God, known as "The Triune God." (II:12)

hope: An expectation of things yet unseen. This expectation is sure when it is based on the promises of God. See also "Christian hope." (I:28)

hymn: A song used in worship. (I:21, II:25)

idol: A false god. (I:14)

immorality: Corruption, contrary to the will of God, especially sexual sin. Galatians 5:19-21 describes some forms of immorality against which Christians are warned. (I:14, 24)

inheritance: All the benefits awaiting those who believe in Jesus, both in this life and in the life to come. (II:16)

iniquity: Another name for sin, especially in the form of injustice. (II:10)

inquisition: A system in which persons holding certain beliefs are searched out, put to trial and punished. (II:19)

inspiration: The work of the Holy Spirit in the authors of the books of the Bible that caused their writings to be the message and Word of God. (I:3; II:17)

Islam: The Moslem faith, the religion that began with Mohammed in 622 AD. (II:19)

Israel, Israelites: See "Children of Israel."

JB: The Jerusalem Bible.

Jerusalem Council: Church council in Jerusalem in 49 AD that declared that circumcision was not a requirement for salvation. Both Jews and Gentiles were to be recognized as Christians on the basis of faith in Christ. (II:13)

Jesus: The Savior, who was born in Bethlehem, Judea, about 4 BC (see Luke 2:10), in fulfillment of Old Testament prophesies. He went about teaching, healing, caring for people and inviting them to enter his Kingdom. He died on a cross for the sins of the world and rose again to rule in the hearts of those who believe in him. He will return some day to rule forever. He is the Son of God in the sense that he is equal with God, and has existed from all eternity. See also "Holy Trinity." (I:8, 10, 28, 29; II:2, 3, 4, 5, 6, 7, 8, 9, 10, 11, 12, 16, 28, 29, 30)

Jew: The name by which the people of Judah became known during the Exile. (I:26)

Judaism: The name by which the faith of the Jewish people became known during the Exile. (I:27)

judges: The persons through whom God ruled over Israel from the time the people entered the Promised Land until Saul, the first king. (I:16, 17)

judgment: Establishing justice by punishing the wicked and recognizing the rights of the righteous. Although human governments exercise judgment, final judgment must be left to God. Revelation 20:10-15 tells of God's judgment on all those who do not repent of their sins. See also "hell," "punishment." (I:9, 24; II:6, 16)

justice: Right and fair relationships among people. Jesus, as well as the prophets of the Old Testament, stressed the importance of justice. (I:24; II:6)

justification: A pronouncement of freedom from guilt. The only true justification is done by God when he pronounces those who believe in Jesus to be free from guilt. (II:14)

KJV: The King James Version, also known as the Authorized Version.

Kingdom of God: The reign of God expressed in the hearts and lives of people both now and through eternity. This term is used widely in Mark and Luke and occasionally in John. Matthew uses the term "Kingdom of Heaven." (II:6, 7, 8)

Kingdom of Heaven: See "Kingdom of God."

knowledge: See "Gnosticism."

koinonia: See "fellowship."

LB: The Living Bible.

"Lamb of God": Jesus, the true sacrifice for sins, who fulfills the meaning of the sacrifices of lambs as described in the Old Testament (see John 1:29). (I:20)

Law of Moses: The rules for living as free people that God gave through Moses to his people. These included the Ten Commandments and other rules and guides for worship. (I:14; II:13)

Law of Retribution: Any harm done was to be "paid back" to the person who did it, "a life for a life, an eye for an eye, a tooth for a tooth." Jesus said that this law was not to be used in his Kingdom (see Matthew 5:39-41). (I:16)

living sacrifice: See "sacrifices."

Lord: "Master," "ruler." One of the names for God. A title of respect for Jesus, as in "Our Lord Jesus Christ." (II:3)

Lord's Supper: The sacred use of bread and the cup as commanded by Jesus. In communion with one another we remember his suffering for us, proclaim his death until he comes, and partake of him in faith (see 1 Corinthians 11:23-26). (II:9, 25)

love: The most important meaning of "love," as used in the Bible, is God's unfailing devotion and care in relation to his creation, and especially to human beings. Human beings are able to express this love only as they respond to God's love. Another meaning of love, as used in the New Testament is "friendship" or "brotherly love" among human beings. The word "love" is not used in the New Testament to describe romantic attraction or sexual desire. (I:6; II:6, 15, 29)

manna: Food for the Israelites which fell on the ground miraculously every morning while they were in the desert. (I:13)

mercy seat: See "Ark of the Covenant."

Messiah: The righteous King, promised by God through the prophets. Christians recognize Jesus of Nazareth, God's Son, as the Messiah. He came into the world to free people from sin and establish his kingdom on earth. (I:19, 28; II:8)

ministry: Service performed by Christians as representatives of Jesus. (II:4, 11)

miracle: Something that happens that has no natural explanation. A sign that God is doing something without using natural methods. Jesus' miracles were signs that the Kingdom of God had come and that he was the King. (II:8)

mission: The responsibility, given by Jesus, to carry on his work; especially to bring his message to the whole world. "Missions" is the program in which the Church engages in order to fulfill its mission. (II:4, 11, 23)

missionary: A person whose profession is to carry on Christ's message as his representative. Missionaries are generally sent out by a church or another group of Christians. There is a sense in which all Christians are missionaries because they all share in Christ's mission, but the term "missionary" is usually reserved for professional or "career" missionaries. (II:11, 13, 23, 26)

Mission Friends: See "Mission Societies."

Mission Societies: Groups of Christians in Scandinavia, known as "Mission Friends," who gave witness to a personal relationship with Christ and who gathered to worship and to support missionary work. They were the forerunners of The Evangelical Covenant Church. (II:23)

Mohammed: Founder of the Moslem religion, born in Mecca in Arabia, about 570 AD. (II:19)

monastery: A place in which members of monastic orders may live, separated from the outside world, to concentrate on spiritual interests. (II:19)

monasticism: A system, common in the middle ages, in which members of "monastic orders" retreated from the world to concentrate on spiritual concerns. The men were known as "monks" and the women as "nuns." (II:19)

monk: See "monasticism."

Moravians: Originally "Bohemian Brethren," followers of John Hus. The movement emphasized missionary work and the joy of Christian living. (II:20, 23)

Moslem: The religion originating with Mohammed. A member of the Moslem religion. (II:19)

most holy place: The inner and most sacred room of the tent of worship in the desert, in which the ark of the covenant stood. (I:13)

Mount Sinai: The mountain, located in the desert between Egypt and the Promised Land, on which God gave Moses the laws for the Children of Israel. (I:13)

murder: The sin of deliberately killing a human being. According to Jesus, hating someone makes a person guilty of murder (see Matthew 5:21, 22). (I:14)

NIV: The New International Version.

new covenant: (see also "covenant") The new agreement, promised by Jeremiah (see Jeremiah 31:31-34), which God made with his people through Jesus Christ, forgiving their sins and giving them a new heart. (I:25; II:9)

New Testament: The second of the two main parts of the Bible. God's message to his people since the coming of Jesus. (I:3)

Nicene Creed: The creed formed by the Council of Nicaea in 325 AD and adopted by another council held in Constantinople in 381 AD. (II:18)

Northern Kingdom: The kingdom formed by the ten northern tribes of Israel that revolted against King Rehoboam in 922 BC. (I:23)

nun: See "monasticism."

obedience: See "faithful obedience."

offerings: Sacrifices made by God's people as part of their worship. Christ offered himself as the true sacrifice for sin (see John 1:29) and God's people now offer themselves and their possessions as offerings of thanksgiving (see Romans 12:1). (I:9, 13; II:26)

Old Testament: The first of the two main divisions of the Bible, God's message to his people before the coming of Jesus. (I:3)

only begotten Son: Refers to God's Son as being in the position of highest authority and equal with the Father. "Only begotten" does not mean that there was a time when God's Son was ever born. He was born into the world as Jesus, but he existed from eternity as God's Son. See also "Jesus." (II:3)

parables: Stories about ordinary things, but which have a spiritual meaning. Most of the parables of the Bible were told by Jesus. (II:6)

Passover: A Jewish festival celebrated every year to commemorate the time when God freed his people from slavery in Egypt. (I:l2; II:9)

penance: "Repentance and sorrow for sin." A requirement, sometimes set up by representatives of the Church, in order to be forgiven. (II:20)

penitential: Name given to certain psalms that describe a person who is repentant and seeking forgiveness. (I:21)

Pentecost: A Jewish festival held fifty days after the Passover. The Holy Spirit came to the Church on the Pentecost ten days after Jesus' ascension. (II:12)

persecute: To cause someone to suffer unjustly, usually because of belief or race. (II:16)

Pharisees: A sect that arose within Judaism after the exile for the purpose of preserving the purity of Judaism. During the time of Jesus the Pharisees had become so strict and legalistic that they missed the real meaning of God's message. (I:29; II:5)

Pietism: A movement within the Church that emphasizes a personal relationship with Christ and a life of devotion to God. The Covenant Church, in its beginning, was influenced by Pietism in the Lutheran Church. (I:23)

pope: "Papa," "father." The bishop of the early church in Rome, who became the head of the entire Church, later to be the head of the Roman Catholic Church. (II:19)

power: The strength and authority of Jesus, which is also available to Christians, through the Holy Spirit, to help them live and witness. (II:3)

praise: To glorify God. An important part of Christian worship. (I:21; II:25)

prayer: Communion with God. Listening to God and speaking to God. An important part of public and private worship. (I:13; II:6, 25, 29)

Prayer, the Lord's: The name given to the prayer Jesus taught his disciples, found in Matthew 6:9-12. (II:8)

Precious Blood: See "blood of Christ."

priest: A minister who offers sacrifices or prayer to God on behalf of the people. (I:13)

Promised Land: See "Canaan."

prophets: Persons chosen by God to show nations and individuals their sin, to call them to obedience, and to present the hope of the Messiah. (I:23, 24, 25)

providence: The care by which God upholds all that he has created and guides all according to his wisdom. (I:11)

punishment: The penalty for sin. God calls sinners to repent so they may be forgiven through Christ, but the final punishment of unrepentant sinners is eternal separation from God. See also "judgment," "hell" (Matthew 5:22; 23:33; Rev. 20:10-15). (I:9, 24; II:6)

RSV: The Revised Standard Version.

ransomed: Another word for "redeemed." (II:3)

reconciled: To become friends again. Through what Christ has done, God has made it possible for human beings no longer to be his enemies but to become his friends. (II:14)

redeemed: To be set free by paying a price. Christ gave his own life to set people free from sin. (II:3, 14)

reformation: An adjustment in which errors are corrected in the Church and it seeks to return to its true purpose and mission; especially, the Protestant Reformation, which began in 1517 AD. Reformation is made possible by the work of the Holy Spirit. (II:20)

reign: To have the authority and power to govern, as a king. (II:6)

relationship: Having congenial communication between persons. Human beings were created for relationship with God, which was broken by sin and may be restored by repentance and faith in Christ. Close relationships are possible among people who also have a relationship with God. (I:4)

repentance: A change of mind that leads to true sorrow for wrongdoing and a turning to God, seeking his forgiveness and the forgiveness of other people. Repentance is encouraged by the Holy Spirit. (I:16; II:14)

resources: The supplies residing in God's creation which are available for human use. (I:7)

resurrection: 1) Jesus' return to life after three days in the grave. (II:4, 10)
2) The return to life of all human beings in the future, the righteous to eternal joy with God and the unrighteous to eternal separation from God. (II:10, 16)

Retribution, Law of: See "Law of Retribution."

reverence: The attitude of awe and respect that is due to God. (II:25)

revival: Restoration to life. The restoration of a vital relationship with God, either in the Church or in an individual. A time of greater interest in a relationship with God among many people, such as "the Great Awakening" in New England. (II:21)

righteous: A life lived in obedience to God. No one is perfectly righteous since all have sinned. Those who repent and believe in Jesus are declared by God to be righteous. (I:9; II:14)

Roman Catholic: The church organization whose headquarters is in Rome and whose head is the Pope. (II:20)

rule: 1) another word for "reign." (II:6)
2) a guiding authority or principle, the Bible. (I:4)

sabbath: A day of rest, every seventh day, as commanded by God in the Ten Commandments. The sabbath is fulfilled in Christians by gathering to worship and fellowship with other Christians and also by the rest that comes by faith in Christ, not just every seventh day but at all times (see Hebrews 4:3-10). (I:13)

344

sacrament: An action, commanded by Jesus, that uses an ordinary substance in a sacred way. We believe that the two sacraments of the church are baptism and the Lord's Supper. (II:9, 24)

sacrifices: Offerings made to God in thanksgiving or to atone for sins. The real sacrifice for sin was made by Christ when he died on the cross. Therefore, Christians do not make sacrifices for sin. To do so would be to reject Christ's sacrifice. Christians make sacrifices of thanksgiving to God to help carry on his mission, the most important of which is the offering of themselves as "living sacrifices" (see Romans 12:1). (I:13; II:9)

Sadducees: A religious and political party in Judaism that rejected life after death and the existence of angels, but which followed the Law of Moses strictly (Acts 23:8). (I:29)

salvation: The work of God through Christ which liberates people from sin and restores them to a right relationship with God. (I:9, 16; II:28)

sanctified: Cleansed and made fit to be in the presence of God and to serve him. Another word for "holy." (II:14)

Savior: Jesus is the Savior. He gave himself completely to the saving of people from their sins and to their restoration to a satisfying and useful relationship with God. (I:28; II:2, 10, 28)

scientist: A person whose work is to try to learn the laws of God's creation through careful study and experimentation and to help make good use of the resources God has given. (I:5)

scribes: Scholars in Judaism, beginning after the captivity, whose responsibility was to study and interpret the Scriptures. (I:27)

Sermon on the Mount: The longest message of Jesus recorded in the Bible, giving instructions for living in God's Kingdom (Matthew 5-7). (II:7)

Scriptures: See "Holy Scriptures." Another name for the Bible.

sign: See "miracle."

sin: All in thought, word and deed that is contrary to the will of God. (I:8)

Sinai: See "Mount Sinai."

Son of God: See "Jesus," also "only begotten Son."

Southern Kingdom: The southern two tribes of Israel that remained true to King Rehoboam when the northern ten tribes rebelled in 922 BC. (I:23)

Spirit: God as unseen and ever present Spirit, known as the Holy Spirit, one of the three persons of the Trinity (see "Holy Trinity"). "Spirit" also refers to the special life or "breath" that God put in human beings when he created them. (I:2, II:12)

Sovereign Lord: God, the ruler of all. Name for God, as used in some versions of the Bible. (I:24)

Spirit of God: Also called "Holy Spirit." See "Spirit."

synagogue: Meeting place for Jewish worship which came into being some time between the exile and the time of Jesus. (I:29)

synoptic gospels: The first three gospels, Matthew, Mark and Luke. (II:2)

TEV: Today's English Version, also known as "The Good News Bible."

temple: The place of worship in Jerusalem, first built by Solomon, rebuilt after the exile, in 517 BC and rebuilt again by King Herod the Great in 19 BC. Destroyed by the Romans in 70 AD. Jesus spoke of his body as a temple (John 2:19-21), and the New Testament teaches that our bodies are temples of the Holy Spirit (I Corinthians 6:19). (I:20)

temptation: An enticement to depart from God's will and to do evil. A test of a person's faithfulness to God. (I:8; II:3)

tempter: The devil, Satan. (I:8; II:3)

Ten Commandments: See "Commandments."

"this world:" The world of unbelievers during this age. Christians have many things in common with "this world," but they must refrain from many things in it, and they enjoy other things that are not a part of "this world" (see Titus 2:11-13). (II:6)

transgression: A sin. Something contrary to God's commands. The disobedience of Adam and Eve was the first transgression. (II:10; see also I:8)

tribe: One of the twelve divisions of the Children of Israel, each one composed of descendants of one of the sons of Jacob. (I:16)

Trinity: See "Holy Trinity."

triumphal entry: The entry of Jesus into Jerusalem, on the Sunday before he was crucified, accompanied by his followers who were singing his praises. (II:8)

triune God: See "Holy Trinity."

trust: To have confidence in someone or something. Personal faith in God. (I:9; II:28)

Twelve Apostles: See "apostle."

twelve tribes: See "tribe."

unholy: Unfit for the presence of God. (II:14)

Virgin Mary: Mary, the mother of Jesus. She gave birth to Jesus by a miracle, without ever having had sexual intercourse. (II:2)

wisdom: The good judgment to choose to obey God and do what is right because this is the sensible way to live. Wrongdoing only leads to trouble. (I:22)

wisdom literature: Literature that emphasizes the value of wisdom. Biblical wisdom literature includes: Job, Ecclesiastes, Proverbs and some of the Psalms. (I:22)

346

Word of God: God's message and promise. The Bible is the Word of God. Jesus is also called "the Word of God" because he has revealed God most fully in his own Person. (I:4; II:17)

world: See "this world."

worship: Ascribing glory to God through praise, prayer, confession of sin, receiving forgiveness, being taught by God's Word and responding to God's call to serve him. Christian worship is a celebration of what God has done rather than an effort to get God to do something. (I:13; II:25)

Picture Credits

American Bible Society: 128 (right top & bottom), 129 (left and top right), 181, 182.

American Values Institute: 213 (bottom right), 217, 227 (bottom left).

Karl Bauer: 252 (inset right).

Pam Bigelow: cover.

Billy Graham Evangelistic Association: 268.

Al Bjorkman: cover, 216, 303, 312.

Russ Busby: 200 (middle right).

Steven Charter: 9 (top left).

Consulate General of Israel: 125 (left).

Covenant Archives: 274 (inset), 275 (right).

Covenant Church, Hilmar, CA: 224.

Covenant Christian Education Department: 97, 311 (left).

Covenant World Mission: 214, 260.

Jim DeGrado: 163, 200 (bottom left), 278, 283, 285, 289 (top left), 290.

David C. Cook: 157, 298, 302.

Steve Elde: 280 (right).

Evangelical Covenant Church, The: 299.

Evangelical Covenant Church, Grand Rapids, MI: 31 (right).

Forest Park Covenant Church, Muskegon, MI: 201.

Graded Press: 26, 340, 63 (bottom left), 73, 234.

P. Grant: 52, 178 (top left), 307 (right).

Jim Jacoby: 16, 35, 36, 48 (bottom right), 68 (left), 83, 89, 110 (inset), 121, 161, 172, 206, 245, 307 (top left).

Jewish Publication Society of America: 54.

Randolph J. Klassen: 152, 153 (windows at Hillcrest Covenant Church, Prairie Village, KS).

Peter Larson: cover.

Bruce Lawson: 38, 190 (middle right), 213 (top left), 222.

Deb Lundberg: cover.

Luoma Photos: 151 (middle left).

Robert Maust: 56, 255.

Bruce Misfeldt: 166.

Nancy Murakami: cover.

Neale Murray: 151 (top right).

Marilyn Nelson and Jean Foss: 275 (left middle).

Wesley Nelson: 4, 173 (bottom left).

North Park College: 29, 61.

North Park Theological Seminary: 211.

Oriental Institute of the University of Chicago: 105, 122 (top left).

Oxford University Press; Guy Rowe, portraits: 43, 47 (right), 48 (top left), 67, 76, 77 (top left), 82, 111 (right), 112 (left & right).

Palphot, Ltd.: 91.

Kenneth C. Poertner: 240, 308 (bottom).

Religious News Service: 9 (bottom right), 12, 14, 17, 27, 30 (inset right), 31, 33, 37, 42, 47 (left), 53, 58, 62, 63 (top right), 68 (right), 72 (right top & bottom), 75, 85, 93, 94, 99 (top), 100, 110 (right), 111 (bottom left), 114, 116 (bottom right), 128 (left), 129 (bottom right), 131, 134, 136 (bottom middle & right), 151 (top left & middle, bottom right), 158, 162, 167, 173 (top right), 189, 190 (top left), 194 (top left, middle right), 195, 196, 207, 208, 223, 226, 241, 247, 248, 249, 252 (left & right), 253, 258, 261, 266, 267 (right), 271, 280 (left), 296 (right), 297, 301, 307 (bottom left), 308 (top left).

Will & Angie Rumpf: 177.

Warner Sallman: 151 (middle right).

G. Douglas Schermer: 274.

Paul M. Schrock: 289 (bottom right).

Scripture Press Publications, Inc.: 44, 104, 107, 154.

Vernon Sigl: 23, 251.

Birger Sponberg: 151 (bottom left).

David S. Strickler: 202.

C. Sundt-Hansen, Royal Castle, Stockholm: 272.

Eric Torgerson: cover, 147.

United Bible Societies: 87, 212.

Robert Vickrey: 193.

Wallowitch: 99 (bottom).

Richard West: 18.

David Westerfield: cover, 8, 13, 20, 57, 72 (left), 77 (bottom right), 90, 115, 116 (top left & right), 121, 122 (bottom right), 124, 132, 183, 199, 218, 227 (top right), 245, 246, 273, 286, 296 (left), 313.